SCIENCE TODAY

In this comprehensive text, key figures in the fields of science and science education critically discuss the role of science in public policy, in the school and in broader public education. Their contributions form an original dialogue on science education and the general public awareness of science, tackling both formal and informal aspects of science learning.

Engaging with the socially contentious areas of this core curriculum subject, as well as the dichotomy between 'science for all' and 'training professional scientists', the authors of these articles uncover the prejudices which haunt the traditional view of science. They offer a range of detailed solutions. The editors argue that a better future for science must involve an open debate on its public role, and this can only happen by breaking down the barriers that divide scientists, schools and the public.

SCIENCE TODAY

Problem or crisis?

Edited by
Ralph Levinson and
Jeff Thomas

with a foreword by
JOHN DURANT

London and New York

First published 1997
by Routledge
11 New Fetter Lane, London EC4P 4EE
Simultaneously published in the USA and Canada
by Routledge
29 West 35th Street, New York, NY 10001

Typeset in Palatino by
Ponting–Green Publishing Services, Chesham,
Buckinghamshire

Printed in Great Britain by
Clays Ltd, St. Ives PLC

British Library Cataloguing in Publication Data
A catalogue record for this book has been requested

Library of Congress Cataloguing in Publication Data
A catalogue record for this book has been requested

ISBN 0–415–13531–1 (pbk)

CONTENTS

v

CONTENTS

Part III Science for all?

Part IV Scientists and the public

vi

CONTRIBUTORS

Henry Bauer works at the Virginia Polytechnic Institute and State University in the USA, where he is Professor of Chemistry and Science Studies. He has published extensively on philosophical and sociological aspects of science and technology, including the relationship between science and pseudo-science, and is the author of *Scientific Literacy and the Myth of the Scientific Method*.

Guy Claxton is Visiting Professor of Psychology and Education at the University of Bristol. Between 1974 and 1990 he lectured on the psychology of education at the University of London. His books include *Educating the Enquiring Mind: Challenges for School Science* and *Liberating the Learner: Lessons for Professional Development in Education*.

Tam Dalyell has been the Labour MP for West Lothian (now Linlithgow) since 1962. He has a particular interest in the House of Commons in political issues related to science and technology and since 1967 has been a weekly columnist for the UK science magazine *New Scientist*, a platform he uses very effectively to raise concerns on a range of environmental issues of the day.

Graham Farmelo is Head of Exhibitions at the Science Museum, London, with special responsibility for the content of the forthcoming Wellcome Wing, to open in 2000. He joined the museum in 1990 from the Open University, where he was appointed Lecturer in Physics in 1977. He is also Adjunct Professor of Physics at Northeastern University, Boston, USA.

Peter Fensham is Emeritus Professor of Science Education at Monash University. His appointment by Monash in 1967, after ten years teaching chemistry at Melbourne University, was the first to such a Chair in Australia. He has been involved in research and curriculum policy in science and environmental education in Australia and world-wide.

Richard Gregory is Emeritus Professor of Neuropsychology at the University of Bristol, where he moved in 1970. Founder of the Exploratory Science

Centre in Bristol, he is now working on establishing a Science Centre focused on astronomy at Herstmonceux Castle in East Sussex. He is a CBE and FRS and his publications include *Eye and Brain*, *The Intelligent Mind* and *The Oxford Companion to the Mind*.

Edgar Jenkins taught chemistry and biology in secondary schools before moving to the University of Leeds, where he is currently Professor of Science Education Policy in the School of Education. He is editor of *Studies in Science Education* and has published extensively on science education. His most recent books include *Investigations by Order?*, a study of the teaching of scientific investigation within the national curriculum of England and Wales.

Les Levidow is a Research fellow at the Open University, where he has been studying the safety regulation of agricultural biotechnology since 1989. He has been managing editor of *Science as Culture* since its inception in 1987 and is co-editor of several books, including *Science, Technology and the Labour Process* and *Anti-Racist Science Teaching*.

Ralph Levinson taught science at secondary schools in London before joinging the Open University as a lecturer in science education. He was editor of *Teaching Science* and has written widely on science and science education. Some of his books for children have won national awards and formed the basis of TV programmes.

Mary Midgley was formerly Senior Lecturer in Philosophy at the University of Newcastle on Tyne. Originally a moral philosopher, she later became interested in problems about the relation between humans and the rest of the cosmos. Her books include *Beast and Man*, *Animals and Why they Matter*, *Science as Salvation*, *The Ethical Primate* and *Utopias, Dolphins and Computers*.

Robin Millar is a Professor in the Department of Educational Studies at the University of York. He moved to York in 1982, after teaching physics and general science in comprehensive schools for eight years; he is currently involved in the initial and in-service training of secondary science teachers. His publications include, *Doing Science* and with Rosalind Driver, John Leech and Phil Scott, *Young People's Images of Science*.

Susan Pringle is Staff Tutor in Physical Sciences at the University of Bristol. She organizes events which take science to the public, from popular and innovative science courses to exhibitions of the university's research. Sue Pringle lectures on the beauty, subtlety and creativity of chemistry.

Hilary Rose is Professor Emerita of Social Policy at the University of Bradford. She has just returned to the UK after spending the last academic year at the University of Gothenberg as guest professor in Feminist Studies and Science Theory. Her most recent book is *Love Power and Knowledge: Towards a Feminist Transformation of the Sciences*. She is currently working on a gender analysis of EU research policy and on the Human Genome.

Joan Solomon graduated in physics at Cambridge University and taught physics, STS and science in secondary schools for many years. She obtained her doctorate while teaching and has written many books and research articles on subjects as diverse as students' perceptions of science, primary technology and cross-European studies. She is now Lecturer in Research at Oxford University's Department of Educational Studies.

Jeff Thomas joined the Open University in 1970, contributing first to a wide range of biology courses. He then helped establish the Centre for Science Education at the OU, which he now heads. His research and teaching interests relate to the science curriculum within higher education and especially the communication of controversial aspects of science. He was co-editor of *Challenges and Opportunities for Science Education* and co-authored *The Sciences Good Study Guide*.

Lewis Wolpert is Professor of Biology as Applied to Medicine in University College, London where he researches on embryological development. He was elected Fellow of the Royal Society in 1980 and awarded a CBE in 1990. He has written and broadcast extensively; he is currently chairman of COPUS, the Committee on the Public Understanding of Science.

FOREWORD

A century ago it would have been inconceivable to publish a book called *Science Today: Problem or Crisis?*. A the end of the nineteenth century, the newly industrialized world regarded science as an unalloyed blessing. If people perceived problems or crises, these were mostly to do with the scarcity of science. By 1950, science had moved to centre-stage industrially, economically, and socially; and for a brief period, it really seemed as if scientifically speaking almost anything was possible. Before long, however, new sorts of problems – problems not of scarcity, but of abundance – began to emerge. In the 'ban-the-bomb' movement of the late fifties and sixties, the student movement of the late sixties and seventies and the environmental movement of the seventies and eighties critical voices were raised about the place of science in the wider society; and today, after a century of extraordinary scientific progress, it is paradoxically true to say that science itself has become problematic.

Science Today addresses some of the key issues that we face at the end of the twentieth century as we confront both the obvious power and the obvious limitations of science. Many of these issues lie at the interface between science and the public, and they have to do not merely with the technical but also with the philosophical, moral, social and political import of scientific research. The movement for the public understanding of science has taken up the cause of closing the gap between scientists and so-called lay people; and in doing so, it has challenged teachers and educationalists to reassess the role of science education in relation to wider cultural concerns about science and technology. There are no easy answers here, and readers of this book will find no pat solutions. Rather, they will enounter contrasting and even conflicting interpretations of the way in which science should be dealt with in the processes of formal and informal education. If, as one of the authors suggests, we are living through a series of 'science wars', then *Science Today* is an informative and frequently provocative guide to some of the key areas of conflict. By avoiding some of the more arcane academic disputes and concentrating instead on the practical arena of teaching and learning, it offers some hope of a way forward in our understanding of the proper place of science in our culture.

John Durant
Assistant Director (Head of Science Communication)
The Science Museum and
Professor of Public Understanding of Science
Imperial College
London

SCIENCE, PEOPLE AND SCHOOLS

An intrinsic conflict?

Ralph Levinson and Jeff Thomas

I know all about elements, compounds and mixtures and that atoms
have little circles and dots and how to use a Bunsen burner but I don't
know what that has to do with anything.

(15-year-old schoolgirl)

One of the major purposes of education, wrote the great critic, Raymond
Williams (1961), is 'that of training the members of a group to the "social
character" ... by which the group lives'. At a general level, being
socialized is an involvement in the problems and struggles of one's fellow
human beings. If this is true of schools then, at the very least, school science
should be preparing students for the scientific issues that occur in their
lives. Few students at school today would recognize the science curriculum as preparing them to make decisions about such things as local
sources of pollution or the ethical questions raised by modern genetics. A
formal education in science leaves a small proportion of students with a
sense of wonder and a wish to pursue the academic subject further in
higher education. Others use it as a route to a variety of careers such as
medicine, engineering and hairdressing. But the majority, like the schoolgirl and her atoms, are left with faint memories of meaningless symbols.

There are numerous critiques of the school science curriculum and, since
the mid-1980s, of the expanding area of the public understanding of
science, but there has been little discussion about the interrelationship
between the curriculum and public understanding. It is this relationship
between the formal science curriculum and people's lives – learning
science as a socializing experience – that is at the core of this book.

Our aim is to ask new questions about science for all, for 5-year-olds and
75-year-olds. We all, however, face a dilemma because it is no easy matter
to bridge the gap between formal science learning and our actions as social
beings in a rapidly changing and uncertain world. Indeed, as we shall see
in the book, it is a thoroughly complex and deeply political task to
construct a formal curriculum that can address the small and large
scientific questions of our lives. This book is directed at people with an

1

interest in the role of education in general, as well as educators and practitioners within the world of science.

Here we describe some of the themes and ideas of the collection of original contributions in the book. Our belief is that a concern about science education raises very broad issues that take the reader far beyond the details of the school curriculum. We consider some of these ideas in what follows, touching on the common elements that run through the different parts of the book; each part also includes a brief introduction to guide the reader.

The Royal Society report (Bodmer 1985) recognized the potential of science education to influence public understanding. 'Public understanding of science has as its base the teaching of science in schools' (Section 1.2). It went on to give its rationale: 'better public understanding of science can be a major element in promoting national prosperity, in raising the quality of public and private decision-making and in enriching the life of the individual' (2.1). As Peter Fensham points out in Chapter 9, better public understanding of science – science for all – has been the aim of a number of countries. While this aim has been expressed through their science curricula, Fensham explains why it has not been realized so far. He goes on, however, to identify some promising leads. In a far-ranging discussion Edgar Jenkins (Chapter 10) teases out the issues and raises the question: 'What is science education for?' His analysis critically examines the prevalent notions of science in education as objective and unproblematic against reworking knowledge – knowledge-in-action – in the contexts of people's lives.

It is worth comparing Jenkins' analysis of knowledge-in-action with an article in the journal *Science and Public Affairs*, where Professor John Postgate (1995) proposes the view of science as a 'cultural experience'. Postgate argues that the sensational presentation of science in the media has not helped people to understand what science is really about – a way of thinking which 'enhances lives, and awareness, and even morality'. The media, according to Postgate, underestimate the viewer's intelligence and natural curiosity. There is nothing exceptionable in what Postgate is advocating but he perceives the understanding of science as a top-down approach – enlightenment delivered from the cognoscenti to the untutored, albeit an intelligent and curious untutored. He says:

> We have to face up to it that, in Britain . . . two generations have emerged into adulthood with little or no exposure to science . . . .
> In consequence the scientifically ignorant component of British society comprises not just the 'broad masses', to slip into old-fashioned politico-speak; it also includes the great majority of writers, journalists, broadcasters, clerics, politicians and administrators; even academics and teachers from the humanities. It encompasses the

great majority of the people who make decisions, who educate children, who set trends and influence opinion. They have little idea of what science is or how it works; indeed most have little serious wish to know: the gulf between C.P. Snow's two cultures has never been wider. The long term solution, of course, is to educate the next generation to at least a minimum knowledge of science. This means educating the educators, too, as the planners of the National Curriculum have discovered. At least that task is in hand, and even elementary knowledge will bring about greater understanding of science and less fear of it. But in the shorter term we have to deal with this huge mass of adult ignoramuses who run our society. How? They are not fools, there is simply a gap in their knowledge. I see no way of bringing a clearer understanding of science to our sadly under-educated public than to present science as a cultural experience.

(Postgate 1995)

Within his provocative analysis Postgate draws a vivid picture of the relationship of science and the scientist to society, the knowledge gap, the role of the media, and ideas of science as culture – themes which are reflected and contrasted in very different ways through the essays in this book.

Science as a cultural tool is the subject of Joan Solomon's Chapter 11. The 'culture' is not that of high science but relates to what is significant in people's lives. In the context of this chapter, looking at the differing notions of scientific culture across Europe, Solomon brings out her own significant pointers towards a more all-inclusive science education. Jeff Thomas (Chapter 12) challenges the meaning of the knowledge deficit model illustrated by the Postgate school of thought. But will greater understanding of science encourage a more positive response towards science as the Royal Society report hoped? Thomas questions what is meant by greater understanding. He provides evidence that becoming more informed about certain scientific issues does not necessarily bring about more positive attitudes; it is just as likely to go hand in hand with a more definite holding of pre-existing views.

What all these contributors do – Fensham, Jenkins, Solomon and Thomas – is to reformulate the problem, to question the old chestnut of delivering science to an ignorant and undifferentiated public. As a result their analysis is fresh, though the solutions they propose are challenging.

So what kind of education would enable these solutions to come about? Tam Dalyell (Chapter 5), who has pursued government policy-makers with scientific questions for many years, warns against expecting anybody other than experts to make decisions about technically complex matters. Given that the issues of the future may not even be anticipated and will involve complex science, Robin Millar addresses this intellectual conundrum in Chapter 7. He formulates ideas for students to gain active insight into technically difficult problems and to understand the issues raised by the media. In a similar vein in Chapter 6, Guy Claxton looks towards the year 2020 – when all the young people today have learned science at school – and argues for appropriate attitudes and experiences in science. His conclusions unsettle the status quo but his logic is compelling.

Some scientists and educators advocate the teaching of science as a politically neutral act. Biotechnology, a development of the late twentieth century with huge research and development input, has strong connections with the science of genetics. Les Levidow points out in Chapter 8 that teaching about contemporary technologies can fall into the trap of supporting politically expedient and commercially profitable solutions in the guise of the public good. A reductionist approach to science, argues Levidow, makes genuine democratic participation difficult because it conceals the values that underlie the problems to be solved.

In contrast, Lewis Wolpert (Chapter 1) makes no apologies for separating the practice of science from the morality of its application. A distinguished scientist and an outstanding communicator, Wolpert applauds the explanatory power of science. 'Science', he writes in his opening sentence, 'is the best way to understand the world'. He elucidates what holds all scientific thinking together and is cautious about how much the lay public can be expected to understand. Chapters 2, 3 and 4 pick up a number of points from Wolpert's opening salvo, including his arguments about the neutrality of science and its unique nature. If it is desirable for the public to understand more about science then we need to understand a little about what science is, and this is the purpose of the first part of the book. Henry Bauer, Mary Midgley and Hilary Rose each discuss the multifaceted nature of science. There are a variety of types of science nestling under the label Science, argues Bauer. He describes the very different practices that take place in the disciplines of science. Explaining how science is held together by the diverse roles of its practitioners, he outlines what everyone should know about the way science works.

Mary Midgley explains how contemporary science came to be characterized by a particular philosophical approach whereas it is a confluence of many intellectual streams. She persuasively argues, on the one hand, against placing science on a level above all else and, on the other, against those, such as Bryan Appleyard, who warn of science as threatening our sense of place in the world.

Science has had an ambivalent press in the latter half of the twentieth century: Frankenstein and Einstein merge and separate, separate and merge. Not surprisingly the scientific community has responded defensively. Within academe, the relationship between scientists and sociologists of science has at best been uneasy and, at worst, tempestuous. Hilary Rose contends that this polarization – those who see science as discovering the reality of nature against the relativism of those who dispute the unique status of science's claims, who may even perceive science as a kind of myth – is unproductive. She occupies distinct ground and looks for new alliances, less confrontational ways of thinking, within and without the scientific community.

So far, the contributions straddle the interface between the formal education system and the way people come to terms with science in our modern society dominated by technology and change. It is vital to explore this relationship. But people learn about science from many informal sources such as newspapers, books, radio, television, idle and purposive talk, museums and science centres. These do, after all, provide the background for the scientific issues that influence us. It is the media where we learn about the global questions such as acid rain, the problems of deforestation, the dwindling ozone layer, cures for ravaging diseases, the unknown effects of synthetic chemicals in the food chain and the perceived threat of biotechnology. Graham Farmelo (Chapter 13) provides a critical overview of these informal sources. Scientists are more and more active with their message and Sue Pringle (Chapter 15) reports on the scientists' responses when engaging with the public. Finally, one arena where science arouses huge interest and excitement is a relatively recent phenomenon – the exploratory. Richard Gregory (Chapter 14), the originator of the Bristol Exploratory and the moving force behind exploratories in Britain, describes their rationale and critically assesses how they can complement the formal role of schools.

The contributors present their ideas from different perspectives and occasionally take opposed views. Our stance is not to attack science or science education but to ask hard questions about something that is so important. The thinking in the book must withstand critical debate. The aim of the book is not consensus, rather it is an attempt to find a framework to solve new problems. We would like to thank the contributors for addressing the questions so energetically. The debate they stimulated should be seen in the context of science as a 'fascinating endeavour, capable of engaging men and women at their best, and enlarging, and enriching the human spirit with its discoveries' (Ziman 1984).

Part I

VIEWS AND CONFLICTS

INTRODUCTION

The first four contributions consist of diverse opinions about key aspects of science.

Lewis Wolpert describes what he sees as the defining features of science, but avoids a definition of its true nature. He points out that there are a variety of ways in which science is pursued but science knowledge has to be consistent across discipline boundaries.

Henry Bauer urges us to recognize the complexity of science. He argues that the different disciplines within science are of deep, tribal significance and culturally determined. Their existence means that generalizations are fraught with difficulty; there are limitless opportunities for confusion and alarm. What is so difficult to define has become such a rich area for dispute.

Mary Midgley and Hilary Rose both expand on the prevalent conflicts within and around science. From a philosophical perspective Mary Midgley notes diverse influences to which science has historically been subject. This provides a basis for her refutation of those who attempt to demonize science as a damaging monolithic force. As a feminist, Hilary Rose examines the conflict between sociologists and scientists, highlighting the sterility of the old arguments. She proposes new alliances for a more socially responsible concept of science.

These chapters pinpoint the contemporary meaning of science in ways that allow the educational implications to be considered later in the book.

1

IN PRAISE OF SCIENCE

Lewis Wolpert

Science is the best way to understand the world. By understand, I mean gain insight into the way all nature works in a causal and mechanistic sense. Science is the only way to understand motions in the heavens, the tides, the movement of terrestrial bodies, the chemical constituents of matter and the nature and evolution of living organisms. There is no other way to understand such objects and processes. That we remain ignorant about many aspects of human behaviour is not a failure of science but a reflection of human complexity. What science cannot do, as Tolstoy pointed out, is to tell us how to live, what is good or bad. It has nothing to contribute to moral and ethical issues; these can, however, arise in relation to the application of scientific ideas. In principle, if we understood more about how society works, it could help us design a just society once we made clear the ethical and moral principles that we want.

But what do I mean by science? I cannot be trapped or forced into a definition any more than I would be willing to define 'life'. Indeed science is in some sense as complex as 'life'. But it is not at all difficult to give some of its characteristics. It attempts to explain natural phenomena in terms of the underlying causes in as economical way as possible – preferably using mathematics. The ideas have to be self-consistent and correspond with reality. They must be tested. It is nice, but not essential, if the theories make predictions – but sciences with a large historical content like geology and evolutionary theory do extremely well. The self-consistency also implies that one branch of science must be consistent with all the others; biological theories cannot contradict chemistry.

In claiming, as I will, that science is a special form of knowledge, I fully realize that scholarly pursuits in the humanities, like history, resemble science, but the differences lie both in the subject matter and the techniques. Not only is history overwhelmingly more complicated, but also it is not subject to experimentation nor can it be easily linked to other sciences like psychology. Also unlike the humanities, ideas in science are value-free. Archimedes' law of floating bodies is simply true. A surprising

9

aspect of science is that almost every important idea can be expressed in fewer than thirty words; how unlike the arts!

This all seems so simple and straightforward, yet attitudes towards science show both ambivalence and polarization. While there is much interest and admiration for science, there is also some fear and hostility. Science is perceived as materialist and dehumanizing, arrogant and dangerous. Reductionism is suspect and uncomfortable, sabotaging all the mystery and wonder of life. This was a theme taken up by D. H. Lawrence in the early twentieth century:

> The Universe is dead for us, and how is it to come alive again? 'Knowledge' has killed the sun, making it a ball of gas with spots; 'knowledge' has killed the moon – it is a dead little earth fretted with extinct craters as with smallpox. . . . The world of reason and science . . . this is the dry and sterile world the abstracted mind inhabits.

Others see its practitioners as a band of cold, competitive and unfeeling technicians wielding power without responsibility. The threats of nuclear war and the genetic manipulation of embryos loom large. Science is also blamed for polluting the environment. On the other hand there is hope, even expectation, that science can provide the solution to our many problems: the cure for cancer and other illnesses, cheap and environmentally friendly nuclear power. There also is considerable enthusiasm for popular science books and programmes which reveal the mysteries of the origin and workings of the universe – including the origins of human beings like ourselves. Science is intellectually exciting.

MISCONCEPTIONS AND COMMON SENSE

There are numerous misconceptions about science that range from thinking that there is some unique scientific method to conflating it with technology; misconceptions which include the idea that it is mainly about the accumulation of facts, uncreative, yet highly competitive. There is even a school of sociologists of science that argue that science is little more than another set of socially constructed myths with no particular validity. For example, in their book *The Golem*, Collins and Pinch (1993) state that scientific disputes are not settled by further experiments but by social negotiations. Collins has even written that the real world has played little role in the development of scientific ideas. These relativists wish to deny the superiority of science in providing understanding. Such views are essentially anti-science and it is a matter of great concern that their views are presented uncritically in so-called science study courses

There is also the illusion that because scientists, in principle, must be willing to accept that fondly held views must be abandoned in the face of new evidence, that all scientific theories are no more than transitory. This fails to recognize that the vast core of scientific knowledge is sound – I can assert with confidence that almost all of chemistry is correct since it has been so well validated by innumerable experiments and syntheses. This is in no way to deny the possibility that at the frontiers of science ideas and convictions are in a state of flux. It is also widely believed that quantum mechanics somehow undermines causality and makes prediction impossible – Heisenberg calling his law the Uncertainty Principle has much to answer for. To the contrary, quantum mechanics makes some of the most accurate predictions in all of science.

Why are there these misconceptions? They have their origin, in part, in the special nature of scientific knowledge. They arise because of science's unnatural nature: neither the ideas nor procedures of science fit with common sense and they almost always go against everyday experience. Science is unnatural because the world just happens to be built in a way that does not fit with common sense, that is with our everyday expectations. I would go so far as to say that if an idea fits with common sense then scientifically it will almost certainly be wrong. And by common sense I am referring to our natural expectations derived from everyday experience. It is how we assess the world we live in on a day-to-day basis. Common sense is complex but is characterized by its naturalness – it is the matter-of-fact apprehension of reality. Thus common sense can never lead to, for example, Newton's laws of motion. While common sense changes with time and is influenced by the particular culture, as far as science is concerned it remains rather similar.

So, science all too often explains the familiar in terms of the unfamiliar. Some examples should help to make this clear.

To any sensible person, it is common sense that the sun goes around the earth, but most of us accept that it is the other way round; yet we accept this more by authority than reasoned conviction or a proper understanding. How many of us could justify the view that the earth is moving around the sun? Again we all believe that the moon causes the tides but the correct explanation is rather more complex. How does one explain that there is a high tide on that side of the earth furthest away from the moon?

Despite our experience of moving objects since birth and Newton's discovery of the laws of motion several hundred years ago, we still do rather badly with quite simple problems. Imagine that you are in a flat field with a gun and two bullets. If one bullet is fired horizontally at exactly the same time as the other is simply dropped, which bullet hits the ground first? Surprisingly they hit the ground at exactly the same time. The rate at which an object falls is independent of its horizontal motion. Unless of course it is shaped like an aircraft wing. One could say that in the case of moving objects, science, through the genius of Newton and Galileo, came to explain the familiar in terms of the unfamiliar. Newton's first law, that

11

the natural state of any object is uniform motion in a straight line, hardly fits with everyday experience

No matter where one looks in science, its ideas confound common sense. It is not even easy to think of how ice cools one's drink in the correct way – cold does not flow from the ice to the liquid. I still remain surprised and a little incredulous when I realize that there are more molecules in a glass of water than glasses of water in all the oceans. And things get much worse when one has to deal with more difficult aspects of physics, chemistry and biology. In the world of subatomic particles, quantum mechanics, black holes and the big bang, everyday analogies completely break down. Part of the problem is that the language of science is mathematics which can be very alienating. Even evolution confounds common sense for many people and rightly so. It requires a special thinking to come to the conclusion that all life has a common origin and that not only are we descended from ape-like creatures but also our more distant forebears were squashy, simple organisms with no resemblance to us. All multi-cellular evolution results from the changes in the DNA which results in changes in the behaviour of the cells in the developing embryo.

Thus at least a part of the antipathy to science probably stems from the difficulties that non-scientists have in understanding science, and this may account for the view held by the humanities, as Max Perutz points out, that they are the carriers of civilization, whereas scientists and engineers are merely the plumbers. There is a certain irony in such a view, for the great triumph of our age, our great intellectual success, is that achieved by science. Even so I am struck by the amount of mysticism and belief in 'supernatural' forces: it is almost as if some people prefer mystery and ignorance to understanding.

Common-sense thinking on its own does not lead to science. One cannot arrive at a scientific understanding of the world by the thinking that characterizes our everyday activities. Doing science requires a special self-awareness and it is often necessary to actually resist common sense since an unfamiliar quantitative rigour is required. There is good evidence that the scientific mode of thought is neither natural nor comfortable. Experimental work by psychologists shows that people rely on a limited number of principles which reduce the complex task of assessing probabilities to simpler judgemental operations. In a very simple example, people expect that a sequence of random events such as tossing a coin is more likely to yield H-T-H-T-H-T than H-H-H-H-H-H, which is, in fact, not the case. The studies show that thinking about probabilities is not only difficult for many people, but also, if the mathematics is a bit complicated, an alienating activity. As Bertrand Russell pointed out, when it comes to assigning causes to events, 'popular induction depends on the emotional interest of the instances, not upon their number'. Science demands that one does deal with dry, statistical data, abandon basic beliefs, and perhaps accept that there is no simple linear cause.

There is, alas, no formula for doing science, no prescriptive scientific method. Philosophers of science have been singularly unsuccessful in finding any formula for the scientific method. The ideas of Karl Popper relating to falsification are greatly overrated, for not only do they not fit with how scientists actually work but also they completely ignore discovery. Indeed, as Peter Medawar (1974) pointed out, scientists get along very well without any philosophy or method. Understanding consistency, and correspondence with the real world is all that matters. Beauty, elegance and simplicity are welcome bonuses.

VARIETY AND DISCOVERY

It is important to realize that there are many different styles of science and scientific research, which is a rich and complex process. Doing physics can be very different from doing biology. Mathematics is not like anatomy. Experimentalists are different from theorists. While I like experimental work, I do not like, and am rather bad at, doing the experiments themselves – I am much better at designing them and analysing the results. I also enjoy it much more. In some ways doing experiments is like gardening. There are those with green fingers for whom everything works; for others, like me, it is best if you do not work too near them. Experimental work can be either the glamorous or dangerously uncontrolled activity many people imagine. It can also be laborious and time-consuming. The ratio of results to effort can be frighteningly small. It usually takes hundreds or thousands of tedious hours of work to obtain a result that can be described in a few minutes. So much of the time is spent in preparation and in waiting.

Experiments in molecular genetics require following something like a very long recipe over several weeks; it is a bit like high-class cooking rather than gardening. They require mixing solutions, pipetting solutions, centrifuging mixtures, spotting them out on gels, and in between each activity, waiting. Each step must be done in a particular time so life is determined by the clock. Then, at last, you develop a photographic plate and there, perhaps, are the results. That is if something has not gone wrong. If it has, then all that time has been wasted. You have to become a kind of car mechanic, trying to find out where the fault lies. Every step should have been recorded in a laboratory notebook and, you hope, the clue will lie there. It may turn out that everything else was right, but the developer was 'off' and that ruined everything at the last step.

I am always struck by the ease with which paranormal phenomena such as levitation and psycho-kinesis are accepted compared with the difficulty of establishing even a very simple piece of knowledge in my own field. Whereas my tiny bit of information takes many man-years, levitation, even though it invokes unmeasured forces and challenges the basis of physics, can be established and apparently accepted in man-seconds. Pseudo-science seems to me a way of getting knowledge on the cheap. The rigorous, painstaking, repetitive means by which conventional scientific knowledge has to be gained is one of the defining characteristics of science.

It may be helpful to give a couple of examples of discoveries in biology to show different styles of research and the relation between theory and experiment. In 1960 Denis Burkitt gave a talk in which he described a tumour, now known as Burkitt's lymphoma, which was the commonest children's tumour in tropical Africa. Anthony Epstein, a virologist present at Burkitt's lecture, concluded that the cause had to be a virus, even though the evidence that cancer could be caused by viruses was at that time regarded with deep suspicion and the possibility that human tumours could have a viral origin was regarded as almost absurd.

From that moment, Epstein dropped everything else and started working on the tumour. 'Slogging' would be a better description. Material from tumours was flown in from Africa, and he and his group used all the standard procedures for isolation of viruses. All of them failed. Failure continued for almost two years; but, although all the laboratory evidence was against the idea that the tumour was caused by a virus, they persisted. 'But it had to be right. It just had the feel of being right. And that's why one carried on.' Then one wintry Friday afternoon a sample arrived from Africa which was cloudy and looked contaminated with bacteria. But Epstein examined it under the microscope and saw that it was cloudy because the tumour had broken up into huge numbers of single cells. Immediately he was reminded of an American group who grew tumours not as lumps, as he had been trying, but by breaking the tumour up into single cells. So he tried to grow the tumour as single cells, and this worked. This was the breakthrough, and soon after he identified a virus growing in the cells – the Epstein-Barr virus had been discovered.

Another example comes from the discovery of messenger RNA in the 1950s. Messenger RNA carries the information for making proteins, from the DNA to a cellular structure, the ribosome, where the protein is synthesized. At that stage everyone was confusing messenger RNA with another RNA which is a component of ribosomes. It required extensive knowledge and imagination to postulate that it existed in order to account for numerous confusing results. Sydney Brenner and François Jacob then did experiments trying to prove its existence. Nothing worked until Brenner realized that they were not adding enough magnesium to their solutions. He had to draw on his wide knowledge and combine it with his experimental skills.

Does luck or serendipity play any kind of role? Often these are invoked almost as a way of minimizing scientific brilliance – it was just the wind blowing in the penicillin mould which gave Fleming his crucial cultures.

14

But would anybody else have recognized the significance of the clear areas on the dish? When Pasteur was told that he had been lucky in his research, he replied 'Fortune favours the prepared mind'. I am always struck by how the good scientists have the greatest share of luck.

The advice from famous scientists on how to be successful again illustrates variety: try many things, do what makes your heart leap, think big, challenge expectations, *cherchez le Paradox*, be sloppy so that something unexpected happens, but not so sloppy that you cannot tell what happened, seek simplicity, seek beauty, never try to solve a problem until you can guess the answer – and so on: perhaps one should try them all. For science is after all a mixture of creative thought and very hard work, much of it tedious. When Newton was asked how he came up with his ideas on gravity his reply was 'By thinking on it continually'. Probably one of the most important abilities is the ability to formulate the problem as in Peter Medawar's famous aphorism – 'Science is the Art of the Soluble'.

The scientific paper presents scientists and science in a misleading way. As Medawar said, the scientific paper is a kind of fraud. The neat format with its 'Introduction' followed by 'Methods', then 'Results' and finally 'Discussion' bears no relation to the way scientists actually work. While the final results must stand up to cold and objective scrutiny, the process of achieving them rarely takes the form of a calm and logical progression suggested by the telling. Purging events of all human emotion, the formal impersonal style totally fails to indicate who actually did what and why. If the effort was a collaborative one, a whole team of widely differing individuals condenses into a faceless, characterless, Delphic oracle of science. The technicians disappear completely. So do imagination and chance, confusion and failure, and the vital conversations in the coffee room and thoughts in the bath. It is, perhaps, hardly surprising that scientists are felt to lack a certain human touch. The illusion that there is such a thing as scientific method has also helped to reinforce this view. There is thus always a sense of surprise and indeed disillusion when scientists disagree. This reflects a failure to realize that at the frontiers of science there are always disagreements. Scientific progress can be difficult and it is essential that there are vigorous debates until the issues get cleared up. There are often at the frontiers different possible interpretations of the same data and even doubts about the reliability of experiments.

Science is very much a social activity. In fact, the individual merely contributes to the collective knowledge, any contribution being assimilated. This social process makes it self-correcting, errors being weeded out. Moreover the individual contribution is in the long run irrelevant, for given a large enough community of scientists, sooner or later, progress will reveal all. If there had been no Watson and Crick then we know that the discovery of the structure of DNA would have soon been made by others. If there had been no Einstein then X or Q would have arrived at relativity. So, quite unlike the artist, your contribution will eventually be made by someone else, and this is not true of *Hamlet* or *The Waste Land*.

You are always conscious of working within a world-wide community. The research papers that you submit to a journal may be refereed by scientists from anywhere in the world. You know personally, or have at least met, a large fraction of your peers. Collaboration is very widespread as one shares expertise. Our own small group, which works on pattern formation in limb development, collaborates with friends in Germany, France, Japan, USA, and of course the UK. But you are also competing, for unlike the arts, a discovery can be made only once. However it is quite often the case that there is simultaneous discovery and then the honours should be shared. There is no point competing if the others are way ahead and it is necessary to know where they are up to in order to help your own research. That is one important reason for going to meetings. This also enables you to meet those in your field and so you learn on whom you can rely.

Much of our scientific life is like that of others outside science. Thus being a scientist is partly about survival, both in the laboratory and within the larger group. Life is great fun if everyone gets on and the work is going well, but awful if there are tensions or your work is going badly, especially if that of your colleagues is going marvellously. As Confucius is claimed to have said, there is no greater pleasure than seeing your best friend fall off the roof. Nevertheless one can have enormous pleasure from learning of a new discovery.

The ecology of laboratory life is highly complex. Conditions are often crowded, equipment has to be shared. Close friendships develop; romances too. Sex is common among the test-tubes. There is no simple way that I know to deal with people who do not get on, or get on too well, and this can be very disruptive to life in the laboratory. Even more destructive for the young scientist is friction with the supervisor. One's early training is essentially an apprenticeship; learning not just techniques but also modes of thought. If the relationship is good, one can identify with particular qualities and acquire a particular style. If the relationship is not so good, a young research worker's whole future may be at stake.

Mark Ptashne of Harvard has spoken of the psychic courage to undertake certain lines of research. Youth certainly helps; so does the support of one's colleagues. But even this cannot always be relied upon. Some survival strategies are common. There is a curious and distinctive brand of laboratory humour which softens and helps one cope with criticism. Murphy's Law is highly respected: if anything can go wrong it will, and usually at the most unexpected stage. Certainly people in laboratories laugh a lot. But most scientists also have to find their own ways of dealing with the demands of this way of life. The thrill of success is rare – the main sensation is that of failure and frustration. It requires a certain spiritual fortitude, quite often, simply to keep going. Many or most of your ideas turn out to be wrong, and months of experimental work can be fruitless. Focus is essential but you hesitate to commit yourself to a programme which, if it fails, yields after months of effort nothing, and leaves you no further than you were before. One needs to have a passion for science.

My first paper in biology was a disaster. I had been working at a marine station in Millport in Scotland on cell division in the sea urchin embryo, and had published in the prestigious journal *Nature* that a substance known as ATP blocked division. This had exciting implications and the next summer I went to a marine station in Sweden to continue the work. To my horror, I could not repeat the experiments. I soon found that I had not, in the original series, carefully enough controlled the activity of the ATP. The result was an artefact I had created myself. I had to publish a retraction and recover from quite a deep depression.

The survival of one's ideas can be very important to a scientist. One nurtures them almost as if they were one's children. No wonder then we scientists can be so resistant to those new experiments or competing ones that will displace our loved ones. The evidence has to be very persuasive to give a hard-earned framework developed over many years. No wonder that it has been suggested that scientists do not give up on their false ideas, their generation simply dies.

My best piece of work also had for such reasons a somewhat depressing immediate sequel. In the spring of 1968 I presented my new ideas on pattern formation in embryonic development at a small meeting in the glorious Villa Serbelloni on the shore of Lake Como. I had been motivated by the conviction – largely an aesthetic one – that there must be general mechanisms for translating genetic information into cellular patterns during development of the embryo. The theory suddenly made sense of an enormous number of different embryological results and I was very excited. The ideas were quite well received at the meeting and some of those there immediately took up the idea and themselves produced novel and testable models. That summer I was in the Wood's Hole Laboratory in the USA and gave one of the very well attended Friday evening lectures.

My ideas were met with silence and at the reception afterwards I was introduced to a leading American embryologist who at once turned his back on me. Next day no one said a word about the lecture. I asked one of my American friends what was going on. 'Well, Lewis, they're all saying, "who in the hell do you think you are?"' It was only Sydney Brenner who was encouraging and helped me through a very dark summer. One has to realize that people do not like being told that they have been thinking about a problem in the wrong way. One also has to face the fact that scientists do not always behave well. There are many examples where new ideas were met with hostility but it is very important to understand that eventually the correct ideas will prevail. In my own case, the ideas I put forward have been widely adopted.

SOCIAL RESPONSIBILITIES

That scientific advance may lead to good or evil ends is undeniable, but the roots of the present anti-science feeling are more tangled than this. In part they simply reflect the ideas of forbidden knowledge and retribution which are deeply embedded in our culture. But even more important is the confusion between science and technology. Science is about understanding, while technology leads to something being made, sometimes based on science. Mary Shelley's Dr Frankenstein is the epitome of the scientist unleashing forces he cannot control, and so powerful is the image that it has become part of twentieth-century popular culture, shorthand and emblem of the dangers of science. These images come not from scientists but from poets and writers. It was Mary Shelley who created the monster, not science.

Science is not the same as technology. While the final product of science is an idea or information, that of technology is a product, something that is used. While much of modern technology is based on science, this link is of recent origin since science had virtually no impact on technology until the eighteenth century. Technology includes the ancient arts of agriculture and metal-making and science made no contribution to those skills. Agriculture was already established in 7000 BC and relied on experience and not on any understanding rather as it does in some remote areas today. It is possible to have very complex technology without any understanding at all. This applies to the great Renaissance buildings and the machines and engines of the Industrial Revolution. The steam engine owed almost nothing to science – it probably could have been built by the Greeks. Quite a lot of technology can be based on trial and error – an example is our own bodies. These are marvellous machines yet evolution knows no science and proceeds only by selecting variants that arise by chance. The great cathedrals were built by engineers who based their construction on effectively trial and error. They may have made use of the 5-minute theorem – when a structure was built and the supports removed, if it remained standing for 5 minutes then it was assumed that it would stand forever.

The relationship between science and technology is not symmetrical since technology had an enormous impact on science which could not have advanced without it. And since science had no real use it is something of a puzzle as to why it should have prospered or have even been invented. Perhaps, like music and drama, it gave intellectual and emotional pleasure.

It is a wonderful feeling to understand how nature works. Humans needed technology but not science. For science we must thank the Greeks.

It is part of the special nature of science that unlike either technology or religion it had a single origin. This is a somewhat controversial view but I believe it is one that can be justified. All science as we know it had its beginnings in Greece. No other society independently developed a scientific mode of thought. The honour of being the first scientist goes to Thales of Miletos, who in about 600 BC took for the first time a detached view of the world and tried to understand it. He wondered what the world might be made of. His answer, which went against common sense, was that it was made of water in various forms. It was a curiosity about nature that was not linked to human needs. This was an attempt to find a unifying principle in nature that could be subject to critical discussion. Moreover it was a personal view. That is, Thales was expressing his own views about nature and not ones held by the society that he lived in. This is the first time in recorded history that an individual had taken such a bold step

The reader may be surprised by my failure to refer to Chinese science about which Needham has written so much (see e.g. Needham 1986). But the Chinese, while brilliant engineers, made a minimal contribution to science. Theirs was essentially a mystical view of the world. Albert Einstein, on receiving a letter from a correspondent asking why it was that science arose only once and in Greece, and then persisted only in the west, replied

> Dear Sir, The development of Western science has been based on two great achievements, the invention of the formal logical system (in Euclidean geometry) by the Greek Philosophers, and the discovery of the possibility of finding out causal relationships by systematic experiment (at the Renaissance). In my opinion one need not be astonished that the Chinese sages did not make these steps. The astonishing thing is that these discoveries were made at all.

Science, I hope to have shown, is very special and provides the best way to understand the world. This imposes on scientists a special social responsibility in addition to those that all citizens have. Because they have access to specialized knowledge whose applications can have an important effect on our lives, they have the obligation to make public both the implications of their work and its reliability. In the case of the atom bomb, I believe they fulfilled these obligations. During the war the scientists advised the British and US governments that it was possible to build a bomb. The decision to build the bomb was taken by the US government and was an enormous engineering enterprise. It was the application of science. As Robert Oppenheimer, who was in charge of building the bomb, made very clear, the scientist is not responsible for the laws of nature. It would be a serious mistake to leave moral and ethical decisions about the applications of science to scientists.

Public understanding of science is an admirable aim. And is it not essential that the public can participate in decisions about the applications of science? Yes ... but there are severe problems. What precisely is it that the enthusiasts like myself want the public to know, since it seems clear that most people can live a satisfactory life knowing little or no science, just as they can without knowledge of law or economics? While they will certainly miss out on the pleasure and intellectual excitement that come from knowing how the world works, how much science do they really need to know in order to make judgements about genetic engineering or global warming? The most important feature for me is that they can have access to science and to scientists. The latter is very important as it is essential that the scientists come to appreciate public concerns about science.

Genetic engineering illustrates some of these issues. Terrible crimes have been committed in the name of eugenics. Yet I am a eugenicist for it now has another, very positive, side. Modern eugenics aims to both prevent and cure those with genetic disabilities. Recent advances in genetics and molecular biology offer the possibility of prenatal diagnosis and so parents can choose whether or not to terminate a pregnancy. There are those who abhor abortion but that is an issue that should be kept quite separate from discussions about genetics. In Cyprus the Greek Orthodox Church has co-operated with clinical geneticists to reduce dramatically the number of children born with the crippling blood disease thalassemia. This must be a programme that we should all applaud and support.

I find it hard to think of a sensible reason why anybody should be against curing those with genetic diseases like muscular dystrophy and cystic fibrosis. Genetic engineering – though the research still has a long way to go – offers the hope that this will be possible by introducing a sound copy of the affected gene into the patient's tissues. As with any new medical treatment there are risks. There is a fundamental difference between knowing how to do genetic engineering and carrying it out on a patient. How that scientific knowledge is to be applied is a subject for wide public debate. The only responsibility in this regard that scientists have is to explain to the public the possible implications of their work and just how reliable the work is. It is not for scientists to take, on their own, ethical decisions regarding the applications of their work.

There is nevertheless a set of restrictions that scientists must accept, that relate not to the areas of investigation but how the investigations are to be done. Many experiments are not permissible because of the risks they involve. More important, others are ethically unacceptable – like implanting a primate's embryo into a woman's womb. Indeed we already have strict regulations as to what animal experiments are permissible and what can be done with human embryos.

CONCLUSION

The distinction between science and technology is essential for a proper debate on ethical issues relating to the applications of science. It may help people to understand science if they are told that it goes against common sense. It may also help if the stories of discovery, warts and all, are widely known. I would much rather that our education system covered less, and that some aspects were covered in greater depth. In spite of all the current emphasis on relevance, the blunt truth is that one cannot understand science unless one knows a reasonable amount at an appropriate level. Science is a special way of knowing and investigating and the only way of appreciating the process is to do it. Only in this way can people come to recognize a key feature of science – there is only one correct explanation for any set of phenomena. Finding that correct explanation can be difficult, painful, exhilarating, exhausting, frustrating, fun and ultimately very rewarding.

2

A CONSUMER'S GUIDE TO SCIENCE PUNDITRY

Henry Bauer

> Unfortunately, the 'metascientists' – the historians, philosophers, sociologists, psychologists, economists and political scientists who describe and analyse science and technology from a variety of different points of view – have not yet come up with a coherent account of just how the research process actually works. Indeed, much of their contemporary discourse seems aimed at proving that there is no such process, that anyway it doesn't work, and moreover that it works all too well on behalf of certain sinister power groups.
>
> (Ziman 1994)

Science – a term I use here to refer to the natural sciences – explains a great deal about the world. But what explains science's success at finding good explanations? A resolution of this conundrum is far from a purely academic matter. Among the concrete issues that call for concrete answers are the following:

1 What should every educated citizen know of or about science?
2 What should science teachers know of and about science? What about science writers? Or journalists in general?
3 How much of society's resources should be devoted to science? To what sort of science – exploratory or applied? In which fields? Physics? Biology? Chemistry? On attempts to find a cure for cancer? For AIDS? For heart disease?
4 What place should science have in the curricula of elementary (primary) schools? Of secondary or high schools? Of colleges?

Those questions are of the widest concern. And there is no consensus over answers. On each and every such issue, politicians, media and public find ample room to disagree. So do the experts even as they each claim authority for their own viewpoint. Those disagreements reflect the lack of unison over the very fundamentals of how science actually works: how reliable its knowledge is, how any given bit of science can best be appraised, how we can judge when science is able to supply a specific recipe for something we want done.

22

The central puzzle, how science has been able to produce such reliable and potent knowledge, has elicited a variety of responses. Some say that science's secret lies in its special method of inquiry, usually said to be reliable and self-correcting (but why should, how can, an inherently reliable approach need perpetual correction?). Others suggest that the secret is empiricism and pragmatism – which fails, however, to capture the role that theories and beliefs play in science. Certain contemporary pundits take the effectiveness of science to be illusion rather than reality. And there are all sorts of other views on the matter as well.

Absent a consensus, it is useful to know what the most prominent camps have to say and why they disagree with one another. I shall describe here the viewpoints about science that are native to various disciplines, as well as an ideological divide that cuts across the disciplines.

DISCIPLINES ARE CULTURES

It is a common presumption that all fields of science – or even all intellectual disciplines – are essentially the same sort of thing: the pursuit of truth, albeit about different topics. In point of fact, this is quite wrong. Each intellectual discipline carries with it idiosyncratic beliefs about what 'truth' even means, about what is valuable and what trivial, about how much or little objectivity is possible, about how certain is the knowledge that can be obtained, and much more. There is good reason to think of the academic disciplines as cultures, whose members have not only a common intellectual task but also many values and many characteristics of behaviour in common (see e.g. Bauer 1990a). Each discipline develops a distinct culture specifically suited to its particular intellectual task – for example differences between pure mathematics and mathematical physics (Quinn 1996). One consequence is that disparate answers may be offered by various disciplines on any given question, say as to how science works: each discipline looks in its own manner for the answer, and each seeks its own sort of answer.

Were disciplinary differences only a matter of different bits of 'true knowledge' available to the respective experts, then disagreements could be settled by recourse to evidence and logic. That unanimity has not ensued despite the adducing of much evidence, and the deployment of much logic by many experts over many decades, illustrates the degree to which cultural differences are at issue. It is just very difficult for physicists, say, even to understand how sociologists can take the sort of stance that they typically do, let alone to engage in fruitful intellectual discourse with them. As with national cultures, each disciplinary culture has its own language or dialect, practices and traditions – each has its own set of things that are taken for granted and customary patterns of behaviour that set members of one culture off visibly from those of another. Among the easily noticed consequences (see Bauer 1990a, 1990b) that have no obvious connection with disciplinary contents are the following:

First, scientists strive to speak (or to appear to speak) off the cuff, using the barest minimum of notes, to demonstrate their mastery of the material. Historians or philosophers, by contrast, read from prepared scripts: should they venture to speak off the cuff, their audience would infer not mastery of the material but that the speaker had not taken the time to prepare a proper paper.

Second, when the professional work of academics is judged by their peers, the manner in which appraisers describe the work is idiosyncratic to each field: in mathematics, for example, individual pieces of work are analysed and rated for creativity and elegance of execution, and direct comparisons with other individuals are typically made; whereas in sociology, the analysis tends to stress such things as the numbers of publications, the prestige of the journals and the roles of co-authors (see Bauer 1988).

Third, practitioners of different disciplines typically differ also in political and religious associations: scientists and engineers are character-istically more conservative and more likely to be religiously affiliated than are sociologists or political scientists or psychologists; but physicists differ markedly from other scientists in these respects (see e.g. Ladd and Lipset 1972).

It is hardly surprising then, though it has remained largely unremarked, that different disciplines have quite different things to say about what science is, how it works, and why (or whether) it has been successful. One point of at least implicit agreement, however, is that science has an impressive record, most especially over the last three centuries or so, of providing definite answers to a host of substantive questions about how the world works. Yet there is disagreement as to whether, or in what sense, the changes in scientific knowledge over these last centuries can legiti-mately be called progress, and if so, in what sense.

On many points the opposing views correlate strongly with the discip-lines within which they have evolved. Other dissensions, however, are found within individual disciplines between experts adhering to disparate schools of thought. Thus within philosophy of science there are various opinions as to how scientific concepts or objects correspond to things in the actual world; within sociology of science too there are many varieties of 'realist' as contrasted with 'relativist' persuasion. There are ideological as well as disciplinary correlates of beliefs about science.

DIFFERENT EXPLANATIONS OF SCIENCE

Broad-brush comparisons as in this chapter must deal largely in stereo-types and pass over nuances and overlaps. I hope that no one will accuse me of pretending, for example, that all scientists think of science in the manner I describe below or that all sociologists hold the views I ascribe to their discipline. But I do claim that these are, as tendencies and by-and-large descriptions, matters of empirical fact familiar to people who have read or heard something of the pertinent disciplinary discourses.

One source of distorted views of science stems not from disciplinary bias but from the historical fact that astronomy and mechanics were the first bits of science to captivate the modern human imagination. Thus physics became the paradigm of 'modern science' on which historians long concentrated to the virtual exclusion of other sciences. Philosophers sharpened their wits on what history of science had most explored; and sociology of science followed. Only in relatively recent times have other sciences come under as detailed scrutiny as physics has received for well over a century.

Explanations by scientists

Another caveat is at once called for. There are substantial differences among the various sciences on several relevant points, for example between geologists and physicists (see Bauer 1992), yet on the issues emphasized here, scientists as contrasted to others do tend to hold something like the following views.

Working scientists accept, through experience if for no other reason, that most scientific knowledge is enormously reliable, 'factual' – corresponding in some valid manner to the realities of Nature. They are already inclined to that view, of course, through learning science in the first place. In school and to college undergraduates, science is taught as indisputably correct knowledge arrived at by the scientific method which guarantees reliability. In graduate work, doing genuine research, science students get the opportunity to recognize what degrees of uncertainty may attach even to some long-accredited facts; yet this remains a gloss of occasional doubt over a large body of established knowledge.

Scientists implicitly believe that through experiments they discover facts; that doing this is what the scientific method amounts to; that scientists more-or-less automatically use the scientific method without needing explicit training in it.

Scientific knowledge is what works, scientists understand. Facts lead to and determine theories. The theories themselves are only heuristic: they get dropped when found seriously wanting (that is, no longer useful) – though up to the very moment of that decision they command unstinted credence. This uncritical, albeit temporary, allegiance gets easily misunderstood by outsiders, who do not appreciate – even though the history of science is replete with examples of it – just how fickle scientists' devotion to any particular theory is. (Individual scientists, of course, just like any

25

other stubborn human beings, may often stick with their own pet theory even when the rest of the discipline has long discarded it; and of course experimentalists are usually more ready to discard any given theory than are the theoreticians.)

To most scientists, it is not theories but techniques that are the biggest deal, for every new instrument or method makes possible studies that were not possible before and leads to ideas that were literally in-conceivable beforehand. For example the polymerase chain reaction has allowed genetic engineers now to contemplate doing things that earlier seemed science fiction. War-spurred advances in microwave technology led to revolutionary advances in radio-astronomy; later developments in electronics have made the search for extraterrestrial intelligence scientific-ally respectable. Several decades ago a question on our Chemistry Honours exam reflected this understanding of the significance of experimentation: 'Every advance in science is an advance in technique. Discuss.' It is a telling comment on the state of science punditry and the matter of disciplinary biases, that only rather recently has the significance of experimental innovation in the progress of science become a 'hot' topic in meta-science; owing in no small part, moreover, to the influence of the physicist Allan Franklin (see Franklin 1986).

Just as non-scientists are naive and ignorant about some aspects of science that practising scientists take for granted, so scientists are naive and ignorant (and disbelieving) of some things that seem elementary to those who study the humanities and social sciences. Thus scientists presume that controversies get settled because logic rules and evidence piles up; whereas political scientists, historians and others are clear that arguments often do not get settled just because the facts have become intellectually plain. Psychologists, too, know of the many ways that human beings have of ignoring unwanted evidence and seeing only what they want to see. So while scientists often have a good intuitive grasp of matters internal to doing science, they can often be naive and ineffective on questions of public policy and public relations pertaining to science.

Scientists do not realize that other disciplines do not deal in or even aim for reliable factual answers: that philosophers may agree over the rules of logic but not over how or whether truth can be established; that historians, philosophers or sociologists do not expect ever to find final answers to which everyone else in their discipline would be willing to assent; that in those fields it is useful, interesting and worth while to remain in dis-agreement even as individuals press their own views vigorously, just as though they believed themselves right and potentially able to convince others of it. In science, when consensus is lacking, that is thought to be owing only to some needed facts still being missing.

Scientists believe that humankind has no finer pursuit than science. So nothing is more important than carrying it on. Thus high-energy physicists have no doubt that a Superconducting Super-Collider (SSC) needs to be built and that whatever it costs must be worth it; and other scientists would not have disputed that, were it not that their own sciences now compete for the same limited funds.

Because scientists take knowledge in science to be openly demonstrable and unequivocally provable, they willingly defer to their fellow experts in the sundry scientific specialities and sub-sub-specialities: all scientists accept what chemists say about molecular interactions, what physicists say about elementary particles and forces, what biologists say about evolution. Naturally, then, they adopt the same attitude on matters outside science. Thus on questions of meta-science, scientists naturally defer (without looking into it very much) to people who carry such labels as historian, philosopher or sociologist of science – unless or until, that is, they become aware that science is being attacked or nonsense about it spoken. (Scientists' incredulity and anger over distortions of science are well illustrated in Paul Gross and Norman Levitt's (1995) *Higher Superstition*. Scientists find it difficult to comprehend that intelligent people could hold the opinions that relativists voice, and are aghast when they come across what is said about science by radical feminists, Afrocentrists or Marxist purists.) Perhaps most commonly adopted by scientists is the realist philosophers' postulate of a methodical, logical science whose theories encapsulate scientific knowledge: it is after all congenial to scientists that science be regarded as an essentially rational pursuit whose method makes their results automatically right.

But most scientists feel no need for an explanation of how or why science works: they just do it, solving problems and making discoveries. Scientists who actually look into meta-science tend to find Thomas Kuhn's (1963) classic *The Structure of Scientific Revolutions* full of authentic insight into scientific activity; in particular, they recognise the verity of Kuhn's insight that scientific revolutions can alter scientific theories without much changing the essence of scientific knowledge, namely how to observe and how to do specific things. For philosophers of science, Kuhn's book was (and remains) controversial. Many sociologists, however, have embraced a relativist interpretation of the book that Kuhn himself strenuously disavows.

Explanations by philosophers

Philosophers of science have concentrated on what philosophy has traditionally covered: analysis of meaning, intricacies of logic, and epistemology. So philosophy of science has focused on scientific theorizing and scientific method. What can make scientific method reliable? What are the criteria for good, better, or best theories? When and why do theories change? Thus, as already mentioned, it has only recently come to the attention of philosophers that progress in science hinges in large part on experimental capabilities.

Philosophy's preoccupation with theory and method has been influenced by the common perception that modern science stems from the Copernican, Galilean, Newtonian episode whose significance lends itself well to discussion in terms of theories: earth-centred versus sun-centred and the religious and therefore social consequences of that. Galileo's role has often been described as illustrating the proper role of method – testing theories by observation – rather than what was really crucial, invention of the telescope and, before that, of the manufacture of lenses. Moreover the view that the essence of science is theorizing and testing theories by crucial experiment happens to be more compatible with physics – elementary-particle physics – than with most other sub-specialities in science.

So philosophers equate science and scientific knowledge primarily with scientific theories. The abhorrence some of them have for Kuhn stems from seeing his work as denying that science exemplifies rationality at work (see e.g. Stove 1982).

Explanations by historians

There used to be two schools, the internalists who looked at the substance of the science and the externalists who looked at the environment in which the science is done; but this distinction no longer (it is often said) applies since it is evident that the two approaches are both indispensable parts of the same story. Yet in practice one still sees work that amounts to internalist because it neglects social circumstances, and also work that is externalist in its neglect of the content of the underlying science.

The historian's trade is to tell authentic stories about the past. Historians are clear that any particular interpretative framework is unlikely to enjoy universal validity, so grand theorizing is eschewed; such maverick theorizers as Toynbee and such amateur synthesizers as H. G. Wells are given little professional shrift. Historians of science have rarely sought to join the disembodied theorizing engaged in by other meta-scientists (though they do like to present stories that show how one or another meta-theory is excluded or not excluded by the evidence).

Not only does unwillingness to venture grand schemes prevent history of science from speaking with unequivocal authority, but also historians concentrate on disparate factors: on ideas, or on social interactions, or on political frameworks – usually within discrete periods of time and specific cultures. Historians habitually and consciously take the modest stance that they are telling only part of a whole story.

The Romantic divide

In the history of human thought one can discern an ancient, now ever-present tension between the belief on the one hand that human intuition and concrete human experience are the royal road to comprehension and the conviction on the other hand that reason, logic and intellectual abstraction are the valid path to understanding. Probably no individual or group has held precisely to either of these extremes, yet history does show periods and places of dominance of the one view over the other. The Scientific Revolution of seventeenth-century western Europe is often taken as harbinger of the eighteenth-century Enlightenment in which rationality in all matters became a guiding principle; used, abused or misused in the service of social revolution, for example, in France. The intellectual 'excess of abstraction that marked the end of the Age of Reason' stimulated the reaction of early-nineteenth-century Romanticism with its emphasis on 'concreteness and the love of common facts' (Barzun 1994). The middle and late nineteenth century then saw a resurgence of 'realism' in response to an excess of Romanticism. At the end of the nineteenth century another predominantly negative response to realism came in neo-romanticism, to be followed in turn by a period of neo-realism (see e.g. Brush 1978).

These sweeping characterizations, of course, express only an apparent predominance of the one attitude over the other. Few if any individuals exemplify the extreme of scientism or the opposite extreme of unmitigated Romanticism. (A dictionary definition of scientism is quite serviceable: the theory that investigational methods used in the natural sciences should be applied to all fields of inquiry, the application of quasi-scientific techniques or justifications to unsuitable subjects or objects.) Both attitudes are simultaneously ubiquitous in people and in societies. Periods of rapid scientific advance are often accompanied by romanticized notions of an anti- or pseudo-scientific sort (see Bauer 1986a, 1986b). Nineteenth-century discoveries in electromagnetism were accompanied by a plethora of electric health-cures and quackery. The realism of natural selection and the tracing of human origins to the animal kingdom came simultaneously with Spiritualism and the enthusiastic investigation of psychic phenomena. The end of the nineteenth century and the beginning of the twentieth saw not only the genuine discoveries of radioactivity and X-rays but also the illusory ones of N-rays and mitogenetic radiation. The Second World War was followed not only by an avalanche of new science and new technology but also by the advent of flying saucers and renewed interest in cryptozoology and parapsychology. Our most modern scientific age also harbours New Age beliefs that counter the cold, hard facts of established science with intuitive, mystical and pantheist concepts.

Among the intellectual disciplines one sees the same cycles as in society at large, though mathematicians, scientists and perhaps philosophers and historians are less likely to partake deeply of Romanticism than are behavioural and social scientists.

Explanations by sociologists

The classical (Mertonian) kind of sociology of science takes a realist view and examines the detailed interactions in the scientific community that have made it pre-eminent as a means of generating reliable knowledge (peer review, criteria for attaining prestige, and so forth). In recent times this approach has been largely pushed aside by the 'sociology of scientific knowledge' which emphasizes that human knowledge is not directly of any real world but only of some consensus reached by specific communities about their world. 'Discovery' is replaced by '(social) construction' (as in Pickering 1984). Scientific practice is thought to be explicable through ethnomethodological studies – observing scientists at work in the lab – rather than by looking at the capabilities of the instruments being used.

At the same time, paradoxical though it may seem, sociologists are utterly devoted to the notion that being scientific means using the scientific method (see Bauer 1992: 128–40). Thus contemporary constructivists and relativists delight in illustrating that scientists do not really practise the scientific method and that, therefore, the natural sciences are no more a matter of hard knowledge and objectivity than are the social sciences.

That belief comes to them naturally, of course. The social sciences do not have the experience that pervades the natural sciences, of dealing with facts that cannot be gainsaid, with operationally unambiguous knowledge and the sort of intellectual consensus that follows therefrom. In the social sciences, schools of disparate viewpoint flourish and coexist as they do not in the natural sciences. Thomas Kuhn's (1963) notion of 'paradigms' is sometimes misappropriated by social scientists to imply that in a science there may fail to be consensus on fundamental matters; one even hears sociology self-described as a 'multi-paradigmatic discipline'. Theory-building is highly regarded (though the testing and discarding of theories is not much in evidence), and sociology of science often harps as much as does philosophy of science on the theorizing part of scientific activity.

INTER- OR MULTI-DISCIPLINARY APPROACHES: 'SCIENCE STUDIES' OR 'STS'

A number of more-or-less organized efforts to blend some of these differences of viewpoint has been made during the last several decades. By the late 1960s, a significant number of college courses (in the USA) addressed social implications of science and technology, often through co-operative ventures among scientists, engineers, humanists and social scientists. Joint ventures by philosophers and historians and sociologists sometimes went so far as the establishment of such departments as History and Philosophy of Science, or Philosophy and Sociology of Science. Full-blooded attempts at inter- or multi-disciplinary scholarship and teaching have led to the founding of units or departments or centres of what is now typically called 'Science Studies' (in Britain) or 'STS' (in the USA). Professional associations too reflect these attempts at synthesis, as for example the Society for Social Studies of Science (founded in the 1970s) or the Society for History, Philosophy, and Social Studies of Biology (established in the 1980s).

However, as the epigraph quoted at the outset indicates, no consensus has yet emerged from these attempts. There is no comprehensive, coherent account of the actualities of scientific activity to which most practitioners and all the parent disciplines, including the sciences themselves, are willing to assent. Indeed, the current scene shows not only some disciplinary merging but also a deep bifurcation. On the one hand – the traditional or right hand – are those who take a realist stance toward science and the world; they include many, perhaps even most philosophers of science and historians of science as well as most scientists and engineers and political scientists engaged in policy studies. On the left stand relativists, constructivists, and debunkers of scientific hubris: social scientists of a theorist rather than an empirical or practical bent together with people in various disciplines with strong ideological commitments to Marxism, radical feminism, and the like.

Once again I pause to note that no such dichotomy should be taken more literally than intended or warranted. Between those left and right hands stretches a well-populated continuum. There are indeed few who would explicitly and seriously propound either extreme view (though there are some). Nevertheless there is quite a clear distinction between the two camps in the *tone* with which science is talked and written about. Those of the right hand are squarely in the Enlightenment tradition, stand somewhat in awe of the success that science has brought to humankind's understanding of how the universe works, and see science as one of the strongest resources for betterment of the human condition. Those on the left harp more in the Luddite tradition on the evils of modern technological society and the science which they Romantically hold (or claim to hold) largely responsible for those evils.

Most of us, of course, harbour some sentiments and attitudes and beliefs from both hands, just as society itself carries concurrent streams of Romanticism and scientism. And just as with society and with individuals, so too with the academic institutions – centres, journals, societies: though incorporating both streams, most of them reflect a predominating set of swimmers of the left or of the right persuasion. By and large, where membership comes chiefly from sociologists, rhetoricians, non-realist

31

philosophers, Marxists, feminists, and the like, then the programme or publication features chiefly a tone that is rather suspicious of science, rather deprecating of it, insisting on its overweening pretentiousness; for example, the early and influential Science Studies Unit at Edinburgh and the journal *Social Studies of Science*. But in those programmes and publications where practising or former engineers and scientists congregate, and practice-oriented political scientists and sociologists, one finds more of a pragmatic concern with putting to good use the unquestioned sound knowledge that science offers, for example, *Bulletin of the Atomic Scientists* or *Bulletin of Science, Technology & Society*.

CAVEAT EMPTOR: ABOUT EXPLANATIONS OF SCIENCE

I began with examples of questions about science for which answers are needed. The most direct way to judge different explanations of science is to test them against such concrete questions: are these met by sensible, realistic answers or by evasion and obscurity?

Using that criterion, common sense can decide among even sophisticated arguments. Here are some questions, more explicit than the earlier ones, that ought to be answerable by people who understand science and might therefore have informed opinions about science policy:

1 What accounts for the success of science over the last few centuries? Why did that begin in seventeenth-century western Europe rather than at some other time or elsewhere? How can we ensure that similar progress will continue?
2 How much of national resources should be devoted to science? How divided between basic and applied? Concentrated in what specialities?
3 What should we teach our children of and about science? Why?
4 What makes for greatness in science? What makes for competence in science? Can we train any or every child to become a good scientist?
5 How come science commands such reliable knowledge and yet seems unable to give us some knowledge that we really want, like cures for cancer and AIDS and cheap sources of non-polluting energy? What determines these limits on scientific knowledge?
6 Why does science enjoy such high prestige at the same time as many are suspicious of or antagonistic to it? Does it really benefit society to harbour a thriving scientific community? In what ways?
7 What exactly is 'pseudo-science'? Why does science pooh-pooh so many subjects that people are greatly interested in, like UFOs and Loch Ness Monsters?
8 Why do we hear so much nowadays about misconduct by scientists? Are they less ethical than other professional people? Are scientists less ethical than they should be? If so, what should be done about it?

Here now are examples of typically unhelpful, biased answers that are offered, and some critical comments on those answers.

Imagine that the first question is met with an answer along the following lines:

> What do you mean by 'success'? Scientific theories are always subject to change. Science has no privileged path to knowledge. Modern science dates to seventeenth-century Europe because it was cultivated there while Europe's military and economic power made the rest of the world subservient. Current scientific knowledge embodies the biases of European, elitist males and serves their interests. If society were differently organized, scientific knowledge too would be different. How to ensure satisfactory progress depends on what you regard as satisfactory, a Eurocentric science or a Third-World-oriented one, an elitist or a democratic one.

That is the sort of answer that relativists have to offer, though they may at times disguise it for tactical reasons. I suggest that common experience and common sense enable us to discard it and to pay no attention to policy suggestions from people who insist on it. Being excessively polite, one might respond: 'How very interesting! But, you know, I've heard quite other things from some historian and philosopher and scientist friends of mine. Let me get you all together, and when you've arrived at a consensus, do let me know and we'll be sure to act on it.'

Imagine that the second question is answered thus:

> Tell us what exactly you want, and give us enough resources, and we'll deliver the goods. Of course, you must also give us continually increasing resources to furbish our infrastructure, because we need to expand our fundamental understanding all the time to make possible the useful applications you ask for. If we're slow delivering what you want, it will only be because you don't give us enough of the needed wherewithal.

That is the sort of answer likely to come from the scientific community. A reasonable response might be:

> How very tempting! But do you have any references as to your qualifications to do all that? I happen to have some historian and sociologist friends who harbour doubts that you can always deliver. They tell me that $20 billion spent in the last couple of decades in a war on cancer haven't made notable inroads into that disease. They remind me that you promised us cheap atomic energy forty years ago and that we haven't got it yet. You told us that *very* cheap, non-polluting energy would come from nuclear fusion, and we've spent billions on that, and now you suggest that we might have a

demonstration power-plant around 2020 or so. Can you convince us that your promises of today are better founded than those of yesteryear?

Imagine that the third question brings the answer,

We shouldn't overburden our children's minds with masses of stuff to memorize. They need only to know that the scientific method has been responsible for science's success, and if they learn it they too can become competent or even great scientists themselves.

Respond to that with quite a diatribe: How does 'the scientific method' help us answer questions 4, 5, 6 or 7? Does it not suggest an answer to question 2 that we have just found wanting? Does it not suggest as answer to question 1, the absurd inference that it took Europeans of the seventeenth century to realize that you need to test the validity of ideas by observation or experiment? Since different disciplines offer disparate insights, in other words, and since there are also marked ideological biases in play, canny consumers will not accept any single answer before they have confronted the relativist with a realist, a practising scientist with a historian, and so on. Such conversations can be enlightening – so are a number of accessible publications that afford useful insights into the history and contemporary workings of science relatively free of the ideological and disciplinary blinders described in the foregoing; for example, see Marks (1983), Knight (1986), Burnham (1987) and Brush (1988). The works of Bauer (1992), Ziman (1978, 1994), De Solla Price (1986) and Stephan and Levin (1992) look at contemporary working in science and are especially recommended.

3

VISIONS OF EMBATTLED SCIENCE

Mary Midgley

ABSTRACT WARS

Why is there so much quarrelling about science? If one came fresh to the question, one might surely think that it was scarcely possible to fight for or against science, any more than for or against language, or history, or work, or human relations, or any of the other very large things that set the scene for our existence.

But of course the role that these large things play in our lives can vary immensely and this variation can cause quarrels in which the names of these abstractions serve as slogans for the most surprising causes. Poetry, for instance, has often needed to be explicitly defended against onslaughts rather similar to those that are often made on Pure Science. The Defences of Poetry that were written by people like Shelley and Philip Sidney have not just served as weapons of war. They have also helped to shape and clarify the role that it plays in our lives. They have altered the idea of poetry itself and in that way have made possible new ways of writing it.

This process has not just been an isolated, internal matter for poets and their readers. It has been an aspect – sometimes quite an important one – of much larger changes in the world. Sidney launched his arguments about the role of poetry within the Renaissance. Shelley launched his within the Romantic Revival, and these were movements that affected all sorts of aspects of European life.

On such occasions, we surely need to be aware of these wider involvements as well as of the local battle among critics. What misleads us, what gives rise to endless wasteful friction, is confusion between the local, internal issues that can be seen from inside a particular profession and the wider ones, which are often hard to grasp at all. Today, this is surely happening about science. During the twentieth century, that large abstraction which is Science has acquired tremendous symbolic importance by being linked with a great range of practical movements which have profoundly altered our everyday life – movements which have been hailed as essentially and typically 'scientific'. The most obvious of these is the general expansion of technology, something which has always produced ambivalent responses and which now causes increasing alarm. But our lives have also been deeply influenced by many other, more detailed policies – policies which have carried the same 'scientific' label and the same sort of significance.

CONCRETE EXAMPLES

Examples are everywhere. There is, for a start, industrial Taylorism, the policy of shaping the manufacturing process so as to treat all workers, systematically and on principle, simply as physical components in the manufacturing process without any reference to their own points of view on the matter. As Henry Ford himself put it, workers must be regarded solely from a functional angle because they were in fact tools:

> The principal part of a chisel is the cutting edge. If there is a single principle on which our business rests, it is that it makes no difference how finely made a chisel is or what splendid steel it has in it or how well it is forged – if it has no cutting edge it is not a chisel. . . . The cutting edge of a factory is the man and the machine on the job.
>
> (Ford 1923)

This project, which was worked out in theoretical terms by F. W. Taylor and his colleagues in the early years of the twentieth century and first adopted on a large scale by Ford, has obviously had an enormous effect, not only on the lives of industrial workers, but also, more indirectly, on the way in which people now regard work (see Doray 1988; Taylor 1914).

What is interesting about this idea is that its inventors did not just recommend it as an effective way of making money. They also justified it on much grander intellectual grounds. They called it pre-eminently scientific, and indeed it was widely known quite simply as 'scientific management'. This claim was not casual, it was meant to carry substantial weight. Scientific status was seen as an adequate defence of Taylorism against any moral objections which might be brought against it.

Taylorism thus served to exempt the treatment of workers from the principles which normally limit the ways in which we can treat other people, principles from which workers had not before this formally been supposed to be exempted, badly though they might in fact often be treated. It served to sideline principles such as the Golden Rule, which tells us to treat others as we would want to be treated ourselves. Equally, it served to neutralize Kant's notion that the good life centres on treating people as people rather than things – as ends in themselves, not just as means to our own ends that we can manipulate at our pleasure. Science, according to Taylor and his colleagues, could simply disprove this sort of contention by demonstrating that workers were in fact just things and could only be treated as such. This is evidently an extremely strange way of settling the question which of these attitudes to people we really ought to prefer. The fact that Taylorists could rely on using the name of science as a moral blunderbuss in this way is a striking testimonial to the prestige that it carried at that time.

Another example is the effort to depersonalize medicine – especially psychiatry – by similarly reducing it to a physical operation on bodies, to be carried out without reference to the uneducated viewpoints of patients or their relatives. Another, again, is behaviourist psychology, which argued explicitly that the subjective angle on human experience could indeed be ignored because it had no effect on conduct. Though this strange view proved in the end unusable for psychology, its ghost still haunts many areas of the social sciences and as long as it prevailed it produced some extraordinary practical advice, especially about such things as child-rearing, advice which had a considerable bad effect on many people's lives.

Yet one more example is Marxism, a thought-system which also claimed to be scientific and used that claim as a defence against moral objections. Though this claim may have been less central for Marx himself than it was for his followers, Engels took pains to build it into his version of Marx's ideas. During the mid-twentieth century a remarkable group of poly-mathic British scientists – J. B. S. Haldane, J. D. Bernal, Joseph Needham and others – developed this notion in many influential popular writings; see Werskey (1988) for this interesting story.

These are not isolated examples. Throughout the twentieth century the claim to be 'scientific' has repeatedly been brought forward as an all-purpose justification for policies to which there were obvious moral objections. Calling these distasteful proposals 'scientific' and 'modern' often served to protect them against criticism, conveying the notion that no reply was needed because it was always laudable to 'drag people kicking and screaming into the twentieth century'. This propaganda was often successful, which is why both terms are now becoming discredited. The reaction against them produces not only the jumble of ideas now confusedly called 'post-modernism' but also a good deal of hostility to science. Nobody, therefore, should be surprised if the public does now tend to see 'science' as supporting ideologies like those just mentioned, nor astonished if it does not always like what it sees.

IS SCIENCE NEUTRAL?

Defenders of 'science' tend to dismiss these accusations against it as unfair (see e.g. Wolpert 1993). But they can give two quite different reasons for thinking so. On the one hand they can say that science is not ideological at all. It is neutral, purely factual, a mere tool that can be turned equally to any use. Or, quite differently, they can say that science does have its own moral programme, and that programme is an admirable one, free from the blemishes of Marxism and Taylorism. Science is then not just a fact-store but an active enterprise devoted to forwarding its own character-istic ideals. Perhaps it may then even be an enterprise so important that it can dominate and guide our whole lives, as its champions have sometimes claimed. We could then accept the words that Pandit Nehru addressed to the Indian National Institute of Science in 1960 – words much-quoted, but a perfectly fair example of a widespread faith:

> It is science alone that can solve the problems of hunger and poverty, of insanitation and illiteracy, of superstition and deadening custom and tradition, of vast resources running to waste, of a rich country inhabited by starving people.
>
> (Nehru 1960: 564)

By 'science alone', Nehru cannot just have meant 'facts alone'. Pure knowledge of facts would obviously do nothing to solve those problems without good will and wise policies. He expected guidance. He expected wisdom. He looked, not just to scientific know-how but to scientific ideals. In some sense, he was calling for a factor that could take the place of religion.

But if this is the hope, it surely becomes urgent to ask just what the special ideals of science are and how ideological prophets such as Taylor and Marx got them so wrong. It is not possible to claim that scientific values and ideals – whatever they may be – have a right to override all other ideals without specifying those other ideals and arbitrating between them. If, for instance, scientific progress seems to conflict on a certain issue with justice and compassion, has it an automatic right to prevail?

'Science' cannot be treated as a conquering invader, an ideology that can simply override existing standards without explanation. Scientific ideals need to be placed in the context of other human ideals, just as scientists themselves have to place their work in the context of their whole lives. The importance of those ideals in that whole spectrum has then to be soberly assessed. It becomes necessary, in fact, to do some serious ethical thinking.

It is not really possible to combine the two defensive strategies of treating science as a harmless neutral tool and hailing it as an infallible guiding star or a cause to be fought for. Its more vocal champions tend, however, to oscillate between these claims. Officially, most of them at present back the modest view that science is inert, purely factual and neutral. That stance represents a strong and natural reaction, led largely by Karl Popper, against the ideological excesses of Marxism. But it is not possible to maintain this position consistently if one still also wants to claim for science any high spiritual status or, indeed, any influence at all on practical affairs.

Historically, too, the main tradition of the profession is against such modesty. The movement which we call modern science was never an inert, unworldly phenomenon of this kind. Its founders and champions in the Renaissance did not present it only as a means of informing people about the physical world but also, boldly and primarily, as a way of changing their attitudes to it. Led by Francis Bacon, they pointed out that knowledge is power. They called for a more confident, interventive or even violent approach to nature. They wanted their new discoveries to lead to active control, replacing the resigned and awestruck submission that had previously inhibited curiosity.

BATTLE LINES ARE DRAWN

At first, there was room for both the attitude of active control and that of submission within the vast, rambling Christian tradition. The Bible had, after all, not only endorsed human dominion over nature but also called on people to respect the world as God's creation. As time went on, however, conflicts developed on many detailed points of fact such as the details of the Creation and the Flood. Although scientists themselves were still usually Christian until the late nineteenth century, public opinion came gradually to amalgamate these conflicts into a supposed general clash between the two abstractions, science and religion. This produces some fairly absurd results.

Thus, when the heroine of Trollope's novel *Barchester Towers* (1857) – who is not supposed to be silly at all – is asked what she thinks of recent scientific theories which suggest that the moon is uninhabited, she replies, 'I really think it's almost wicked to talk in such a manner. How can we argue about God's power in the other stars from the laws which he has given us for our rule in this one?' Similarly, from the other side, Peter Atkins (1992), declaring the 'omnicompetence of science', feels that his work will have been done if he can only get rid of religion and soars to remarkable metaphoric heights to do so: .

> Science's cautious, publicly monitored gnawing at the cosmic bun is a far more honest approach to universal competence than religion's universal but empty gulping and the verbal flatulence that passes for theistic exposition. . . . The stern and stony eye of science seeks answers that are not grounded in the fundamentality of purpose.
>
> (Atkins 1992: 32)

This way of thinking reifies and indeed personifies those two concerns in a way that tends to make clashes between them look final and non-negotiable. It then seems that such issues can be settled only by war. It was doubly unfortunate that, although many of the early Christian fathers had

endorsed symbolic rather than literal readings of the Bible, their descend-
ants during the Reformation (both Protestant and Catholic) largely came
to insist on a literal reading which did indeed bring them into conflict with
the science of their day, thus generating an unprofitable warfare of
abstractions in a way that would have shocked St Augustine.

Once this has happened, it becomes extremely hard to deal with these
clashes one by one in a rational fashion, on their merits, and extremely
easy to class them all wholesale as triumphs or disasters of war. It is very
interesting to see the workings of this process in the row which arose over
Brian Appleyard's (1992) lively and attractive book *Understanding the
Present: Science and the Soul of Modern Man*. Appleyard's chief aim was to
examine the role that the idea of science played in present-day thought
and to see what might be wrong with it. His discussion was undoubtedly
thoughtful and serious. The book produced vigorous discussion from all
sides and many people agreed with the author's expressed alarms about
the current influence of science. However, in the preface which he has
added to his second edition Appleyard writes that he was astonished to
get a violently hostile reaction from many scientists, who accused him of
launching a 'New Ignorance Movement'. Until then he had not realized
(he says) that he was attacking an institution.

WHO OR WHAT THEN IS SCIENCE? TROUBLE WITH DEMONS

What kind of entity, however, did Appleyard suppose that he *was*
attacking? Throughout the book – which contains a great deal of fascinating discussion – readers are constantly confronted with this puzzle.
Appleyard is often just as anthropomorphic as Peter Atkins in the things
that he says about science. In his prose, science keeps doing things which
one would think could be done only by a person. For instance it 'possesses
an intrinsically dominating quality'. It 'now answers questions as if it were
a religion'. It is 'incapable, whatever it may pretend, of co-existence'. More
alarmingly, it has 'made exiles of us all. It took our souls out of our bodies'.

Passages like these are written in the mythic mode. They accept the
convention used by scientistic writers like Atkins of treating science as a
potent figure, a kind of demon. Anything written in this style has an
extraordinarily strong and primitive appeal. In such sentences, deep
speaks unto deep without the inconvenient interruption of serious
thought. These passages sell books all right, but there is always a price to
be paid. An author who uses this kind of language, even for two or three
sentences in the course of a book, can be sure that those are the sentences
which will be remembered and that critics are likely to respond to them
at the same gut level – as they have done in this case.

Most of Appleyard's book is far more subtle and reflective than this. It contains some really valuable discussions of the nature of science and the many ways in which it has affected us. But he seems to have swallowed his own rhetoric to the extent of regularly treating the various abstractions he deals with – science, liberalism, environmentalism, religion – as though they were monolithic, given, immutable wholes rather than loose, jumbled ways of thinking which are constantly changing and developing along with the society that uses them.

By personifying and oversimplifying this cast of characters, by separating them so drastically from one another, he ends up with a tragedy that looks as foredoomed and unavoidable as a play by Racine. In theory, Appleyard is trying to find a new way of thought that can replace the demonic and discredited scientific outlook. But this project is constantly hindered by excess of drama:

> Science made us; science broke us; it is time to start making repairs. . . . Science inspired a version of the universe, of the world and of man that was utterly opposed to all preceding versions.
>
> (Appleyard 1992)

This, for a start, is an extraordinary claim. It quite ignores the continuity of Renaissance science, not only with Greek thought but also with the rationalist element in Christianity. The idea of an ordered universe organized by a single creative mind has always pervaded Christian thought about the world, as it does that of Judaism and Islam. It was as crucial a part of Newton's and Galileo's worldview as it was of St Thomas's. And the fact that Christianity was a 'religion of the book', a worldview centred on the truth of a single sacred story, prepared the niche into which science subsequently stepped.

Indeed, this same unlucky notion of one given monolithic truth, rather than the patchy, piecemeal struggle towards truth which we actually deal with, lies at the root of the science-versus-religion rivalry today. Narrow-minded fundamentalism – the claim to a monopoly of truth, the inability to see how much room is left for other aspects of it – has been a blot on both sides of this debate. Though it does not dominate either of them in a way that could possibly justify Appleyard's despair, its past excesses do provide him with the quotes that lead him to think that no movement is possible. (Peter Atkins, now almost an isolated coelacanth, still does his best to maintain this tradition today.)

In this way and many others, the continuity of modern science with its predecessors is strong. Renaissance science only looks like a complete innovation if you insist on treating it as a new character in the drama – a demon who has just stepped onto the stage. However, Appleyard's main charge against it is still to come. He goes on:

41

Most importantly, it denied man the possibility of finding an ultimate meaning and purpose in his life within the facts of the world. If there were such things as meanings and purposes, they must exist outside the universe describable by science.

(Appleyard 1992)

But this separation of facts from meaning and value was not a product of science. It came from a mistaken philosophical tradition, which in turn reflected wider trends. The first false step in this tradition was Descartes's drastic division of human beings into two separate and disconnected components, mind and body. This cleavage, which was indeed partly designed to protect science from outside interference, did cause it to become gradually separated from the rest of thought. But the worst effects of the split did not flow from what science then did in isolation. They came from the confusion that surrounded the status of mind and its relation to matter.

Since Descartes's idea of a world divided into radically disconnected halves seemed incomprehensible, theorists set about trying to reduce one half to terms of the other and debating about which half should prevail. At first some serious thinkers (Leibniz, Hume, Hegel) tried to dissolve matter away by showing that it was really a form of mind. Gradually, however, hopes shifted to the opposite enterprise of proving that mind was really a form of matter. This materialist contention became increasingly attractive with the growing success of physical science. Much of its strength, however, has always come from simple opposition to religion – a consideration of a quite different kind which often exercises a force irrelevant to the real issue.

Today, we are gradually managing to recognize that both kinds of reduction are unworkable. It is not realistic to draw the sharp line between mind and body which seemed to make them necessary. The proper unit is the whole person. But our whole way of thinking has been deeply shaped by this tradition of mind–body warfare, in particular by the very influential form given to it in the early nineteenth century by Auguste Comte's doctrine of positivism.

Comte simply proclaimed that matter was all that we had to deal with. The only proper kind of thought must therefore be scientific thought which dealt in facts about material objects. Any other kind of thinking was merely a temporary product of our primitive, childish state of development. All civilizations (he said) passed through three intellectual stages – religious, metaphysical and positive or scientific – shedding at each stage some of the superstitions which had led them to look for anything other than scientific facts. All forms of thought other than science were, then, superficial and inadequate. History and ethics, for instance, must be reduced to statements of scientific fact, and anything in them which resisted that process must be abandoned.

This extraordinary fantasy – itself visibly a piece of prophetic meta-physic – caught on partly because, when it was proposed, hopes for the sciences (especially for the new social sciences) were unrealistically high. More deeply, however, it succeeded because it seemed to offer an all-purpose weedkiller which would remove traditional religious ideas that obstructed the development of thought in many areas. This was the time when the word 'scientific' began to be used as a loose term of praise which was almost equivalent to 'non-religious' or 'anti-religious', without neces-sarily bearing any clear relation to any actual science.

Enthusiastic theorists eagerly tried to put Comte's scheme into practice, but as they did so its inherent difficulties became obvious. At first, they proceeded by colonizing large non-scientific areas of thought in the name of science. They built large, supposedly scientific systems such as those by which Marx and Spengler scientized history and Freud claimed to organ-ize psychology. These were at first widely respected and successful. Gradually, however, it became clear to scientifically minded persons that these schemes bore little relation to any known science.

At this point, positivist policy went into a rather startling reverse. It abandoned colonization in favour of isolationism. Karl Popper, defining science much more narrowly, now drew in its boundaries in a way that excluded from it, not just Marx, Spengler and Freud, but a great deal of the social sciences as well, while leaving the humanities still unconquered. Modern positivism thus quietly dropped Comte's ambition to make the whole domain of commonly recognized thought scientific.

It did not, however, part with his flattering notion that only scientific thought is truly rational. The effect is to suggest that all thought which lies outside science also lies outside reason. While history is now rarely mentioned, this ban was expressed quite explicitly against both ethics and metaphysics. The project of reducing ethics to a set of scientific facts, which had not proved very successful, was dropped in favour of simply de-claring the whole of ethics, along with metaphysics, to be meaningless nonsense. This ukase can be found expressed in handy form in that highly metaphysical and prophetic manifesto of logical positivism, A. J. Ayer's (1936) *Language Truth and Logic*. Although not all positivists wished to endorse this rather emotive wording, they standardly did (and still do) accept the idea of a 'fact–value gap' which was also a frontier between the rational and the irrational.

THE ROLE OF PHILOSOPHY

In modern times, scientists have largely followed Popper in simply endorsing the split between facts and values. (Popper never questioned this aspect of positivism, though he attacked a good deal of its scientific methodology.) Scientists were undoubtedly reacting against ideologies

such as Marxism which tried to bestride that split. But modern special-
ization, too, makes the split popular with scientists because it absolves
them from dealing with matters about which they do not feel confident.
Of course it is also true that Descartes had the position of science in mind
when he designed the split in the first place. Appleyard is indeed right
that the immense prestige of scientists today leads to their being credited
with prophetic status on such matters – even though, when they are
wearing their neutralist hats, they insist that science is impartial and
purely factual.

Positivism, however, is still itself a philosophical doctrine, not a part of
science. Ought the guns, then, perhaps to have been turned against
philosophy instead? It would certainly be possible, and no less convincing,
to rewrite much of Appleyard's book in that way, making philosophy the
chosen demon. No doubt it is true that philosophers such as those
mentioned do carry some responsibility for today's distresses. But it would
surely be bad faith to make much of this, since these positivistically
inclined philosophers, from Hobbes through Comte to Bertrand Russell,
were campaigning against ecclesiastical oppression which was indeed a
real and serious evil. In the UK especially, there would be something comic
about suggesting that a people so robustly philistine as the British, so
resistant to intellectual stimuli, have been the helpless victim of a philo-
sophic conspiracy. The philosophy, in fact, has reflected the life of the age
and the ideas grew from many sources.

COLD WINDS FROM A WIDER WORLD: THE
MEANING OF LIBERALISM

If we were indeed looking for a single source of modern moral confusion
– if we were forced to confine ourselves to one candidate for that role – it
might seem that another good candidate for the demon's role would be
exploration, the process of world-discovery for which the Renaissance is
so famous, and which set off the process of European colonization. This
widening of horizons, which Appleyard scarcely notices, was surely a
central cause of the main evil that he attributes to science. The trouble was
not just that the European discovery of distant lands led to brutal
exploitation and oppression of their inhabitants, corrupting the colonizers
as well as hurting the colonized. The moral damage which that exploitation did could perhaps, at a pinch, be seen as an accidental,
unnecessary consequence of exploration. But what was no accident; what
could not fail to follow on these voyages was a widespread awareness in
Europe of the plurality of cultures. This is the source of Appleyard's other
demon, liberalism, a force which – in the weakest arguments of his book –
he desperately tries to conflate with science.

What he is really campaigning against here, and quite rightly, is cultural relativism – the idea that nothing sensible can be said about value-judgements except that they vary with the culture. They are therefore undiscussable and all in some sense equally 'valid', so that 'it is all a matter of your own subjective point of view'. The distinction between facts and values is here taken to mean that only facts can be rationally considered, values being some kind of steam which entirely eludes thought. Appleyard does not seem to distinguish at all between this kind of slop and serious liberalism of Mill's kind, which centres on a very strong and well-defended value-judgement, namely the judgement that political freedom is itself something good, both as an end and a means, and that this good is more important in human life than has often been supposed; see Mill's essay *On Liberty* (1859: ch. 2).

From Mill's angle, differing value-judgements are indeed bound to arise in the world and should initially be respected, both because those holding them merit personal respect and because the truth is so complex that no one has a complete monopoly of it. Elements of truth may be found on both sides of a disagreement. Rational moral discussion which will attempt to bring together these partial truths is perfectly possible and is indeed an urgent duty. It is a main function of toleration to leave space for such discussion.

This position of Mill's not only does not support a general refusal to discriminate between values but also is quite incompatible with it. Appleyard, however, does not seem even to have heard of this well-known view. His idea is that goofy relativism of the kind just mentioned necessarily follows from accepting the fact–value gap, so that – since science owns all the facts – the expansion of science is bound gradually to crowd out the space left for moral thinking:

> Given the seductive effectiveness and persuasive power of science, over time it is clear that this line will tend to move further and further over to the scientific lobby. The pressure on the other side will be decreased as science continues to conquer because of its corrosive and restless refusal to co-exist. So I have two points here; all moral issues in a liberal society are intrinsically unresolvable, and all such issues will progressively tend to be decided on the basis of a scientific version of the world and of values. In other words they will cease to be moral issues and will become problems to be solved. The very idea of morality will be marginalized and, finally, destroyed.
>
> (Appleyard 1992)

THE LEGACY OF NAIVE SCIENTISM

This idea that science is in some sense 'omnicompetent', that it does indeed contain all proper and serious thinking, and will eventually oust all competitors from the intellectual world – an idea that is sometimes called scientism – is not, of course, an invention of Appleyard's but a legacy from crude positivism. It is a diagnosis and prediction that have been eagerly pronounced by scientistic prophets throughout much of the twentieth century. A recent version (Atkins 1995) may be of some interest:

> Scientists, with their implicit trust in reductionism, are privileged to be at the summit of knowledge, and to see further into truth than any of their contemporaries. . . . Scientists liberate truth from prejudice, and through their work lend wings to society's aspirations. While poetry titillates and theology obfuscates, science liberates. . . . Reductionist science is omnicompetent. Science has never encountered a barrier that it has not surmounted or that we can at least reasonably suppose it has power to surmount and will in due course be equipped to do so. [*sic*] . . . Science, with its currently successful pursuit of universal competence, should be acknowledged king.
>
> (Atkins 1995)

B. F. Skinner also systematically took a similar line, especially in his last book *Beyond Freedom and Dignity* (1973). Thus, recommending science in general and his 'scientific' behaviourist psychology in particular as the only cure for the world's evils, Skinner writes that we cannot

> carry on, as we have in the past, with what we have learned from personal experience or from those collections of personal experience called history, or with the distillations of experience to be found in folk wisdom and practical rules of thumb. . . . [Science must be invoked instead]

> We need to make vast changes in human behaviour, and we cannot make them with the help of nothing more than physics and biology. . . . *What we need is a technology of behaviour.* We could solve our problems quickly enough if we could adjust the growth of the world's population as precisely as we adjust the course of a spaceship, or improve agriculture and industry with some of the confidence with which we accelerate high-energy particles, or move towards a peaceful world with something like the steady progress with which physics has approached absolute zero. . . . But *a behavioural technology comparable in power and precision to physical and biological technology is lacking*, and those who do not find the very possibility ridiculous are more likely to be frightened by it than reassured. *That is how far we are from 'understanding human issues' in the sense in which physics and biology understand their fields*, and how far we are from preventing the catastrophe towards which the world seems to be inexorably moving.
>
> (Skinner 1973, emphases added)

H. G. Wells in his day made similar proposals that government should be handed over to a scientific elite who alone had the knowledge needed to handle it. The difference is, of course, that the prospect which these prophets viewed as a matter for hope and celebration fills Appleyard with horror. Here too he is not alone. Whatever may have been happening to science itself, there is no doubt that this dream of a general takeover of society by scientists has become less and less attractive to thoughtful people – including many scientists themselves – as the century has worn on and that it has eventually begun to appal a wider public. Serious science-fiction, once full of euphoria, deals now chiefly in dystopias and warnings. Very few scientists today share Wells's urge to take over the government. Does it follow that Appleyard's alarm is misplaced, that people have seen through the whole silly project? To some extent I think they have, but by no means completely. Scientistic propaganda has been very successful and much of it will outlast its authors. Whatever else he was, Skinner was a publicist of genius and his ideas still live. Moreover, the confusions that underlie his position are so deep that it can be really hard to think one's way out of them.

For instance, the problem about arbitrating between conflicting value-judgements, especially those involving different cultures, is a real one, a problem which needs to be resolved separately, each time that it arises, by great good will and careful co-operative investigation. We are constantly puzzled by disagreement about crises, not only about familiar contro-versial topics such as marriage laws and education but also about newer ones such as environmental pollution, transport policy and climate change. Though science can of course help us to get the facts right here, there is no obvious way in which it could be invoked to resolve the clashes of values which arise. Where (for instance) personal freedom needs to be controlled if environment is to be protected or art competes for funds with medical care, we have to use serious moral thinking to balance the various ideals involved. Skinner's promise to solve such difficulties by behaviourist psychology was mere bad faith.

Many people, however, are indeed puzzled by the fact that these difficulties are there at all, by the constantly recurring need to face unresolved moral conflicts. They have somehow imbibed the view that, in a scientific age, such awkward problems ought not to exist. They expect science to do what Skinner promised and provide a simple way of dealing with them. This puzzlement does often lead to a kind of paralysis which is indeed expressed in the goofy relativism that Appleyard mentions. If science does not help, they tend to think that the trouble must be past cure.

Thus, the prominence of science does cause a difficulty here, not because of anything particular that scientists do, but because of the wild over-estimate of its capacities that has grown up, partly unavoidably and partly through deliberate propaganda, in the course of the last two centuries. But what part does Appleyard's other villain, liberalism, play in this malaise? What rescuer does he want to invoke to save us from it? At times it almost looks as if he is denouncing permissiveness from the right and will ask the US Cavalry in to restore law and order by censorship. But he is actually much too sharp to suppose that this would help, and anyway what bothers him is not so much public disorder as intellectual anarchy, the moral bankruptcy that paralyses judgement.

STABILITY, MYTHIC AND OTHERWISE

What Appleyard wants, then, is the kind of stable background to life and thought which he takes Christianity to have provided in the past, a solid context of agreement within which life had an obvious meaning and disagreements could be much more easily settled. The wish is reasonable enough but there is something fatally unreal about the way in which Appleyard expresses it.

In the first place, he greatly exaggerates the monolithic certainty which obtained in that past epoch. Despite the best efforts of churchmen to produce both an apparent and a real unity, Christianity was always a vast, sprawling system, full of muddle – much of which was often fertile – and riven by all kinds of disagreements. These clashes came to a head in the Protestant Reformation a century before modern science began to be widely known. Even if that science had never developed, those disputes would surely have led to wars of religion and – along with exploration – would have produced the kind of pluralism that Appleyard deplores. Christians were involved, too, in conflict with outside religions such as Islam, and the Crusaders' swords do not seem to have provided a better way of resolving that clash than the fuddy-duddy liberal devices that are used today.

Appleyard expresses his nostalgic exaggeration of Christian solidarity in a strange and significant graphic example. He writes:

> The cathedral at Chartres was completed thirty years before the *Summa*. It is, perhaps, the most eloquent of all expressions of mediaeval humanism and the Gothic spirit – an *overpoweringly consistent* celebration of an all-inclusive intellectual synthesis. After many visits Chartres still renders me speechless with the certainty and unity of its vision. The building is obviously beautiful but also *brutal in its single-mindedness*.
>
> (Appleyard 1992, emphases added)

You could say the same, of course, about the Parthenon. The point of such great buildings is to convey a single-minded message. This certainly does not mean that their builders passed their lives in a state of chronic oppressive agreement. As it happens, Chartres is quite exceptional among cathedrals in having been very quickly built, so that it actually does have this unified effect. (A glance at other cathedrals – Gloucester, for instance, or Ely – could lead one to assess Christianity quite differently as showing amazing flexibility in responding eclectically to unexpected challenges.) Appleyard's comment shows, however, a fatal ambivalence, an uneasiness about the idea of that very solidarity which he is officially demanding. In fact, by exaggerating the narrowness and triumphalism of serious Christian thought he makes religion, as well as science, seem incapable of development. Thus it becomes another foredoomed, Racinian character, a stereotype in his drama, useless for any kind of rescue.

Other possible rescuers get similar treatment, notably environmentalism, which he says has (most reprehensibly) also frozen itself into an unusable stereotype, having

> expanded to become an entire moral, social and political orthodoxy. As such it has joined forces with a whole range of other anti-progressive movements which advocate the abandonment of economic growth and the return to 'natural' ways of life. . . . Their conception of meaning and purpose is wholly negative.
>
> (Appleyard 1992)

How is that for a sweeping, fatalistic dismissal of a major issue?

CONCLUSION

I have been using Appleyard's very interesting and lively book, in a way that I hope is not too unfair, to illustrate the crucial role that rhetoric and symbolism play in our current confusions about science. My chief aim is to draw attention to these powerful imaginative factors, so that we can be on our guard next time they start to carry us away, and can sometimes exert ourselves to divert them into better channels. If we can just calm down and stop ourselves using words like 'science' and 'religion' as mythic abstractions, we will probably get on a good deal better.

Other contributors to this book are dealing with the various errors which tend to make us reify 'science' into a single entity. I have concentrated here rather on the dramas in which that single entity can seem to be involved once it has been formed. I think, however, that these dramas are not a secondary matter. They are already part of our culture and have a strong attraction for many of us, so they may well be among the causes that drive us to oversimplify 'science' as if it were a single thing or person in the first place.

In diagnosing the present state of these visions, Appleyard seems to be stuck in something of a time-warp. Our imaginative life has changed a lot since the positivistic picture that he conveys was coined. That picture did indeed show 'science' as a monolithic entity which was somehow secluded from the realm of practical choice, a kind of pure scholar in an ivory tower, but a scholar who, in spite of his isolation, had somehow a monopoly on useful knowledge and could be entrusted with all important decisions. This was the vision that led eminent scientists in the forties to disclaim any responsibility for nuclear weapons, claiming that science dealt only in providing factual knowledge. The use that politicians might make of that knowledge was then 'the responsibility of society' – a body to which, apparently, they did not belong.

Since that time, not only nuclear weapons but also environmental damage have made this stance look increasingly absurd and repulsive. The social responsibility of science has become far more widely accepted. Indeed, it is now something that few people would be bold enough to disown in public. Moreover 'the environment' is not, as Appleyard so quaintly suggests, just the name of an idol worshipped by some weird Californian sect. It is the name of a great range of urgent practical concerns which now occupy about half of *New Scientist* every week and fill the time of an increasing number of scientists. These people know that their business is a matter of life and death for all of us, and so does a large part of the general public.

Appleyard was expecting a religion. He was also expecting that religion to resemble an unreal model of medieval Christianity. So he seems to have missed this development entirely. It is, however, the place where a usable outlook is growing up, one in which scientists regularly co-operate with the rest of the public without the slightest need for war. That growth, however, is still young, and it is true that some of the absurd forms of scientism which Appleyard describes are still very strong. Their first component – the belief that 'science' is an entity formed in isolation and not accountable to the ordinary standards of society – has taken a considerable knock. It no longer looks reputable. But the second absurdity – the excessive trust in science as compared with other forms of thought, the belief that it has answers to all questions on all aspects of life – is still powerful. It will take much longer to die away.

Books like Appleyard's can still be useful in exposing these things. But those who write them need to be quite clear that they are talking about myths that have gathered round the idea of science and not about the doings of a bizarre entity called 'science' itself. Otherwise they merely prolong a war of which we have had far too much already.

4

SCIENCE WARS

My enemy's enemy is – only perhaps – my friend

Hilary Rose

Compared with the USA, cultural struggles in the UK have been less a generalized attack than a series of assaults – one of the most conspicuous being on the sociology of scientific knowledge – known to its practitioners as SSK. Perhaps this transatlantic difference derives from the scale of the lurch to the right in the USA, by comparison with the slow implosion of the right in the UK. The attack on SSK claims to come from something that its protagonists speak of as 'Science'. From the standpoint of this single entity – which I shall describe with a capital 'S' to distinguish it from the heterogeneity of the sciences and their methods – SSK is criticized for taking a constructivist stance and repudiating a realist theory of scientific knowledge.

In the US version of these wars, the self-appointed defenders of Science are seeking to police the boundaries of knowledge, and to resurrect canonical knowledge of nature, against the attempts of the Others (who include feminists, anti-racists, psychoanalysts, post-colonialists, leftists, multi-culturalists, relativists, post-modernists, etc., in all our bewildering diversity) to extend, transform or maybe even dissolve the boundaries between the privileged truth claims of Science and other knowledges. (Gross and Levitt's (1995) *Higher Superstition* is the tip of the iceberg. Members of the US scientific elite attacking one or more of the critical Others include Gerald Holton (1993) and even Thomas Kuhn (1963), the author of *The Structure of Scientific Revolutions*, who, though himself criticized, has cast off SSK as his progeny.) But first, just because any of 'us' may find ourselves among the Others under attack, I must emphasize that this commonality may not automatically generate bonds of solidarity between this 'us'. My enemy's enemy is – only perhaps – my friend.

For example some (usually post-modernists) have claimed such an alliance between themselves and feminists, while numbers of feminists have claimed that post-modernism depoliticizes and weakens feminism. Jane Flax (1993) writes of her distress as a feminist psychotherapist and theorist at a bruising attack on her post-modernism by a feminist audience.

51

Conversely, from a critical realist standpoint, the editor of *Race and Class*, A. N. Sivanandan (1995), criticizes the attempt by an anti-racist post-modernism to construct a new non-racialized subjectivity for white working-class youth. This literary turn may diminish discrimination, but cannot meet the challenge of racist violence on the streets.

In such times alliances between 'us' are likely to be provisional and built; the innocent appeals of an old ungendered and 'unraced' solidarity of class are no longer available; gone too is the 'innocence' of universal sisterhood. Instead, while not abandoning commonality, recognition of complexity and the need to pay meticulous attention to context, not least our own, are the name of the game. Positioning myself within a particular reading of the feminist critiques of science – and they are plural and diverse – I want to analyse the attacks on SSK and its response. Who is speaking is as important as what is being said and in what location the debates take place.

THE EYE OF THE CULTURAL STORM?

The most recent debate about the nature of scientific inquiry, which has been grumbling away in the background for some time, is in many ways an extension of the old assumption within the Anglo-Saxon tradition that Science equals the natural sciences. The concept of *Wissenschaft*, which holds all of systemic inquiry together in other cultural traditions, is simply not available in an Anglo-Saxon context. This background grumble took centre stage with a public debate held at the 1994 meeting of the British Association for the Advancement of Science (BAAS) between Harry Collins, a leading sociologist of science, and developmental biologist Lewis Wolpert, Chairman of the Royal Society's Committee on the Public Understanding of Science (COPUS). Collins, together with fellow sociologist Trevor Pinch (1993), had published *The Golem: What Everyone Should Know about Science*, and Wolpert (1993), *The Unnatural Nature of Science*. These rival and polarized texts claim to extend the public understanding of science, the former by claiming that science is socially constructed, the latter by its insistence that scientific knowledge has unique truth claims derived from its capacity to hold a mirror to nature visible to its illuminati.

As reported by the *Times Higher Education Supplement (THES)* the confrontational debate made a considerable impression on those who witnessed it as an extraordinarily vituperative event. To the extent that considerable sections of the academy have given up those highly adversarial and masculinist exchanges, long criticized in feminist circles, as fostering the non-meeting of minds (Moulton 1983), the debate was a return to a past from which we are not yet free.

PUS: THE CONTESTED TURF

The ground under contest is the Public Understanding of Science (or to give it its unlovely acronym, PUS) which formed the title of a report produced by a Committee of the Royal Society chaired by Walter Bodmer (1985). The problem, as perceived by this elite grouping, was that science was losing its popularity. The report sought to overcome this by proposing that a more scientifically literate public would be more supportive. The Royal Society's Committee for the Public Understanding of Science (COPUS) was set up under Bodmer's chairmanship, with the mission of encouraging scientists to assist the public in understanding science. A whole battery of science festivals, hands-on experiences for children, prizes for authors of books which enhance PUS, Science, Engineering and Technology weeks for schoolchildren and research awareness for industry were brought into being. However, the Bodmer credo, that the increased public understanding of science bred trust and thereby support, was indeed a matter of faith. A number of both quantitative (Durant *et al.* 1989) and qualitative (Irwin and Wynne 1996) social science studies have pointed to the association between increased scientific literacy and increased scepticism about science. These findings have had no impact on the COPUS credo and in 1995 it relaunched itself into its second decade with a continuing commitment to one-way communication. The job of the public is to listen and learn.

Communicating science to the public through the media is a long and honourable tradition, pioneered in the 1940s by the Marxist, geneticist and brilliant essayist, J. B. S. Haldane, with his regular column in the *Daily Worker*. Before that the lecture hall was the chief form. In the second half of the twentieth century this task of communication has become largely the task of professional science writers, who have extended it into popular science magazines (*New Scientist, Focus*), the broadsheets and television.

Recruiting scientists themselves into public understanding of science activities as an officially sanctioned activity is relatively new in the UK. Radical and feminist scientists have of course long been at this game, but from a critical standpoint. What remains peculiarly difficult for the British is to move beyond communication as monologue. Unlike some other countries such as Denmark, which has a strongly democratic approach to technical decision-making and takes for granted dialogue between the producers of, for example, new biotechnology, and the public as end-users, Britain, apart from one cautious experiment at a biotech consensus forum, remains incredibly apprehensive that a non-technical expert should have an opinion and start talking as well as listening. Such anxiety has two origins: the first is the pathological commitment to a culture of secrecy endemic to British society; the second is specific to scientists and reflects a deep anxiety about letting others talk about scientific matters. Science is one of the few cultural activities where the practitioners have always sought (indeed rather successfully) to stay in charge of the story about science. Despite very few practising scientists in the Anglo-Saxon context having any training in the history and philosophy of science, there is more than a whiff of an ideology of the authority of the ultimate expert who is alone qualified to say what is and what is not Science. Historians and philosophers, it goes, are all very well in their place, but the ill-concealed subtext is that their place lies in being deferential to the natural sciences. The dream of the 'happy marriage' was for many symbolized in the mutual admiration between the distinguished immunologist Sir Peter Medawar and the equally distinguished philosopher of science Sir Karl Popper.

Twin groupings born in the late 1960s, one outside the academy, the radical science movement, and one within, the new post-Kuhnian social studies of science (T. Kuhn 1963), broke with this deference. Science, in this analysis, was not outside culture, independent, uncontaminated by the social, and 'pure', but was itself an integral part of culture. The social studies of science, whether radical, feminist or mainstream, understood themselves as having a more or less critical, and no longer deferential, relationship to science.

Struggles over the social standing of science are not confined to visible debates; the strategic positioning of key actors in the committees which bring together Science and Society is far from accidental. Within the life sciences one of the fiercest debates, which has mobilized particularly, but not only feminists, concerns the potent link between the new reproductive technologies and the new genetics with their claims to diagnostics and therapy. Together these threaten to determine not only which foetus shall survive but who shall mother. As the disciplines of embryology and genetics have come under intense public scrutiny, the elite geneticists and embryologists have mobilized as very visible players within the PUS discourse. Thus following the 'test tube baby' debates of the 1980s, the Warnock Committee was established by the UK government to consider the ethical issues raised by human embryology and to suggest any necessary regulation. Incidentally even the Thatcher administration recognized that this was a woman's issue and in addition to the predictable clutch of theological ethicists, scientists, etc., actually allocated half the membership to women – a first for any such committee of the Great and the Good. (Of course these were rather carefully chosen women thus unlikely to rock the patriarchal boat whether of science or anything else.)

None the less one of the most interesting appointees to the Warnock Committee was Anne McLaren, an embryologist and experienced committee woman, but also that very rare phenomenon (4 per cent) a woman Fellow of the Royal Society. McLaren herself, perhaps because of her radical political background but also her gender, was rather different from her male counterparts, in that she was able to engage in dialogue with various different publics, not least with feminists. She energetically entered the public arena advocating a solution which both permitted research to proceed and simultaneously allayed mainstream anxieties. In large measure it was her position which was eventually adopted by the majority of the committee. In recognition of her work McLaren was awarded the Royal Society's Faraday Medal in the Public Understanding of Science.

That the first chair of COPUS was the geneticist and leading figure within the International Human Genome Organization, Sir Walter Bodmer (also awarded a Faraday Medal), and that the second was Lewis Wolpert is expressive of this desire of scientists from disciplines under criticism to stay, at least strategically located, if not in charge of the Science story. The location of the committee responsible for research on the Ethical, Legal and Social Aspects of the new genetics within the Medical Research Council, rather than with either of the bodies responsible for Social or Humanities research, is expressive of this cultural defensiveness. My own judgement is that this very British strategy of natural scientists, not only in staying in detailed charge of their own discourse, but also in seeking to control the discourses of other disciplines about PUS, is not simply misconceived, but it will for good reason increase distrust. Indeed the House of Commons (1995a) Science and Technology Select Committee report on *Human Genetics* has taken on the argument that the Ethical, Legal and Social Aspects of the new genetics should not be under the exclusive control of the Medical Research Council and has recommended that it is jointly managed with the Economic and Social Research Council. The struggles around the public understanding of science go on at a number of levels and places, not only in the head-on confrontation as in Golem versus Unnatural Science.

GOLEM SCIENCE

Drawing on the mythical Jewish figure of the Golem, a clumsy but powerful fool with 'emeth' or truth written on its (and sometimes his) forehead, Collins and Pinch (C&P) set out to explain the political role of science and technology. For them science is a Golem, wobbling in their text between gender neutrality and masculinity. I have many sympathies with C&P's political project, which is to increase the public understanding 'about' science rather than merely to increase the public understanding 'of' science, as in the COPUS model. I might use different language but we share a common sociological impulse that people are expert in their own lives and that a desirable cultural and political objective is to move to a dialogue between the several publics and the sciences.

Their book discusses seven case studies of scientific controversies, from the worm-runners (a 1960s claim that tissue from the brains of trained worms could be injected into the bodies of untrained worms and that memory was thus transferred) through experiments to prove relativity, to cold fusion theorists. Set plain the C&P thesis is that 'the scientific community transmutes the clumsy antics of Golem Science into a neat and tidy myth'.

For me the central theoretical problem is the lack of reflexivity in C&P's sociological stance. Thus while they show us the scientists as actively socially constructing their 'neat and tidy myths', we are invited to believe that their own sociological accounts of science are real. They tell us that their subjects construct science, while they offer one true sociological story which everyone should know. Arguably they thus reproduce for sociology the authoritarian scientific voice they criticize. Worse their tactless use of the word, 'myth', to describe the slow patient work of laboratory scientists, pretty much forecloses the possibility of dialogue with them. For 'myth', used in what appears to be a vague everyday sense here, includes any narrative having 'fictitious' or 'imaginary' elements.

Sociobiologist Richard Dawkins is quick to pick up the 'myth' word and to attack relentlessly.

> It is often thought clever to say that science is no more than a modern origin myth. The Jews had their Adam and Eve etc.... What is evolution some smart people say, but our modern equivalent of gods and epic heroes, neither better nor worse, neither truer nor falser.... There is a fashionable saloon philosophy called cultural relativism which holds in its extreme forms that science has no more claim to truth than tribal myth: science is just a mythology favoured by our modern Western tribe.
>
> (Dawkins 1995: 31)

Collins' claim, that SSK is only methodologically relativist, does not quite match up to the ontological slippage taking place in SSK which renders it vulnerable to Dawkins' attack. A more sophisticated – and politically more sensitive – account of science as stories about nature is also used by Donna Haraway in *Primate Visions* (1989). But as a fully reflexive scholar, she also has the grace to acknowledge that her accounts are also stories. The more general point that I want to make by contrasting C&P with Haraway is that there is a tremendous range of positions available within the social studies of science.

What separates the feminists from mainstream SSK is that feminists are committed to building alliances, and consequently are sensitive to the delicacy of the relationship between the feminist critics of science and feminists in science. While C&P deliberately rule out the possibility of their scientist subjects entering into negotiation with their sociologically realist account of science, feminists are willing to listen to those voices, and some (both feminist and non-feminist) want to include Nature herself as part of the actor network. Apparent oxymorons bind the feminist discourse: feminist science, feminist empiricism, feminist objectivity, feminist rationality. These mark out a normative discourse and delineate it from the deliberately scientistic discourse of mainstream SSK. While sensitivity does not guarantee success, there is much more attention among the feminisms to choosing language which is likely to foster dialogue as against that which is likely to foreclose it. By contrast C&P's sociology of science shares more than a little of the same clumsy Golem-like qualities of the scientific Golem they want us all to know about.

There are always problems with popularizing research and in using case studies to resolve theoretical issues. Thus I read the original case study on, for example, the worm-runners, rather differently, and think that C&P go rather beyond the original claims. The worm-runners' thesis had hilarious and very obvious social possibilities, not least for educational practice – should we eat or mainline the professors' brains? As such it produced lots of media discussion and some wonderful cartoons. However, its reception within the biological community, as against its presence in the popular scientific weeklies always looking for a controversial story to maintain readerships, scarcely matches the notion of the establishment of 'a neat and tidy scientific myth'. Indeed a conversation with the sociologist David Travis, who carried out the original research into this controversy, confirmed that practically all the neuroscientists he interviewed were deeply sceptical about the worm-runners' claims, both for theoretical reasons within biological discourse and because they did not trust the accounts of the experimental procedures.

C&P assert that both the psychologist McConnell's worm and the pharmacologist Ungar's later rat-based claims for memory transfer have not been disproved by what they speak of as 'decisive technical evidence' (Collins and Pinch 1993: 25). But the very notion of decisive technical evidence begs the question, for it sets aside the possibility of theoretical biological criticism and trust in scientific craftsmanship. Although the unrepeatable experiment plays a part in resisting the establishment of a scientific fact, not least when carried out with the theatre of multi-authorship or multi-location, the production of a fact is not convertible to one decisive moment but requires a not always tidy cumulation of evidence. Hence it is entirely possible for me to take considerable pleasure in C&P's own meticulous empirical work showing the processes of constructing scientific facts at the micro-level, while still not finding myself compelled by their broader theoretical conclusions.

C&P's case studies set to one side the larger context in which scientific claims are made. Dorothy Nelkin's (1987) *Selling Science* by contrast reminds us of the lure of press releases in a grant-funded research system especially where there might be potential commercial developments. Today's version of the memory transfer hopefuls may be the current hunt for 'smart drugs' and associated big bucks. While some have already gone down the 'smart drug' claim drain, the more modest likelihood increasingly under discussion among the neuroscientists is whether it might be possible to intervene chemically to slow down the terrible neural degeneration associated with Alzheimer's. The point I am driving at, which C&P seem to allude to in some sentences where they acknowledge expertise, but exclude in crucial others as when they sum up Golem science as 'myth making', is that science is concerned with the test of performativity. As a cultural project modern western science has never been content only to represent nature, but also, and always, to act upon it; hence performativity is not a criterion that can be lightly set aside. It is this (whatever the applicability of the self-same criteria to a number of his own social claims) which enables Richard Dawkins to explode with: 'Show me a cultural relativist at thirty thousand feet and I will show you a hypocrite. Airplanes built according to scientific principles work' (Dawkins 1995: 32).

The understanding that science is socially shaped finds increasingly wide cultural acceptance, but it does not follow that because scientific claims are socially shaped they are interchangeable with myths or even stories. What is called the good science / bad science debate remains – just as it does in sociology or for that matter plumbing and dressmaking. The trouble with Collins is that where fringe science is concerned, it is as if he wants to make heroes (never heroines) insisting that because they have the tools of the trade and appear to follow the procedures, no one is allowed to say that the plumbing leaks at every joint. Ian Hacking suggests that the social constructionists focus on the early stages in the construction of scientific facts, but that they leave the scene too early, so that we are 'left with a feeling of absolute contingency. They give us little sense of what holds the constructions together beyond the networks of the moment, abetted by human complacency' (Hacking 1992: 131).

Indeed Collins has appointed himself as the defender of fringe science. Thus when the biologist Jacques Benveniste made his homeopathic claims in *Nature* he was given the full theatrical treatment. The editor John Maddox plus a magician and a scientific fraud-buster visited Benveniste's Paris laboratory to witness a replication experiment. While most biologists were as sceptical as *Nature* about the claim, many thought that *Nature*'s style was bullying and offensive. The combination of what was referred to as the editor, his magician and his rabbit was robustly criticized in the ensuing correspondence. Collins, however, claimed that this was epistemology in action and that replicability could not prove or disprove the claim.

C&P insist that they are concerned with the political role of science and technology; well, so am I. But their refusal to acknowledge the now substantial body of feminist scholarship which has explored the sexualized and racialized representations of nature constructed by an androcentric and Eurocentric science (articulating the social processes through which women have been excluded from science and how, even when they enter, their contributions are erased) is also political. Their construction of the political is pretty much synonymous with Sandra Harding's concept of 'weak reflexivity' as they persistently restrict their analyses to the 'micro processes of the laboratory explicitly excluding race, gender and class relations' (S. Harding 1991: 162). For genuinely smart field workers, their inability to see such social relations at work is quite an achievement. More mischievously, were I a feminist sociobiologist, I might ask whether there was something on the 'Y' chromosome.

Inability to see feminist research is not exclusive to C&P, but has been a general weakness of British mainstream SSK, and would include the work of Mulkay, Bloor, Barnes, Woolgar, and Ashmore. Nor did Latour as the most authoritative voice across the Channel do any better until his enthusiastic appreciation of Haraway (Latour 1993). In his work on reproductive technology Mulkay begins to cite a small number of feminist texts (Mulkay 1995); Woolgar is beginning to acknowledge feminism in relationship to constructivism (Grint and Woolgar 1995). Shapin (1995), now working in the USA, is clearly much more aware of the feminist literature even if he feels unable to integrate it into his otherwise extensive review of the field.

Until these hints of conversion, this highly professionalized grouping has been singularly hostile to normative critics of science (whether anti-racist, left, feminist or deep ecologist) dealing with them by erasure and silence. By contrast *Science*, the powerful voice of US science, has for some years had an annual issue devoted to feminist debates in science, and even *Nature*, its UK counterpart, reviewed Evelyn Fox Keller's (1983) brilliant biography of Barbara McClintock, while the lead British SSK journal *Social Studies of Science* did not. Instead their sociology, despite their claim to be interested in the political role of science, has chosen to mirror science's claim of being a gender/race-free culture. C&P's radical impulse concerned with the political role of science and technology is so hedged in by professionalized and pale male constructions of the political that its capacity to build alliances with other critics, whether within or without the sciences, is severely restricted. Arguably the unquestioned success of this highly professionalized British approach to SSK (quite apart from the flak it is drawing from some natural scientists) is beginning to run out (Knorr Cetina 1993). There are hints that more normative approaches such as those of feminism look to be more fruitful.

More optimistically this exclusivity of mainstream SSK does not imply that the Others cannot borrow their intellectual tools. These will unquestionably need adapting, as Audre Lorde's epigrammatic question 'can the master's tools tear down the master's house?' does not go away. There are also encouraging cracks in the masculine culture of science studies, as feminist research students wishing to work on the social studies of science and technology pressure the departments from below. Gradually the departments are beginning to hire feminists and the possibility of whole new conversations comes into existence. My reading of *The Golem* is that it contributes to these new conversations almost despite itself.

UNNATURAL SCIENCE

The Unnatural Nature of Science (Wolpert 1993) is, for anyone with more than a cursory familiarity with current philosophy of science, an astonishing essay in that it sees no gap between the word and the thing. Some scientists simply do not appreciate the lethal criticism of the mirror theory offered by the Picasso joke. A man troubled by Picasso's portraits with eyes facing both frontwards and sideways asks the painter why he does not paint realist pictures. To make his point clear the man takes out a photograph of his wife and says: 'Like this'. The artist looks at the photo and mildly observes: 'Small, isn't she?'

Scientists, unlike post-modernists and other ontological relativists, believe that there is something 'out there' and that by following the practices of science they can represent that thingyness faithfully. This realism, while a crucial belief for everyday laboratory practice, is not transferable into a mirror theory of representation with the simplicity of the man with the photograph. Such a theory would have a hard time within the philosophy of science and an even harder time within the new ethnographic accounts of science classically represented by Latour and Woolgar's (1979) *Laboratory Life*. Many laboratory scientists report their pleasure in this book as a meticulous mapping of the socio-technical process through which scientists take the inscriptions/printouts emanating from their equipment and gradually turn them into scientific facts. They acknowledge that persuading other scientists working in the area that these are the only possible interpretations of the inscriptions – that these are indeed the new facts – is at once both technical and deeply political. But Latour and these scientists both know that while science is always social, it is not only the social which writes the science (Latour 1993).

Numbers of scientists show no special discomfort with the idea that science is not independent of the culture in which it is produced. The biologist Robert Banks has observed (at a 1994 conference in Durham) that 'Biology is grossly biased towards those organisms which closely resemble ourselves, or which irritate us, like ecoli'. (Just so I thought, given biomedicine's historic preoccupation with the male body and the female reproductive system and brain, but did Banks have that in mind?) But equally, natural scientists insist that science is also not independent of observation and experiment on the natural world. By contrast Lewis Wolpert seems to need his Science to act with a more profound certainty, thus perhaps it is not by chance that two of the more influential voices to support him – the physical chemist Peter Atkins and sociobiologist Richard Dawkins – are committed to militant atheism with a positively nineteenth-century fervour. The elision between science and social progress possible in that century began to dissolve in the middle of the next. Thus while C. P. Snow was making the heroic masculinist claim of scientists as 'the men [sic] with the future in their bones', as usual Minerva's owl was leaving. That old certainty about both scientists and the future began to erode in the atomic explosions over Nagasaki and Hiroshima. These came, and not only for Robert Oppenheimer, to represent the scientists as knowing sin. Nostalgia for a lost innocent past where heroes made the future cannot help in our present cultural uncertainties.

Wolpert's central argument is that modern science has strongly defined boundaries; that it is unique as a way of knowing nature; that its roots lie entirely in ancient Greece; and that it is radically different from something he speaks of as common sense. He thus sets aside historical accounts such as that of Martin Bernal (1988) who is concerned with the black African roots of Athenian science, and dismisses as technology the ethnosciences, whether those of the Chinese (monumentally documented by Joseph Needham (1986) and his colleagues), the Egyptian, Indian, Islamic or the Mayan – to name but a few of the many seeking attention. Post-colonial sociologist of science Mammo Muchie argues that because modern western science is hegemonic, it appears as natural and universal. Its achievement is to appear as a culture of no culture. In similar vein to the feminist arguments I was trying to make for a re-visioned rationality, Muchie spoke (at a 1994 conference in Durham) of the exclusion of emotion and ethics. Against such arguments for the possibility of other more localized and more environmentally and socially responsible sciences: Wolpert insists that there is only Science.

Science, he claims, is unnatural knowledge in that many of its truths run counter to everyday beliefs – i.e. common sense – for instance that the sun goes round the earth or that heavy bodies fall faster than lighter ones. However, common sense is a culturally relativist concept, today's 'common sense' is all too often yesterday's 'good science'. Or by common sense does Wolpert want to invoke the counter-intuitive, which is surely the stance of every systematic approach to knowledge from the arts to the sciences and by no means the unique property of any single one?

As a sociologist I would want to argue that not least because we live in a deeply scientific and technological culture, 'lay' people, and outside our narrow expertises we are all 'lay', pick up particular areas of science, typically those which are important or have some special interest for them and that they make sense of this knowledge within their expertise concerning their own context. Often people do this without claiming that their knowledge is 'science' but instead speak modestly of 'hard facts' or 'reliable knowledge'. Thus in my own PUS research on people with a cholesterol genetic disorder (autosomal, so handy for a researcher interested in gender), both women and men knew more about saturated and unsaturated fats than was revealed in a parallel quantitative study ascertaining public levels of scientific literacy. But because women have still different responsibilities in family life, they have both greater knowledge of food production and of the problem of catering for the individual idiosyncrasies of family members. This new knowledge was integrated into a more holistic understanding by women whether or not they had the genetic disorder. Knowing and caring meant that they gave practical culinary support to affected men partners. By contrast men without the disorder, with their differently gendered familial responsibilities (so knowing less and caring less), gave less support to affected women partners. In the same series of sociological studies of PUS, Wynne's Cumbrian sheep farmers rapidly acquired a richer appreciation of radiation in the food chain than the Ministry of Food and Agriculture scientists (Irwin and Wynne 1996). For that matter effective natural scientist PUS practitioners perceive their publics as having tacit knowledge of say probability theory, or of biomedicine, but also recognize that as non-scientists, they often do not equate their knowledge with mathematics or science. The practitioners use this perception as a building block for their pedagogy and do not draw a sharp line between science and common sense.

By contrast Dawkins, Wolpert and Atkins are as one in their contempt for SSK. Dawkins dismisses SSK as just 'Chic drivel'. Wolpert's view of the sociology of science is matchingly scathing: 'I've never come across anything that wasn't either obvious, trivial or wrong. I think they have made zero contribution.' Atkins resists the very idea of science as a social construct: 'The universal character of science, by which I mean its independence of lasting national, racial and religious and political influences, must argue strongly against science as a social construct' (THES 30 September 1994).

At another level I cannot see why C&P and the mainstream SSK in Britain are so under attack. They never question, as do feminists and anti-racists and sundry others, the larger political role of scientific knowledge such as that of sociobiology, the eugenicist cultural push within the new genetics (Duster 1990) and the 'IQ racket'. (Arguably, in addition to radical critics, that strand within the British Scientific elite which pretty much equates psychometrics with astrology has done more to weaken the IQ claims than SSK.) Sociobiology's endorsement of rape, polygamy, male violence, male dominance and so on, to say nothing of the outpourings of scientific racism, from say Jensen through to Brand since the early 1970s, surely merits criticism both from within their own canon and without.

For example, after a passage about genes reproducing, Dawkins continues: 'The world is full of organisms that have what it takes to become ancestors'. As a sociologist interested in biology I might be sceptical, but I would have to leave effective critical analysis to a biologist. For good reason I would look to biologists willing to enter that debate such as Beckwith, Fausto Sterling, Gould, Hubbard, Lewontin, Rose. But when Dawkins goes on to make what appears to him to be a self-evident claim about the social: 'A body that actively works as if it is trying to become an ancestor ... that is why we love life and love sex and love children' (Dawkins 1995: 2), then social scientists need to engage. While the cadences of the sentence flow easily, if this purports to be a realist account of the social we have surely entered the sociological counterpart of the *Hello!* magazine. Does such crude biological reductionism in its cheerful sentimental universality purport to explain everyday life in Oxford, let alone mass rape and genocide in Bosnia?

Today we have rather a peculiar situation in which a handful of scientists speak for all of Science with absolute ontological certainty, whereas we are to be denied the pleasure and intellectual interest of hearing 'working' scientists talking about the messier, more provisional discourse of particular sciences, and the tremendous difficulty of doing 'good science'. But the business of mediatrics seems to be to promote adversarial debate about Science as a monolithic entity which minimizes the possibility of any complexity, any interchange of views and positions merely become more entrenched.

My (optimistic) hunch, however, is that outside these adversarial arenas, there is a widespread cultural understanding that science is a human activity and as such is socially shaped, and that both the boundaries and the nature of science are continuously subject to change over time and place.

Beyond the unproductive soundbites promoted by the media there are quieter and more serious arguments which matter to our culture, as to whether the post-modernist turn is depoliticizing, whether we can or must give up the truth claims of science, what are the possibilities of a local concept of objectivity, and whether and how the abstract rationality of science can be replaced by a new socially and environmentally responsible concept of rationality. Should the gently squabbling 'we' – which at present includes only a handful of natural scientists – be endeavouring to engage in dialogue with many more, admitting the scientist as collaborator rather than as object (Labinger 1995)?

Or should we set aside these debates and try to examine the new ideas about the changing production system of knowledge (Gibbons *et al.* 1994) so that it is moving towards 'post academic science' (Ziman 1995), and if this is the case what does it mean for our cultural practices? At my most optimistic, I read these changes as opening the possibility of many new actors entering the production system of science, which could indeed

include those Others historically excluded by modern western science –
not least Nature herself. If the old Science and even the sciences have lost
public trust, the only effective and creative response is to try to reshape
the sciences democratically by bringing the other Others in. There is
nothing mechanical or guaranteed about these possibilities as the new
production system could, as in the emergent Conservative British model,
seek to exclude everyone except industry and the technoscientists, but this
new system is developing in a context where dreams of localized,
embodied, responsible knowledges press from multiple currents in both
the South (Shiva 1989) and the North (Haraway 1985; S. Harding 1991;
Rose 1994; Schiebinger 1993). Dreams come into existence not I think
through binary confrontations, but through multiple conversations and
complex alliances. For my part, anyone who is prepared to help make
space and enter seriously – and pleasurably – into such conversations and
alliances, is my friend.

Part II

DEMOCRACY AND THE CURRICULUM

INTRODUCTION

Tam Dalyell (Chapter 5) identifies issues of major concern to the whole book and to Part II in particular: can the formal curriculum, whether in school or higher education, enable its students to participate fully in public policy decisions in science? His views reflect common agreement about the purpose of an education in science. The following chapters show how far short of the ideal we currently are.

Both Guy Claxton and Robin Millar tackle the issue of curriculum change. Both have major concerns with current practice and have imaginative proposals. Guy Claxton (Chapter 6) focuses on the year 2020, emphasizing the uncertainty of defining knowledge objectives in a changing world. Starting with a thorough critique of science education as it happens in schools, he moves on to propose a way forward based on attitudes and personal skills that students will need to cope with science in an unpredictable future.

Robin Millar (Chapter 7) discusses on democratic decision-making, reflecting Tam Dalyell's point about the complexity of the science involved in issues of science policy. Millar also discusses the uncertainty of knowledge: not only might experts disagree but the process of science itself cannot be cut and dried. Like Claxton, Millar critiques the formal science curriculum but from a different perspective. He suggests that there is a core knowledge essential to any scientific understanding and proposes new areas to address the role of science education within a democratic society.

Les Levidow (Chapter 8) takes a close look at biotechnology education, which has strong links with the science of genetics. He explores the way in which commercially driven values can become incorporated in school texts. Levidow argues that science educators have to reflect on, and question, the values inherent in science, and look at alternatives to the dominant sciences and technologies, if their students are to be empowered.

5

INTEREST IN SCIENCE AND PUBLIC POLICY

Some thoughts

Tam Dalyell

I like to start with the positive and the good. While any estimate of the level of interest in science is necessarily anecdotal, my hunch is that interest in the subject is far, far greater than pundits and Jeremiahs would have us believe.

I say this out of two sets of experiences. First, there is the number of people who will initiate conversations arising out of science programmes on BBC2 or on Channel 4 – and, to be fair, from BBC1's *Wildlife on One*. Time and again, when I have seen the same programme, I am struck by how much has been retained by the viewer compared to that which has been retained from watching a political programme. Alas, a huge proportion of political pontificating goes in the one proverbial ear and rapidly exits from the other ear. Points and nuggets from scientific programmes actually lodge in the memory. Be this true of television, it is even more true of 'Steam Radio'. Crisp broadcasters like Jessica Holm on the *Natural World*, and the contributors to *Medicine Now*, for example, perform a real service to the cause of arousing interest in science. Perhaps it is only a pity that the multiplicity of media outlets does not make it possible for authoritative gurus of the stature and calibre of Sir Julian Huxley or Dr Jacob Bronowski to emerge – purveyors of scientific education to a whole generation in the 1950s.

The second set of circumstances which emboldens me to suggest that public interest is at a vastly higher level than conventional wisdom suspects relate to my thirty years' experience as a weekly columnist for *New Scientist*. I never cease to be amazed not only by the amount of written and oral feedback that returns to me, much of it from non-scientists, but also by the way in which I am used, legitimately, as a receptacle for information. Curiosity about 'how the world works', and in particular about 'how our own biology works', has never been so quickened.

Politicians – and I am no exception – are sensitive to the charges of complacency. Do I hear readers saying *sotto voce* 'How can this MP fellow be so complacent?' Well, that is a matter of taste. But it is not just my view: there is objective evidence to support what I am saying.

Given the level of public interest that I believe exists, one might suppose that the question of public participation in science is not a difficult one to address. On the contrary, it is a very difficult question indeed. It assumes that it is highly desirable that people should understand public policy decisions in science. At the risk of being dubbed elitist, I am agnostic as to whether it is all that important that people should understand public policy decisions – unless they want to, in which case they have a right to an explanation. Let me give an example. In the 1966–8 period, the first House of Commons Select Committee on Science and Technology delved into the issue of Reactor Types. Should we continue with the Magnox System? Should we put our eggs in the basket of the Advanced Gas-Cooled Reactor? Should we opt for the High Temperature Reactor being developed at Winifrith in Dorset? Should we join with the Canadians in developing the CANDU Reactor, which at that time looked like being the most reliable and cost-effective reactor in the world? Or should we turn to American developments, or try to forge a partnership with Electricité de France? At the end of eighteen months' hard work, I rather doubted whether the opinion of a baker's dozen of MPs on the Select Committee, albeit under the chairmanship of the late Arthur Palmer (himself a distinguished power-engineer), really added to the sum of human knowledge. Still less was a *vox pop* opinion on the topic worth anything whatsoever. Only a nuclear engineer could make a worth-while assessment of that question. Public understanding of such an issue is sheer myth.

The question of whether there should be a public understanding of the merits and demerits of nuclear, versus those of oil, coal and gas, is a quite different problem. This is because it is an argument which by no means wholly depends on a technical assessment. And this is true of other scientific and technologically related questions in the public eye, such as genetic engineering.

What people have above all to assess is the validity, the weighting attached, to the questions which ought to be put. The question that is uppermost in the mind of the member of the public concerned will determine his or her attitude. 'What solution will give jobs to the over 40s?' points a solution in the direction of coal. 'What solution is least unhealthy for those working in the industry?' would, in the light of the fact that the price of coal is often the price of pneumoconiosis, and too often the price of life itself, point to a solution other than coal. 'What solution points to the use of the cheapest source of power in the short term?' points to oil. 'What solution is most expensive in the long term from the point of view of the planet's scarce resources?' points against oil. 'What solution provides the most convenient source of power for cooking in the home?' might point in the direction of natural gas. 'What solution is going to deplete most rapidly the world's supply of chemical feedstock for future generations?'

points away from using natural gas. 'What solution is best for considering the planet's natural resources?' points in favour of nuclear power. 'What solution will build up the most difficult waste to reprocess or dispose of?' might point in the direction of a non-nuclear solution. Public understanding depends often on the ability to formulate, if not the right question, at least the question that is most relevant to the person who frames it. In this sense, political awareness and a keen sense of social responsibility are rather more important than a knowledge of science.

It is, however, necessary to have sufficient knowledge to avoid unreal solutions and cop-outs. The easy notion that wind-power or wave-power, whatever their small-scale virtues, can fuel huge advanced-world megalopolises just will not do. This is something which school-leavers should understand: facts, such as that to provide the same amount of power as one medium-sized power station, it would take 35,000 windmills, at some distance from one another, over 400 square miles of land or sea. So can these skills – let us tag them the 'skills of scientific discrimination' – be taught at school? My answer is an emphatic 'yes'. In this regard one should note the pertinent comments of my parliamentary colleagues on the Education Select Committee in July 1995 after listening to a variety of views from parties involved in science education and science policy (House of Commons 1995b: para. 66).

> The debate on public literacy with regard to science and technology needs to be extended and its implications for the curriculum considered. Witnesses from the Science Museum in London believed that 'a systematic review of the science curriculum from the perspective of the public understanding of science is long overdue'. Evidence received by the Science and Technology Select Committee during its inquiry into Human Genetics also makes the case for better public understanding of particular aspects of science (House of Commons 1995a). For instance, the Royal College of Pathologists argues that the extent to which secondary schools provide education in the basic principles of genetics should be assessed and 'very probably strengthened'. The National Consumer Council argued that better understanding of this very important aspect of scientific development required in turn a proper grasp of 'basic science, biology and mathematics'. This would 'help an individual put genetic information into an understandable context' (House of Commons 1995b: para. 68).

There are arguments from many quarters as to what is needed and what is the best way to go about it. It appears that there may be some agreement on the 'what' but little consensus on the 'how'.

Finally, a thought or two on the appreciation of science at school. Early enthusiasm, as the science writer Jim Baggott (1995) eloquently put it, for science's great questions, may be lost under the weight of its 300-year legacy. No amount of entertainment can hide the simple fact that to become properly qualified, to ask questions and hold an opinion, young people must first have a sound basis of knowledge and skills; in a world where information is so much more accessible and the corpus of knowledge is growing so quickly, this is a monumental task. Moreover, it can suddenly dawn on those in their late teens that the kind of science that they are required to do has scant association with those questions which held their interest when they embarked on a serious scientific course.

Politicians, when mentioning science at all, too often put it almost entirely in terms of how science can be of huge benefit to the nation's economy, and ability to compete commercially in a tough world. Can we then be surprised that the original enthusiasms for science can be quickly dampened? We might do better to pontificate more on the sense of wonder and purposes of science, and my experiences of innovations, such as the Launch Pad at the Science Museum teeming with inquisitive children, is that we are moving in the right direction.

6

SCIENCE OF THE TIMES
A 2020 vision of education
Guy Claxton

In this chapter I want to make some comments about science, then about education, and finally to put these two sets of considerations together and see what implications they have for the way we teach science to young people. Though what I shall have to say about science and education seems to me rather straightforward and unexceptionable, I suspect that it will not be so for everyone who reads this book. I would hope that when I come to put them together and make some suggestions about the kind of science education which we should now be working towards, perhaps with our eyes on the year 2020, that what I have to say will seem more sensible than radical. We shall see.

THE NATURE OF SCIENCE

Science, viewed as a body of 'knowledge', is more accurately seen as a set of languages or 'maps' than an incontrovertible edifice of truth. One might say, for example, that 'Hydrated copper sulphate crystals are blue, turning to an amorphous white powder when heated', and in doing so, seem to be simply stating a fact or reporting a reliable observation. But if I ask what 'copper sulphate' *is*, or *why* it should turn white when heated up, it rapidly becomes plain that, really to understand this simple 'observation', I have to learn a much more extensive language; to be able to read a map of this corner of 'reality' which is full of symbols and conventions, just as an ordinary map can be read only if I understand the conventions of contour lines, or the use of different colours to denote different kinds of roads.

Once we see that sciences are maps, or collections of maps, two other things about science emerge. First, just as there is no one 'best' map of London, say, no 'true' representation, so scientific theories and languages are also, necessarily, multiple and complementary. A 'perfect' map of London would *be* London – and its very completeness would render it useless. A map has to symbolize, simplify and distort if it is to be of any practical value. The map of the London Underground is a brilliant map precisely because it leaves out almost everything. Just so with the maps of the Periodic Table and the motions of the planets.

Maps are good only in so far as they enable people to fulfil their purposes; they are judged by their utility, not their veracity. The maps of science are good in so far as they enable us to predict, explain and control the behaviour of the material world. The languages of science are valuable if they allow us to talk interesting sense about interesting things, to have new thoughts about how things might be that have not yet been sensed, and to solve problems that are amenable to technical solution. Science, we might say, comprises a loose-knit family of ways of knowing, but there is no reason at all to suppose that this powerful, articulate, precise, explicit, predictive, practical family comprises the whole clan. There are other domains of human experience, other human purposes, for which these maps and dialects are not best suited, and this is not a failing of science, any more than it would be a failing of the technical argot of cricket that one could not talk in it of 'goals' or 'free kicks'.

The second point to emphasize is that, outside mathematics, the languages of science are saturated with metaphors and symbols borrowed and adapted from the vernacular. Scientific maps, like all maps, are works of human invention, and they must needs borrow from the known to chart the unknown. Whether it be atoms as billiard balls, electric current as a teeming crowd of electrons, or *Homo sapiens* as a naked ape, scientific theories are closer to poetry and art than the rhetoric of science frequently admits. Thus Werner Heisenberg (1971) could describe Niels Bohr – a 'scientist' if ever there was one – as using

> classical mechanics or quantum theory as a painter uses his brush and colours. Brushes do not determine the picture, and colour is never the full reality; but if he keeps the picture before his mind's eye, the artist can use his brushes to convey, however inadequately, his own mental picture to others. Bohr [has formed] an intuitive picture of different atoms; a picture he can only convey to other physicists *by such inadequate means* as electronic orbits and quantum conditions. It is not at all certain that Bohr himself believes that electrons revolve inside the atom.
>
> (Heisenberg 1971, emphasis added)

Ivan Tolstoy (1990) also invokes the spirit of Bohr:

> As Bohr said, 'When it comes to atoms, language can only be used as in poetry. The poet, too, is not nearly so concerned with describing facts as with creating images.' The same is true of cosmological models, curved spaces and exploding universes. Images and analogies are the key.... Not you, not I, not Einstein could interpret the universe in terms wholly related to our senses. Not that it is

incomprehensible, no. But we must learn to ignore our precon-
ceptions concerning space, time and matter, abandon the use of
everyday language, and resort to metaphor. We must try to think
like poets.

(Tolstoy 1990: 16)

Heisenberg's mention of 'an intuitive picture' is instructive, for here again
the process of 'doing science' (as described above; not as technical tinkering
and routine problem-solving) differs from its public face. Certainly science
relies on a subtle interplay of dispassionate observation and rational
deduction – which distinguishes its maps and methods from those of
'common sense' on the one hand and philosophy on the other. But the stool
will not balance without its third, vital, leg: that of intuition and imagination. The generation of ideas through hunches, analogies and intuitions is
as essential to science as the extrapolation and the testing of them. It is not
the absence of poetry that defines science, but the ways it interacts with
reason, and the purposes and criteria to which its products are subject.

In a survey, eighty-three Nobel laureates in physics, chemistry and
medicine were asked about the role of intuition in their research (Marton
et al. 1994). Of these, seventy-two were in no doubt about its importance.
(To complement the physicists' perspective offered by Heisenberg and
Bohr, I shall quote here from laureates in medicine and biology.) Michael
Brown (laureate in 1985), for example, said:

And so . . . as we did our work, I think, we almost felt at times
that there was a hand guiding us. Because we would go from one
step to the next, and somehow we would know which was the right
way to go. And I can't really tell how we knew that.

(Marton *et al.* 1994)

Several of the respondents commented on the fact that intuition, to work
well, seems to need a certain attitude of mind, one in which the exercise
of deliberate, purposeful reason is suspended, and a different, more
leisurely way of knowing gently encouraged. Rita Levi-Montalcini (laureate in 1986) said:

you've been thinking about something *without willing to* for a long
time. . . . Then all of a sudden the problem is opened to you in a flash
and you suddenly see the answer.

(Marton *et al.* 1994, emphasis added)

And Konrad Lorenz (laureate in 1973) spelled it out even more clearly:

This apparatus . . . which intuits . . . plays in a very mysterious
manner, because . . . it sort of keeps all known facts afloat, waiting
for them to fall into place, like a jigsaw puzzle. [Scientific creativity
is no guarantee against the *mixing* of metaphors, it seems.] And if

73

you press, if you try to permutate your knowledge, nothing comes of it. You must give a sort of mysterious pressure, and then rest, and suddenly BING! . . . the solution comes.

(Marton *et al*. 1994)

It appears that the way of knowing that is most conducive to idea-generation, especially the discovery of fruitful images, models and metaphors, is leisurely, poetic and unpremeditated; very different from the way of knowing in which subtle implications are extracted and elegant and watertight experiments designed.

Science, in sum, is both a content and process. As content, the most appropriate analogies for science itself are maps and languages, whose value inheres only in their ability to facilitate the human purposes, preeminently, of articulate explanation and technical control. Conventional sciences, being essentially reductionist and analytic, work well in domains which are amenable to such approaches – roughly, those enshrined in the school physical science curriculum – and badly when applied to 'dissipative structures' (Prigogine and Stengers 1984), microorganismic systems, global ecology or, indeed, living bodies. (Dissipative structures are chemical systems that behave like biological systems in that they 'evolve', under suitable conditions, into more complex patterns.) Different terrains and different purposes require different maps: 'complementarity' is to be expected.

As process, science is loosely characterized by an interplay of observation and experimentation, deduction and intuition, governed by criteria of coherence, elegance, and parsimony, which result in interesting speculation, productive explanation and/or successful prediction. This core cognitive cocktail, the proportions of which depend on the nature and maturity of the science in question, is mixed, consumed and judged within a context of personal, social, political and financial pressures which influence the process in a variety of ways (see Figure 6.1). Collins and Shapin (1986) and others have clearly shown how the research that gets done reflects the (non-scientific) priorities of those who fund it; and how the way it gets accredited – published in prestigious journals, for example – is influenced by all kinds of informal, intuitive judgements that percolate through the scientific community.

It follows that the public image of science, and especially that which informs the vast majority of science education, is wrong or misleading at almost every point. With the exception of the odd lesson about Brave Little Galileo and the Stupid Old Church, and a nod at 'phlogiston' and 'caloric', the social and historical context are ignored in favour of a routine transmission of a body of (true, unequivocal) knowledge. Likewise that which *is* new, contentious and equivocal – the Gaia hypothesis, chaos theory, qualitative biology – is rejected (precisely because it is 'unproven')

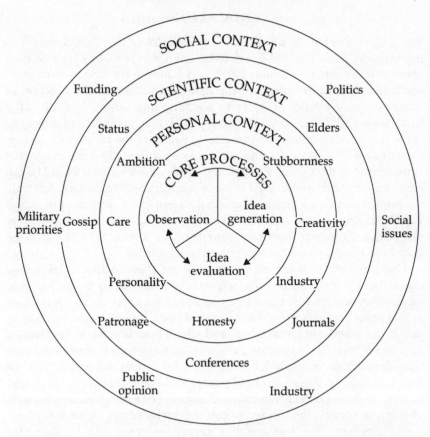

Figure 6.1 The nature of scientific activity
Source: Claxton (1991)

in favour of the dull, desiccated roll-call of 'core concepts' with which we are all familiar. The theory-ladenness of both 'facts' and 'observations' may be acknowledged, but is then simply disregarded. The essential role of poetic, intuitive modes of mind in science is ignored in favour of a naive acceptance of scientific language as literal and transparent. The place of values, purposes and vested interests in science is generally overlooked, as is its role as a discourse of power within its cultural setting. The exposure of science and technology as villains of the environment, just as much as its heroes, is a minor embarrassment, if it is mentioned at all. (The cleverness of toasters or foetal heart monitors tends to be explored rather more fully than factory farming and genetic engineering.) The widespread assumption that science does not just own the epistemological high ground, but is actually the only (valid) epistemological game in town, goes, for the most part, unarticulated and uncontested.

EDUCATION

But I do not wish to dwell here on describing the shortcomings of mainstream, post-National-Curriculum science in schools: I have written about this elsewhere (Claxton 1991), and I am not the first to have done so. Rather I want to turn from the nature of science to the function of education as a whole, in order to see how and why – if at all – the distortions and deletions should be rectified. It is not sufficient merely to show that science education does not do justice to the realities of science; there may well be good educational reasons for defending the image that is presented to the young. Perhaps the 'truth' about science would be too complex, or too destabilizing for most young people to handle. After all, we protect them, as a matter of principle, from many aspects of the adult world for which we judge them to be unready. Or maybe it simply does not matter. To answer these questions, we have to face, for a moment, the hoary old question of what on earth education is for.

'Child-rearing' is what adults provide for their society's children to equip them to live successfully, responsibly and happily in the world in which they will find themselves as adults. 'Education' is the formal part of that provision which could not be relied upon to come about on its own, just in the process of growing up, and which therefore has to be planned and prescribed. The 'education system' which any society finds itself with thus depends on a whole lot of different influences: what image of the future is held by those who hold power and wield influence; the degree of inertia which prevents education changing fast enough to keep up with changes in society; the dominant cultural assumptions about what 'success', 'happiness' and 'responsibility' mean, and about what learning may be supposed to happen 'naturally' in the course of growing up, and what cannot be trusted to do so.

So, with the intention of seeing what may be desirable and appropriate, rather than starting with what we have got, let me put on my long-distance visionary spectacles – the ones with 20–20 foresight – and try to discern what education as a whole may need to be moving towards. Where better to start than with a cliché: we live in an age of uncertainty, and that uncertainty can be confidently expected to grow. We can say very little about the year 2020 – except that we can say very little about it. Its technology, its jobs, its patterns of employment, unemployment and self-employment, the nature of leisure, lifestyle and 'family life', its social and geographical mobility, its religious and spiritual forms, its national and international politics, its multi-ethnic balances and tensions, its environmental and ecological concerns . . . none of it is in the least predictable. How to equip the babies that are being born today with the ability to live well under such conditions as the young adults of 2020, is, it seems self-evident to me, the only serious educational issue there is.

It is equally obvious that we cannot give them what they will need if we cannot anticipate with any confidence what it will be. We cannot give them the tools when we do not know the jobs. But what we can – I say must – do is give them the capacity and the confidence to be tool-makers: to be able to fashion and refashion their tools for living and working as different challenges and opportunities emerge and change throughout their lives. Someone once defined 'intelligence' as 'knowing what to do when you don't know what to do'. The next great challenge for education is to put the development of intelligence, in this sense, at the top of its 'research and development' agenda. Our top priority, not just at the level of some cheerful snap-on rhetoric, but in reality, has to be to re-cast education so that it helps all young people – not just the academically adept – to become good learners: to develop, we might say, their learning prowess.

We used to think that intelligence or 'learn-ability' was a (relatively) fixed dollop of general-purpose ability that God gave you when you were born, the size of which could be accurately diagnosed on the basis of answers elicited under stress to a variety of mental puzzles. We now know that intelligence is much better seen as a tool-kit of diverse learning skills and attitudes, one which almost everybody is capable, given the right help, of acquiring (Howe 1988). To refer to students as 'bright', or 'less able', as if this were the same kind of thing as saying that they had red hair, or a quick temper, is to lock them into an old-fashioned view in which learn-ability is something you manifest, not something which you can grow.

What does this New Look intelligence mean? How can we unpack this high-sounding aim so that it becomes more clear what exactly we are trying to achieve? I have tried to do this elsewhere (Claxton 1990, 1994, 1996a) in terms of a new 'Three Rs': resilience, resourcefulness and reflection. (In what follows I am drawing on my 1994 article 'The next challenge for education', published in *Teacher's Post*. I am grateful to the Post Office for permission to quote from that piece.)

Resilience

Resilience is the ability to stick with learning when it gets difficult. When you are learning, there is always the risk of making a mistake – asking a silly question, getting it wrong. You may very well feel confused as you try to sort out what is what. And you are quite likely to experience some apprehension or anxiety. That is how learning feels, so to be a good learner you need to be able to tolerate these possibilities and emotions.

If, on the other hand, you have learnt that it is vital to your self-esteem to succeed, to understand, to be in control, and to feel cool, calm and collected at all times, then your resilience as a learner will have been undermined. As soon as things stop running smoothly and a bit of uncertainty creeps in, you will begin to get rattled, and instead of learning you will have to start protecting yourself and covering up. We know only too well how people behave when they do *not* feel equipped to cope with learning. They become invisible and pass the buck. They feel ashamed, upset or angry. They create diversions, blame the system, or stop trying (Thompson 1993). If all else fails, they go missing. Once the rot sets in, and learning becomes a misery, then damage-limitation is the top priority. The school, the society and most crucially the people themselves all suffer.

The first requirement for an education system that wants to help young people become good learners, therefore, is that it protects and strengthens their resilience. They have to see learning as a challenge, not as a threat. Any school that places too much emphasis on successful achievement and fast answers, and which outlaws the feelings of learning, may look good in the league tables, but it is not a learning school. Aiming for achievement, in conventional terms, may, at the same time, develop learning prowess; but it may also damage or stunt it. It depends on the implicit messages of the learning 'subtext' that necessarily accompanies any particular 'text' that forms the object of study.

Resourcefulness

The second feature of good learners is their resourcefulness. Given the willingness to see learning situations positively, and not to bolt at the first sign of difficulty, the next thing is to know what to do when life (or school) lobs a learning invitation your way. Good learners are equipped not just with one way of tackling problems but with a varied repertoire, so that if their initial approach turns out to be unequal to the task, they always have an alternative up their sleeve. Different people learn in different ways, and different learning jobs require different tools and approaches.

For example recent research has revealed that not all situations are best dealt with via a head-on, problem-solving kind of approach (e.g. Berry and Dienes 1993). Complex, messy kinds of situations may be more amenable to a strategy in which you take time to play around with them, rather than trying to figure them out consciously (as the Nobel laureates, quoted earlier, well knew). A few years ago you may have had the humbling experience of failing to master the wretched Rubik cube, while a young acquaintance seemed to crack it with relative ease. In such cases we learn better when we stop trying to understand and simply 'mess about' with the task, paying sustained, relaxed attention to the way it behaves, without at the same time seeking to formulate explicit ideas about it. Young people have a greater facility with messing about, and greater implicit faith in it as a learning strategy, than do adults, who have often been taught to put all their learning eggs in a single basket labelled 'Figure it Out and Show Your Working'; and who thus feel discomfited when they do not have an instant mental handle on the situation.

In general a good learning tool-kit comprises the ability to see what is there, rather than what you think is there, or would like to be there; to maintain attention to things that do not immediately reveal or explain themselves (i.e. 'concentrate'); to ask useful questions, both verbally and via non-verbal interactions; to gather data through reading, and to organize it in productive ways (which may be haphazard and idiosyncratic as well as systematic); to experiment, play and practise; to allow intuition and imagination to work on things in their own unhurried and unfocused way; to think things out carefully and logically; and to observe the way other people go about doing what you would like to be able to do. Of course you have to have a reasonable (but not infallible) working knowledge of what kinds of learning challenges each of these is likely to be good for. (You will not find the meaning of life in a book, nor will you get the right time by meditating.)

The tools of learning cannot be taught directly. Some people, once they realize that we can learn how to learn, immediately start thinking about how to analyse learning into its components and turning these into a new 'curriculum', as if intelligence were composed of bits of mental Lego that could be trained separately and snapped together. But human minds are not machines that can be assembled out of pre-cast blocks and cogs. They are integrated systems that have to be grown rather than engineered. Learning ability develops out of first-hand experience with a diversity of interesting challenges. Education for learning has to avoid the blind alley of isolating and training 'competencies'.

Reflectiveness

The third ingredient of good learning is reflectiveness. As you are engaged in learning, you need to be able to monitor how things are going, to take stock from time to time, and to decide, in the light of the whole picture, whether to plough on, change tack, or even drop it for a while. Knowing when to quit is as vital a skill for the learner as it is for the poker player. Good learners have to be good managers of their own learning, and this needs self-awareness. But this ability to manage your own learning is not something that can be taught directly, any more than learning itself can. If you put young people in a learning environment where everything is predetermined, where they have little control over what, when, where, why and how to learn, where 'success' is defined and measured by someone else, and where the choices that are offered are trivial or cosmetic, then they have no chance to develop the skills and awarenesses of good learning management. Self-discipline and self-awareness grow only through responsibility. Education for learning has always to be asking how little has to be predetermined, not how much. Teachers have to cultivate the art of backing off. The more we try to make education fool-proof, the more we will produce people who are foolish as learners.

SCIENCE EDUCATION

Let us make a crude distinction between Science, with a capital 'S', and science with a small 's'. Science with a big 'S' is what professional Scientists know and do. It involves mastery of specialist languages and maps, and the ability to use high-tech methods and machines. Science with a small 's' is the low-tech vernacular equivalent: it is the ability to combine observation, experimentation, imagination and deliberation creatively and flexibly in the pursuit of solutions to personally relevant problems. In the light of the foregoing discussion, I would argue, as aims of science education, that it is essential for everyone, in an uncertain world, to be able to operate as a vernacular scientist; it is useful for everyone to understand something of the real world of Science, and to feel confident of their ability to find out more about specific Scientific issues that affect or interest them directly; and that it is not necessary for everyone to go through the protracted and diluted apprenticeship in the rudiments of classical Science which currently forms the basis of the school science curriculum.

In fact, in so far as this apprenticeship teaches some (most?) young people that Science is boring, hard, technical and remote – which all the research shows is exactly what it does – it undermines the achievement of the first two aims, and should be discarded. Of course there comes a point in the lives of some young people when they make career- or university-related choices that put them on a track towards becoming Scientists, and at this point they will certainly need to begin to master canonical bodies of knowledge (languages and maps) and increasingly sophisticated techniques. But the evidence seems clear that the imposition of this track on all young people is not worth the candle: it does more harm than good. The risks, in terms of dulling interest in the Scientific issues of the day, and in stunting the development of young people's ability to be good vernacular scientists, outweigh the benefits. There is no justification for forcing them to grapple, over several years, with Newtonian dynamics, photosynthesis, Boyle's Law and the Periodic Table, if the net gain is a mediocre GCSE and the net loss is damage to their resilience, resourcefulness and reflectiveness, and to their self-confidence as finder-outers about Science as they go along.

Much curriculum development in science education since the early 1960s or earlier has attempted to fiddle with the presentation of these core concepts and theories, without seriously questioning their sacrosanct status. Introducing Newton's frictionless universe with a brief discussion of roller-blading, or Ohm's Law by talking about Jean-Michel Jarre's laser show, is just seduction if, below the surface, nothing has changed. Instead of the dead hand of traditional physics, chemistry and biology – however warmed-over and sugar-coated – I have proposed the following skeleton of a 2020 science curriculum for discussion and elaboration (Claxton 1991).

At primary school – as is the case with much good practice at present – the emphasis should be on developing children's intuitive understanding of scientific thinking, as well as its role and value. At all costs they must be protected from the ever-lengthening tentacles of traditional Science which currently threaten to reach ever further down the age range. Learning the Scientists' names for things does not matter at this level; what does is getting a feel for the power of combining observation, imagination, deliberation and experimentation – or, to put it even more simply, looking carefully at something (a piece of pumice stone floating; milk going sour), and asking How come? So what? What if? 'How Come?' requires you to use your imagination to dream up a story about what you see. 'So What?' elaborates the story to explore its logical implications. 'What if?' links those deductions to further observations or tests that one could carry out to see if the story holds up. This can be done – is best done – without a single test-tube, or any reference to formal Science. Insist on the 'proper' names, measurements and ways of communicating and you will, for many children, kill the spirit of scientific thinking. At this age, re-inventing the wheel is perfectly acceptable, because it is the inventing, not the wheel, that is at stake.

In the early years of secondary school, science should be divided into four main themes. First and foremost is the inquiry theme, which continues and deepens the project-centred approach of the primary school. Students work individually or in small groups on projects of their own choice, under the general supervision, guidance and modelling of a teacher – or preferably an older student Science specialist in the school, who would gain valuable experience from the role. (As any science teacher will tell you, it is the naive questions of the beginner that are often the hardest to answer, the most challenging.) A central role for the supervisor here is guiding the development of students' reflection on the process of inquiry, so that their ability to monitor, evaluate and differentiate between their own learning strategies, in the light of events, becomes an habitual and instinctive resource. 'Where are we going?' 'What have we found out?' 'What else could we try?' 'Is it worth carrying on?' These are all questions which good, intelligent learners hold in their minds continually. Students should be encouraged to take on projects where they are going to have some interesting explorations – before discovering that in this particular case the scientific approach fails (perhaps because terms are too ill-defined, or because the question is ultimately one of belief or value rather than empirical observation). Mapping the limitations of scientific thinking is as important as developing its power.

As educator, the teacher's role here is not didactic but Socratic: the teacher acts as a midwife to the birth of students' own theories, and encourages their testing. Just how powerful this can be – not least in transforming student interest and engagement – has been demonstrated many times. In a study by Mark Cosgrove at the University of Technology, Sydney, for example, groups of unexceptional 14-year-old boys were working with one of the good old stand-bys of the school lab, the circuit board, on which simple electrical circuits containing batteries, switches, bulbs and resistances can be assembled (Cosgrove 1995). Even though the content here is conventional, and not self-generated or controversial, the teacher adopts a clearly Socratic role, not giving students the accepted definitions and formulae, but skilfully helping them to draw out, put to the test and improve upon their own intuitive images and metaphors for the behaviour of the electric current.

The boys discovered for themselves that the key to their difficulty lay in the assumption, enshrined in their intuitive analogies, that current had to be used up in order to overcome a resistance – which it is not. In order to resolve the problem, they generated new metaphors which made the crucial – and Scientifically 'correct' – distinction between the whatever-it-is that flows round the circuit, and the quite different whatever-it-is that pushes it around: what Scientists refer to as 'current' and 'voltage'. For example, if electricity is likened to a convoy of lorries, their fuel gets used up as they drive along – and more gets used up if they have to go up steep hills – but the goods they are carrying do not. By working this out for themselves they are experiencing what Latour (1987) calls 'science-in-the-making'; they are acting as proto-scientists, and developing their abilities to think scientifically in the process. Cosgrove comments that these 'ordinary' students

> showed that they were capable of mature and sustained thinking. They relished the opportunity to reason through to a conclusion and to take part in extended debates and discussions (in which there was strong reliance on the evidence provided by tests they [had planned and carried out themselves] to discriminate amongst the possibilities they proposed. After a time, these students showed the capacity to take some control of their learning. They gave up asking the teacher for all the answers, *confident that they could work problems out for themselves.*
>
> (Cosgrove 1995: 307, emphasis added)

While the class teacher observes, with some surprise:

> The thing that impresses me is how far they have come. . . . They are automatically sieving out what does not fit with what they have seen. And they are only accepting and hanging on to what they see. . . . And only ideas which might be right are accepted and tossed

around. They are not interested in me telling them any more. They
have moved right away from, 'What's the right answer?' . . . What
they really want from me is for me to say, 'That sounds like a good
idea' or 'What if this was tried?' And they go off and think. They are
not interested in whether you think it is right or wrong.

(Cosgrove 1995: 307)

From the traditionalists' point of view, this is cause for a lot of harrumphing
about 'mastering the basics' and even 'dereliction of duty'. But for teachers
interested in developing students' abilities as learners – their resilience,
resourcefulness and reflectivity – this is music to their ears. Here, in
microcosm, is genuine science – and Science – in the doing and the making,
with all its ingredients of observation, imagination, deliberation and
experimentation being deployed to good effect. Here is Science as a useful
human invention, subject to dispute and erected on the metaphorical
foundations of everyday life; as a map that is purpose-built and which
changes over time. And here are students who are not just force-fed with
the dried fruits of past Scientific labours, but tracking the growth of that
fruit, and understanding for themselves why and how it grew as it did.

The second theme for early secondary school – Key Stage 3 – also
develops the work of Key Stages 1 and 2, and focuses on practical
understandings of how things work. If the first theme is proto-science, this
is proto-technology. Developing intuitive, working knowledge, and confidence in taking things to bits and putting them back together (and also
knowing the limits of one's ability to 'do it yourself') is a useful life-skill.
Designing and making machines out of readily available bits and pieces
to get useful jobs done again builds confidence and capability. Under no
circumstances should a concern with technology be used as a Trojan horse
in which to smuggle back the old baggage (as, I am sorry to say, it often
is at present).

The third theme should be aimed at developing students' ability to be
critical consumers of Science. This means understanding both the power
and the limitations of Scientific discourse; being able to discriminate
between Science and Scientism – the illicit attempt to give warrant and
status to one's claims by presenting them as if they were Scientifically
proven or justified; and developing the disposition to do so in the course
of daily life. (Ernest Hemingway, you may recall, was being hounded by
an interviewer, in the early 1960s, to identify the essential characteristic of
a 'great writer'. Finally cornered, he agreed that there was just one, 'a built-
in, shock-proof crap detector'. This is also what every citizen needs in a
Scientific age.) Advertisements and newspaper claims should be routinely
run through the crap detector. '9 out of 10 owners who responded said
their cat preferred Whiskas'. To what: Tabasco sauce? Fresh salmon? Who
were the sample interviewed? What proportion failed to answer (and

why)? What inducements (if any) were people offered to take part in the survey? Who carried it out? Were the interviewers impartial or Whiskas employees? Where was it conducted: Athens? Chipping Norton? And so on. Good learners now, as in the year 2020, will need to be able to see through the claims of Science to truth, universality, and trustworthiness, while at the same time not jumping out of the frying-pan of awe and gullibility, in the face of Science's smugness and superiority, into the fire of an equally dangerous and simplistic cynicism, or into the arms of the pseudo-certainties of the New Age.

If this theme is to have maximum bite and benefit, it has to be opportunistic, capitalizing on the events of the day, while they are 'hot' in young people's minds. The decommissioning of Shell's Brent Spar storage platform would have made an excellent focus for all kinds of discussions ranging from the technical to the ethical, for example; as would a news item about a legal battle to switch off an irrecoverable coma patient's life-support system, or French nuclear testing in the South Pacific. This, of course, demands flexibility, enthusiasm and general-purpose scientific (and Scientific) *nous* from the teacher. What it does not require, however, is omniscience – because the point is not for the teacher to have all the answers, but to orchestrate the asking of good questions, and to explore ways, in practice or in principle – of finding things out.

The fourth and final theme, which should not take up more than a quarter of the available time, is a study theme, which is the only time teachers are allowed to actually teach, in the old-fashioned sense of the term. This should focus on a small number of currently contentious areas in Science, exploring both the Science of it – the theories and the data – and the way the debate is being conducted. I have mentioned some of the contenders earlier: they include James Lovelock's Gaia hypothesis, chaos theory, the evolution of consciousness, parapsychology, neurology and neuropsychology à la Oliver Sacks, and Rupert Sheldrake's theory of 'morphic fields'. (Sheldrake's (1994) *Seven Experiments that could Change the World* would form an excellent source-book here, not because he is right, or even because he exemplifies good Science; on the contrary, his rightness and his Science are highly questionable, and, just for that reason, ideal material for students on which to cut their teeth.) I simply do not believe anyone who says that in order to be ready to tackle these 'hard' issues, you need to have sat through years of electromagnetism, chemical bonding and the kinetic theory of gases. As Peter Fensham has said: 'There appears to be no inherent need to spend four, six or eight years of slow build-up of this sort of scientific knowledge' (Fensham 1985).

Beyond the age of 14, the content and methods of Science must be allowed to resurface – but by then, if I am right, an unshakable foundation of confidence and competence in scientific thinking will have been laid, which would not be capable of being undermined by some genuinely hard stuff. Indeed the 'hard stuff' would be less hard, by virtue of the greater resilience, resourcefulness and reflectiveness which all students would be bringing with them. By delaying study of the conceptual and methodo-logical apparatus of formal Science until a strong facility with vernacular science has been established, everybody wins.

We need finally to return to one common objection to presenting Science as human-made maps and languages: that young people are cognitively and/or emotionally unable to cope with the implied uncertainty and condi-tionality. 'You may be right about Science', they will concede, 'but school students need the security of a firm grounding in the basics, presented as "the truth", before they are ready to cope with a more complicated picture'. Or – a stronger version – they might argue, with M. R. Matthews (1995) that opening up a view of science as a human construction is the thin end of a highly dangerous wedge that can only result in a slide into the black pit of post-modern relativism, and The End of Civilization as We Know It. (This presentation of Matthews' position is no caricature, much as it sounds like one: see Claxton 1996b.) While I have much sympathy, especially for parents, with the former argument in the moral domain, their fears for 11-year olds, say, in the cognitive sphere are groundless, and reactionary. Studies by Ellen Langer and colleagues at Harvard (e.g. Langer *et al.* 1989) have shown that students ranging in age from 9 to 22 are not disconcerted by being taught in a way that makes the uncertain status of knowledge evident; and are able to use what they have studied in more creative, flexible and intelligent ways if they have been so taught.

> If children are initially introduced to information in a conditional way, they appear to be better able to deal with that information creatively, if circumstances change. . . . [Students] taught 'absolutely' were good at reciting back what they had been given, but were limited in their ability to creatively *and spontaneously* use that information. . . . Children taught conditionally are *more* secure be-cause they are better prepared for negative or unexpected outcomes.
> (Langer *et al.* 1989: 144, 147, 141, emphases added)

To put it in Langer's more general terms, knowledge understood as the absolute truth or objective reality tends to be treated by people in a parrot-like and mindless fashion. Knowledge understood as a useful, provisional human construction is available for flexible reappraisal and creative play. And children as young as 9 are perfectly able to handle this latter approach, and to benefit from it.

CONCLUSION

If we are to begin to ask questions about schooling of the requisite depth, and to put in place a system that will adequately address the real-world needs of the citizens of the year 2020 – all of them – we have to shift our attention from the content of learning, whether this is seen as 'concepts' or 'competencies', SATs or GNVQs, to the processes, feelings, capabilities and qualities of good learners: to the development of learning prowess. The implications of this shift are subtle and immense; we are only just beginning to appreciate what will have to change if this essential goal is to be met. Teachers' language (especially with respect to 'ability') and attitudes (especially with respect to assessment, feedback and the evaluation of engagement over achievement) will certainly have to change, as will their classroom organization and their views of themselves as learners. But school organization, the public examination system and parental expectations will have to change too. The debate is critical and overdue. Neither politicians nor, sadly, teachers' professional associations, seem to have grasped either the profundity or the urgency of the situation.

Science education occupies a key position in this debate, for if it would only release its anxious and stultifying grasp on its traditional content, and encourage young people to develop their resilience, resourcefulness and reflection within the scientific domain, by acting as vernacular scientists, it could lead the way in developing a new education for learning. And if it were to accept that Science reflects one among several valid and valuable ways of knowing, each of which can be misunderstood, abused or misapplied; that it is a human construction of incredible power, in the hands, all too often, of people with moral myopia and a dangerously materialistic squint, then it might regain some of the ethical and epistemological credibility which it has lost.

7

SCIENCE EDUCATION FOR DEMOCRACY

What can the school curriculum achieve?

Robin Millar

Although the products of science and technology play a major part in our everyday lives, they are, for the most part, taken-for-granted and 'invisible'. As a result, one of the ways in which we become most directly aware of the impact of science and technology is through media reporting of socio-scientific issues, that is, social issues with a significant scientific or technological dimension. Among the many such issues which have arisen in recent years are concerns about BSE (bovine spongiform encephalopathy) and meat products, arguments about the disposal of radioactive waste from the nuclear power industry, worries about global climatic effects of carbon dioxide emissions and debates about the use of genetically engineered organisms.

One of the commonest, and also one of the more persuasive, arguments for seeking to improve public understanding of science springs from a concern about the public response to such issues. In a democratic society, the argument runs, the public accountability of science depends on people having an understanding of science which enables them to recognize what is at issue in a socio-scientific dispute, reach an informed view, and participate in discussion, debate and decision-making.

This is not, of course, the only argument for improving public understanding of science. Others appeal to the practical utility of scientific knowledge, or the cultural significance of science as a form of knowledge (for a fuller discussion, see Thomas and Durant 1987). In this chapter, however, I want to focus on the democratic argument for promoting better public understanding of science. I will begin by asking: what understanding of science do people need in order to respond appropriately to socio-scientific issues which enter the public domain? From this discussion, I will draw out the idea that some understanding of the nature of scientific knowledge is necessary. I then go on to discuss some recent attempts in the UK to teach about the nature of scientific knowledge within the school science curriculum. This leads to a more general discussion of the implications of trying to communicate an understanding of science which recognizes, and can account adequately for, the consensual nature of core knowledge and the openness of socio-scientific issues. My focus will be on formal school science, but the issues apply equally to the portrayal of science more generally.

RESPONDING TO SOCIO-SCIENTIFIC ISSUES: WHAT DO PEOPLE NEED TO KNOW?

In order to understand a media account of a socio-scientific issue, it is clearly necessary to have some understanding of the science content involved. This content, however, changes from one socio-scientific issue to the next, and it is impossible to predict the science content of future socio-scientific issues. The detailed knowledge needed to understand even a small subset of recent socio-scientific issues would overfill the school science curriculum – and might be wholly inappropriate for dealing with future issues. As regards science content, what the school curriculum should aim to provide is the framework of fundamental core ideas which provides the basis for acquiring a more detailed understanding of specific issues as and when they arise. So, for example, Andersson (1990) argues that an understanding of the possible links between pollution from vehicle exhausts and damage to forests depends on an understanding of the scientific model of a chemical reaction as a rearrangement of atoms to form new molecules, with nothing being destroyed or created. Therefore, he concludes:

> The concepts used . . . – atom, molecule, chemical reaction – should be part of the mental equipment of every pupil by the time he or she leaves school. They are key concepts that help build a rough model of various situations, for example, one's own working environment. These concepts enable us to form a general picture and provide a basis for further enquiry about the details.
>
> (Andersson 1990: 53–4)

Other 'framework' ideas of this sort might include: the germ theory of disease; the gene model of inheritance; ideas about energy, entropy and the direction and limits of change; the transfer of energy and information by radiation.

Such knowledge may be necessary, but it is not sufficient, for understanding a socio-scientific dispute. To see better the range of understandings demanded, it may be helpful to consider a specific example. I will choose, simply because it happens to be in the news at the time of writing this chapter, the controversy over French nuclear weapons testing in the Pacific. An article in *The Independent on Sunday* (10 September 1995: 12) explains that 'French scientists claim there is no risk of radioactive contamination because a nuclear explosion creates intense heat which vitrifies volcanic rock, so sealing radiation emissions in a glass "sarcophagus".' It then goes on to report the views of 'an expert in volcanic rock at the British Geological Survey': The question, she said, is whether the rock will retain its integrity or whether it will fracture – and over what timescale. . . . 'What the French are clearly assuming is that the heat will turn the rock to glass and it will self seal. This needs to be tested in the laboratory and modelled on computers.'

Several features of this dispute are common to most socio-scientific issues which enter the public domain:

1 There is disagreement between scientific experts.
2 Data relating to the situation are incomplete and/or uncertain. Key 'facts' are not known or are contested.
3 The situation is complex (it involves not just highly advanced physics and chemistry and their associated technologies, but also geology, vulcanology, ecology). It is also messy (there are many variables, which cannot be fully controlled; the conditions are quite unlike laboratory conditions), and locally specific (the outcome depends on specific characteristics of the local rock structures).
4 The outcome in the actual situation cannot be determined by experiment. Instead approaches such as computer modelling have to be used to apply laboratory knowledge to the complex real-world situation. The structure of these models and the values of parameters used are a matter of expert judgement. Different views and predictions are stated in terms of probabilities, rather than certainties.
5 The core scientific knowledge which bears on the situation (in this case, for example, about radioactivity and radioactive processes) is not disputed, but is agreed by all the protagonists.

Science educators have increasingly argued that, in order to understand disputes of this sort, people need a subtler appreciation of the nature and status of scientific knowledge, through a better understanding of the methods of scientific inquiry and of science as a social enterprise. Giere (1991) argues that a person reading an account of a scientific episode needs to approach it with a model of scientific inquiry like that shown in Figure 7.1 in mind: scientists propose theoretical models and hypothesize that these match the real world, in some respects and to some degree of accuracy; reasoning from a model leads to some specific predictions about what will be observed; these are compared with data from observation or experiment; the extent of agreement either increases or diminishes our confidence in the model. A theoretical model is a conjecture and hence tentative. It is not simply a description or 'picture' of the real world.

In a similar vein, many science educators have stressed the need to teach scientific explanations as 'models', and not as descriptions of the world. In other words, there has to be time, in science teaching, for some reflection

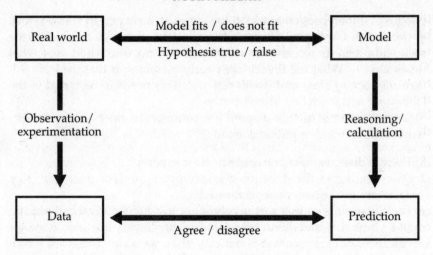

Figure 7.1 The structure of a scientific episode involving a theoretical model
Source: Giere (1991)

on the nature of scientific knowledge itself; a metacognitive and epistemological strand is necessary, not an optional extra (for a fuller
discussion, see Driver *et al.* 1996, esp. chs 2 and 10). Collins and Shapin
(1986) argue for teaching about the social influences on theory choice and
knowledge construction in the sciences. They argue that the science
curriculum communicates a '"received model" of scientific rationality',
which leads learners to think that 'unbiased methods of investigation will
reveal unambiguous, unique and repeatable true facts about the natural
world' (p. 73). This provides, in their view, no resources for interpreting
disagreements between scientific experts, other than ascribing bias or
incompetence to one or both. They suggest that practical work by the
pupils might be used to draw out key ideas about scientific practice: that
data are inherently and inevitably messy and do not lead unproblem-
atically to 'the truth', and that consensus does not simply emerge but must
be negotiated. Millar and Wynne (1988) report examples of precisely the
sorts of attributions of bias and incompetence to which Collins and Shapin
(1986) refer in an analysis of media reporting and comment following the
Chernobyl disaster. They argue for a curriculum which emphasizes 'the
processes by which scientific knowledge is obtained and validated', but
against any simplistic representation of these as a knowledge-generating
algorithm. Shapin (1992) suggests that the science curriculum should
include some studies of 'science-in-the-making', drawing on either historical or contemporary case studies, an approach which has a lengthy
pedigree within the liberal education tradition (M. R. Matthews 1994).

Returning, then, to the nuclear testing dispute, it is certainly the case that many of the claims made by the scientists involved are tentative and based on conjecture, and that understanding this is important in making sense of the dispute. The dispute is about how likely certain outcomes are. The uncertainties are about the models which are used, on both sides, to try to apply scientific knowledge to a particular, local situation. Hence there is ample scope for differences in interpretation of the data, and it becomes difficult to avoid the conclusion that the wider commitments of the protagonists influence the weighting they give to different pieces of evidence and to different models. Models of this sort, however, are very different in nature and status from the models of core science, such as the atomic/molecular model of chemical reactions, or, in this case, the accepted model of radioactive decay processes. It is clear that a substantial core of knowledge of this sort is not under dispute. Most of the science content taught in school, however, is within this generally agreed core. If we are to emphasize that scientific explanations are based on tentative models, we must face the question: do we really want school students to regard these core ideas as tentative? Harré (1986: 3) asks rhetorically: 'Could anyone seriously doubt that the blood in the human body circulates? ... Does it make any sense at all to doubt that water is predominantly H_2O?' Are we really to teach pupils that core ideas like the atomic/molecular view of chemical reactions are tentative? If such ideas are tentative, then 'non-tentative' is at risk of becoming a null category!

There are, in addition, pedagogical issues here. Is it wise, from the perspective of effective teaching and learning, to portray demanding and difficult ideas as tentative conjectures? Is this likely to increase students' motivation to undertake the challenging mental work of coming to terms with these ideas, so that they can use them as tools for their own thinking about new problems and situations? And there is also a moral dimension. In so far as teaching about, say, the germ theory of disease is intended to provide students with understanding which can be practically useful in taking decisions about their own health, is it responsible to portray generally accepted core knowledge as tentative conjecture? On pedagogical grounds alone, I would want to argue for the straightforward teaching of core science, to younger pupils at least, as 'how things are'.

The challenge then – as the solution cannot be to imply that explanations and ideas 'emerge' from observation, or can be 'read off the book of nature' – is to help students to see how a conjecture can attain the status of agreed knowledge. As science educators, we need to recognize, and then convey to learners, that, in the real world of practical action, logical entailment is not essential for 'certainty'. But there is a tension here, and we would do well to recognize it explicitly. The science curriculum aims to teach students a body of consensually agreed core science and, at the same time, to help them develop the understandings needed to respond to socioscientific issues. The methods and approaches best suited to each of these aims are almost certainly different – and may even be at odds. Teaching and learning both elements involves an understanding of the nature of scientific knowledge. The challenge is to provide a consistent account which can explain both the accepted status of the core, and the uncertainty of science in socio-scientific issues.

In the next section, I will outline some of the approaches adopted in the UK for teaching students about the nature of scientific knowledge. Then, in the final section of the chapter, I will consider how well these meet this challenge.

HOW HAS THE SCIENCE CURRICULUM ATTEMPTED TO TEACH ABOUT THE NATURE OF SCIENTIFIC KNOWLEDGE?

The principal means by which science curricula have, historically, sought to convey to learners something of the nature of scientific knowledge is by drawing attention to the methods and procedures of scientific inquiry. Through hearing about historically significant inquiries, watching a teacher conduct practical investigations, or carrying these out for themselves, students are expected to develop an understanding of the kinds of evidence and reasoning used to build up the corpus of scientific knowledge. Often such learning is taken to be tacit, though some courses and approaches have argued for making explicit the key elements (as the course developers see it) of the scientific approach to inquiry.

Arguments that school science education should stress the methods of scientific inquiry are common within the science education community. At a very general level, an emphasis on inquiry is seen as a means of avoiding the aridity of portraying science in the classroom as a body of established knowledge which cannot be contested and to which the learner can make no critical or creative input, but must merely assimilate. This image of science is seen, with some justification, as responsible for turning many young people off science. One strategy for addressing this which has a long history is to base learning on first-hand practical exploration by the students. The Nuffield curriculum projects of the 1960s revived the ideas of the late-nineteenth-century pioneer of chemistry education, H. E. Armstrong, in advocating 'guided discovery learning'. The key idea was that by carrying out a carefully prepared series of practical investigations, under the guidance of the teacher, learners would 'discover' for themselves the major concepts, laws and theories of established science. Not surprisingly, the classroom reality was rather different, and provided striking evidence, if any were needed, of the shortcomings of an empiricist and inductivist view of scientific knowledge and its acquisition: students failed to 'discover' what they were meant to, and many treated inquiry as a game, recognizing that the teacher knew the answer in advance (Atkinson and Delamont 1977; Wellington 1981). None the less, the Nuffield developments had the effect of increasing the amount of practical work done by students, and of shifting the emphasis from 'verification' of established principles towards more open exploration.

In interpreting more recent science curriculum history in the UK, the national surveys carried out in the 1980s by the Assessment of Performance Unit (APU) (Archenhold 1988) are a significant landmark. First, by adopting an assessment framework in which the ability to design and carry out open-ended scientific investigations (such as finding out which of a number of paper towels absorbed water best, or how the period of swing of a wooden board suspended at one end depended on its length and breadth) was seen as the culmination of science performance, the APU gave impetus to curriculum approaches which emphasized methods of scientific enquiry. Second, the striking evidence provided by the APU of the low levels of performance of 15 year olds in written questions requiring the application of basic scientific ideas to simple everyday situations – evidence which has been supported and greatly extended by a considerable body of subsequent research (see, for example, Driver *et al.* 1994), and which resonated with many comprehensive school teachers' day-to-day experience – created a climate in which it was attractive to teachers to emphasize the value of learning outcomes of the science curriculum other than content knowledge.

'Process science'

A strong strand of advocacy emerged in the UK in the late 1980s for 'process science'. This was not a new idea; an important precursor was an elementary science course, developed in the 1960s by the American Association for the Advancement of Science (1967), called *Science – A Process Approach*. An influential British government official policy statement began from the premise that 'the essential characteristic of education in science is that it introduces pupils to the methods of science' (Department of Education and Science (DES) 1985: 3). It proceeded to portray these methods as beginning with observation, followed by a search for patterns in these observations, leading to the generation of hypotheses to account for these patterns. These are then tested by experiments designed for the purpose. Around this time, several groups of science educators began to advocate, and to develop, science programmes designed primarily to develop pupils' 'process skills' rather than their scientific content knowledge. The 'process skills' they identified included the ability to observe, classify, predict, hypothesize, and so on. The director of one such course development justified the 'process' emphasis by claiming that the rapid pace of change in scientific knowledge meant that 'a knowledge-led curriculum has little relevance' (Screen 1986: 13). Instead, he argued, there are

> qualities of science which might be termed 'the primary or generic qualities' which will be of value when the facts are out of date or forgotten. If any qualities or generic skills are transferable then the processes must form a substantial proportion, and any preparation of young people must take into account the transferable skills which they will need to succeed.
>
> (Screen 1986: 13)

Other courses of this period similarly based their framework and structure around the notion of 'teaching' and 'developing' a similar set of 'process skills'; assessment packages to evaluate students' 'process skills' were also produced.

The 'process approach', however, has a number of serious weaknesses (for a fuller discussion, see Millar and Driver 1987). First, it is an oversimplified and misleading account of scientific inquiry. The idea that science begins with unbiased observation fails to take adequate account of the widely held view that all acts of observation are influenced by the conceptual baggage which the observer brings to the situation – that observation is, to varying degrees, theory-laden. The empiricist idea that patterns 'emerge' from inspection of the data, which is also the error at the heart of discovery learning, fails to recognize the imaginative steps involved in proposing explanations: we do not simply infer the Newtonian explanation of motion from the myriad examples of moving objects which surround us, nor the chemist's explanation of reactions from our experiences in the kitchen or the school laboratory. Nor does it help to move the emphasis to the testing of explanations: to imply that hypotheses can be tested by experiment in the school laboratory (with limited resources and by non-expert investigators) is to trivialize the notion of 'severe testing' which underpins the hypothetico-deductive view of science, by treating the collection of reliable data, and its interpretation, as unproblematic.

Second, the 'process approach' is blind to the fact that the so-called 'processes of science' are general cognitive skills which all of us routinely perform from infancy. Developing a stable view of the world around, learning to use words for classes of objects (like apples, or chairs), acquiring language and social competence, all depend on acute observation, the ability to classify, make predictions and hypotheses about the future behaviour of objects, other people and one's self. So it is more than a little problematic to claim that the ability to engage in such 'processes' needs to be taught or can be developed by formal instruction. The aim of science education is not to develop such skills but rather to help students see how to *use* ways of thinking and reasoning which they employ routinely in other contexts in science domains too, and to motivate them to want to do so.

Science investigations

The National Curriculum does not take a 'process approach'. The working group who drafted the first version of the Science National Curriculum in 1988 endorsed the emphasis within the science education community at that time on scientific methods of inquiry by proposing attainment targets dealing with *Exploration and Investigation* and *Communication* which together carried a higher weighting than *Knowledge and Understanding*. Not surprisingly, however, they were unable to specify ten levels of increasing performance (as the assessment framework for the National Curriculum demanded) in terms of 'processes' and 'process skills', and opted instead for a more general depiction of a hierarchy of levels of learners' performance on open-ended practical investigations, of the sort used by the APU (see p. 93). An attainment target dealing with the ability to plan, carry out, interpret and evaluate the results of such investigations has been maintained through the subsequent revisions of the National Curriculum. In the current version (1995), Science Attainment Target 1 (Sc1) is entitled *Experimental and Investigative Science*. It is one of four attainment targets, with a weighting of 50 per cent at primary school stage and 25 per cent at secondary. It is, of course, expected that teachers will also continue to use more prescribed practical tasks in teaching the content required by the other attainment targets, covering biological, chemical and physical topics.

The first Science National Curriculum (1989) portrayed investigative work in science as largely concerned with exploring relationships between variables. So, for example, pupils might explore how the length of a rubber band depends on the weight hung on it (the variables being weight and length) or how the bounciness of a squash ball depends on its temperature (variables, rebound height and temperature). This variables-emphasis is also evident in the APU's choice of investigation tasks, and can be traced back to Piaget's view that the ability to reason about multivariate situations indicated attainment of the formal operational stage of reasoning. Because investigations of this type can vary in the number and nature of the independent variables involved, variables tasks are also attractive to anyone who has the job of trying to write statements of performance on a ten-level scale. This emphasis on variables quickly came to dominate school science investigations and the additional guidance provided for teachers by the National Curriculum Council was entirely about variables in investigations.

There were many problems with this first version of National Curriculum Sc1. Its philosophical basis was criticized. It was argued that it presented a narrow view of science investigation which was more suited to physics than chemistry or biology, embodied an empiricist view of science, starting from observations and looking for patterns, and limited the notion of a 'science investigation' to variables-type tasks (for a fuller critique, see Donnelly 1994). Many of the tasks proposed were also criticized as being largely low-level empirical investigations, with little theoretical content (or, at least, little at a level accessible to the students): students might investigate, for instance, which of a number of paper towels would be best at mopping up a spill, or how the diameter of a ball of Plasticine affected the time it took to roll down a slope. Science was being reduced to consumer testing of objects and materials, or the discovery of empirical relationships of no theoretical significance. Practically, teachers found the assessment and record-keeping requirements impossibly complex. Under pressure from the practical rather than the philosophical problems, the government asked the National Curriculum Council to revise the science curriculum. The 1991 revision of Sc1 had three strands, dealing with the ability of pupils to

- ask questions, predict and hypothesize
- observe, measure and manipulate variables
- interpret their results and evaluate scientific evidence.

The first and third strands were, in part, an attempt to address the criticism of the inductive emphasis of the previous version – by stressing that a hypothesis or prediction came first, and that data were collected in the light of this. The emphasis on variables-type tasks, however, was even stronger and became increasingly seen as restrictive. So, in the most recent revision of the National Curriculum (1995), the idea of an investigation has been broadened to include a range of open-ended practical tasks, not just those involving relationships between variables; the emphasis on predicting and hypothesizing is reduced, while that on the collection and evaluation of evidence is increased.

In addition to an attainment target on scientific investigating, the first version of the National Curriculum also contained an attainment target (AT17) dealing with understanding of *The Nature of Science*. Students were to be helped, through consideration of historical and present-day episodes in science and through reflection on their own practical work, to 'develop their knowledge and understanding of the ways in which scientific ideas change through time and how the nature of these ideas and the uses to which they are put are affected by the social, moral, spiritual and cultural contexts in which they are developed'. There was little accumulated experience, however, within the science-teaching community of how best to teach such ideas, and few suitable resources to support such teaching, so there was only muted opposition when AT17 was assimilated, in much diluted form, into the attainment target on investigative work, as part of the 1991 revision of the National Curriculum. It now survives, in the 1995 version of the National Curriculum, only as one of five general guidelines in the preamble to the detailed programmes of study.

The evolution of the National Curriculum to date, then, has seen a steady reduction in emphasis on historical and contemporary case studies of scientific change and controversy, leaving first-hand practical investigation as the principal means of teaching students about the methods of science. This, as I will argue in the concluding section, is a major weakness if we are serious about helping students to understand socio-scientific disputes.

HOW CAN WE TEACH ABOUT SCIENCE AS PRACTICE?

Earlier in this chapter I suggested that the central problem in teaching about the methods of science in the school curriculum is to provide a consistent account which encompasses both core science and science in socio-scientific disputes. Can experience of carrying out scientific invest-igations, of the sort envisaged by National Curriculum Sc1, teach students the necessary understandings? For two reasons, I think the answer must be 'no': the rhetoric and the practices associated with investigative work are likely to convey some misleading and unhelpful ideas about scientific inquiry; and there are important ideas about inquiry which are unlikely to be developed through first-hand practical investigations.

Many of the criticisms of earlier versions of Sc1 (discussed above) continue to apply to the current version. Weaknesses may have been addressed, but have not been entirely eliminated. The practical investiga-tions which schools have come to use in their teaching portray science in rather naive empiricist terms, as the exploration of relationships between variables which are themselves seen as arising 'obviously' and unproblem-atically from the context. The implicit message is that science develops from rather atheoretical practical inquiries. The relationship between observation and explanation is largely unexplored. The implication that data collected by students using the resources of a school laboratory, often within a very short span of time, can be used to draw reliable and valid conclusions, conveys the misleading impression that collecting data about the natural world is a quick and straightforward business.

Encouraging the view that learners can, through their own practical investigations of the world, obtain answers to their own questions, also leads to quite significant problems when practical demonstrations and standard 'experiments' are used to provide warrants for accepting well-established ideas and explanations in core science. Providing good class-room demonstrations to support such teaching is often, as most teachers know, a matter of careful stage-management, choice of parameters and manipulation of apparatus. If illustrative practical work of this sort is

97

carried out by the students themselves, it is likely, as I have commented earlier, that many will fail to see what they are meant to see or to produce results which display the intended pattern. Classroom demonstrations of this sort, whether carried out by the teacher or by the students, are not 'severe tests' of core science explanations. If a student 'discovers' that magnesium loses weight when burnt in air, or obtains a pattern of results 'showing' that the acceleration of a trolley is not proportional to the net force applied, then our understanding of combustion or of Newton's Second Law is not challenged. It is misleading to make claims in what we say about practical work in the teaching laboratory, which, if taken seriously, would lead to the conclusion that they should be.

Rather classroom demonstrations are contrived and essentially theatrical events, designed to display, with as much clarity as possible, a phenomenon or pattern about whose occurrence and interpretation the scientific community is agreed. Observations or measurements which do not fit this are, quite properly, taken as evidence of flaws in the apparatus or its handling. In such a situation, the teacher's task is to negotiate with the students an interpretation of the observations which accords with the accepted view, drawing on ideas like 'experimental error' where appropriate. Negotiation is necessary, not because the students' views and data are of equal status with the accepted account, but because the explanation does not simply 'emerge' from the data and intellectual work is required by students to take on the scientific way-of-looking at phenomena. Coming, for example, to see combustion as the adding-on of something from the air rather than the loss of something, or the charging of plastic rods as transfers of invisible electrons from rod to cloth or vice versa, requires that the learner imagine a world containing new entities and interactions.

We should also note that, for precisely the same reasons that a classroom experiment cannot ever refute established knowledge, neither can it provide an adequate warrant for accepting it. Its function is rhetorical, a theatrical event, a public display of how things can be contrived to follow expectations. The rhetoric of science investigation, however, is that students are able, using their own resources, to answer their own questions about the world. It is scarcely surprising that few act as though it were so: questions about 'what's supposed to happen' and whether results are 'correct' persist. Thus the warrants given by teachers to students for accepting different pieces of scientific knowledge as 'reliable' alternate between an emphasis on first-hand evidence and an acceptance of authority, in ways which are wholly inconsistent.

If we are to fashion a more consistent account we need to find ways to re-integrate a central feature of scientific inquiry which is largely missing from Sc1 and has been steadily reduced through the successive revisions of the National Curriculum. This is the imaginative and essentially risky step involved in proposing explanations. An understanding of the relationship between data and explanation is essential both for understanding core science and for approaching socio-scientific issues. So helping students to read accounts of scientific episodes in terms of a framework like that proposed by Giere (1991: see Figure 7.1) needs to be an explicit aim of general science education. This involves understanding that the theories we propose as explanations of our observations are conjectures, made on the basis of available data, but never completely determined by it. Theories do not emerge from the data; there is always an element of creative speculation. They do not report the data, but propose explanations of it. Theorizing involves imagination and guesswork and risks being wrong. Understanding this aspect of science involves recognizing theory as separate from data, and being able to relate theory and data appropriately – to say, for example, whether given data agree or disagree with a given theory (or with several), and to draw logical conclusions from this.

There is evidence from research, however, that these are steps which many students find difficult and younger ones may not be able to accomplish (D. Kuhn *et al.* 1988). A large-scale study of the understandings of 9–16 year olds in England of aspects of the nature of science (Driver *et al.* 1996) also found little evidence that many students thought of scientific knowledge in this way. New approaches and materials will be needed to develop the necessary understandings. There is much work still to be done.

But if we portray explanation as essentially conjectural and tentative, how then can we account for the accepted status of core science? We cannot duck this issue, for the peculiar thing about science – indeed its uniqueness as a knowledge form – is that its core claims about the world are consensually agreed by everyone who has considered them seriously. The answer, I think, lies in recognizing that scientific consensus, where it exists, is a result of the inability of those working with the phenomena in question to entertain any other interpretation of things. Faced with the evidence, they can see no other way to make sense of it. And that, of course, is what we normally mean when we say we are 'certain' of something. The meaning of words like 'certain' and 'sure' (and 'true' and 'real') is sustained by their everyday usage; the contexts of use determine the meaning, not vice versa. In this sense, scientific knowledge *is* socially constructed, while constrained by 'the way the world is'. It is a product of work, over a period of time, by a group of people. (For a fuller exploration of this line of argument, see Ogborn 1995.)

The implication for science education is that we need to make clear that the explanations of core science arise from data and evidence collected over a long period of time, by many people, going far beyond what can be presented and replicated in the school laboratory. In this respect, the metaphor of 'the pupil as scientist' is deeply misleading. Practical work by students, whether open-ended or teacher-directed (the difference is of degree, not of kind), has the role of providing an opportunity for learners to think and talk about a phenomenon from within the 'mental landscape', and using the linguistic terminology, of an imagined model, with their interventions making sense, and the observed outcomes being interpreted, in the light of this model. It is of central importance in science education because acting on the world in terms of an imagined model provides the most powerful means of making the terms of the model become 'real' for the learner.

Science in socio-scientific disputes differs from core science in that consensus has not, as a matter of fact, emerged. At school level, it seems to me that this lack of consensus is best accounted for in terms of the complexity of the contexts of application, their local specificity, and the general difficulty of obtaining valid and reliable data on the natural world. It is these which provide the 'space' for expert disagreement, and for social and personal commitments to impinge. Relating this to the curriculum, it is first essential that students come to appreciate the sheer difficulty of obtaining valid and reliable data about the natural world. Here first-hand practical investigation can clearly play a role. The latest revision of National Curriculum Sc1 is helpful in placing greater emphasis on the student's ability to evaluate the support which collected data provide for the conclusions drawn. Students need to understand ideas like accuracy, reliability, validity, which have to do with the relationship between a measurement or observation, and the 'truth'. These ideas apply generally to systematic inquiry, not only in the sciences, and centre around the notion of evidence and the quality (or persuasiveness) of evidence. The curriculum implications are that practical work needs to give greater emphasis to uncertainty and error. Estimations of accuracy, reliability (the need to repeat measurements) and validity (are you measuring what you think you are measuring?) need to become much more commonplace. We should avoid any suggestion that there is an infallible method, or algorithm, for gaining the sort of knowledge which can convince other people.

Second, rather than emphasize the conjectural nature of the models of core science, we might do better to draw attention to the models which are used in trying to relate core science understandings, developed in the laboratory, to the peculiar features of a specific 'real world' situation: in the case of French nuclear testing, modelling the effects of a large explosion on local rock features, or modelling the possible movement of matter through the local rock structures. The status of such models is very different from that of the models of core science: they are altogether more tentative and uncertain. An understanding of modelling in this sense, gained through considering simple models of populations or of the economics of a small business, might give students a clearer insight into the choices and decisions involved, and hence into the issues involved in real socio-scientific disputes. (For a fuller discussion of modelling in the curriculum, see Mellar *et al.* 1994.)

Third, it is striking that accounts of many socio-scientific issues, including the French nuclear testing example, demand the ability to interpret statements of probability and risk. These are topics which are almost wholly absent from the science curriculum at present. We need to consider how they can be introduced at school level. Work to develop suitable materials to introduce and explore these ideas with school students has not really begun.

To summarize, then, if one major purpose of science education is to equip students to respond to socio-scientific issues, this requires an understanding of the nature of scientific knowledge. Such an understanding cannot be developed solely through investigative practical work, though this can make a contribution, by providing insight into the problems of data collection and the relationship between data and explanation (or evidence and theory). Other learning contexts are necessary, including case studies, historical and contemporary, both of the production of agreed core knowledge and of scientific disputes, to highlight the ways in which consensus is created and to identify the features of disputes which result in an absence of consensus. Students also need experience of using and building simple models, and some understanding of probability and risk. Much work is needed to explore the extent to which these ideas can be introduced and developed within the school science curriculum, which remains, for most adults, the major source of their scientific knowledge about the world, and a significant influence on their understanding of science itself.

8

DEMOCRACY AND EXPERTISE

The case of biotechnology education

Les Levidow

People have felt both fascination and unease about biotechnological developments which promise – or threaten – to transform our world irrevocably. Biotechnology has met controversy over the problems it selects to be solved and over its proposed solutions. Since the 1980s a wide-ranging debate about 'risk' in biotechnology has involved environmental, socio-economic and ethical concerns. The term 'risk' denotes not only tangible harm, but also a threat of violating social norms or imposing a sinister control upon nature and society.

As well as sustaining interest among school students biotechnology education could enhance access to this debate and help to develop an informed citizenry. It could strengthen efforts at democratizing techno-logical decision-making, for example in setting agendas for research and development (R&D). Educators may well hold such aims, though other considerations guide the materials available for biotechnology education.

Partisan aims are often acknowledged by funding agencies, such as the European Commission. According to one official, the European Com-mission seeks to correct any 'misinformation' responsible for public fear about biotechnology (cited in Levidow and Tait 1992: 102) – thus implying that information is correct only if it dispels fears.

In 1996 the European Commission substantially increased its grant to an industry-sponsored Task Group on 'Public Perceptions of Biotech-nology'. According to the Group's chairman, public understanding 'is essential if European biotechnology is to remain competitive world-wide, while at the same time retaining public confidence and trust' (European Federation of Biotechnology (EFB)). Thus the Group embraced the political-commercial aims of the biotechnology industry as the prime criteria for a correct 'public understanding'.

To enhance public understanding, educators try to make biotech-nological concepts more accessible. It is assumed that technical ex-planations can be separated from socio-political-ethical issues, which are acknowledged (if at all) as supplements to the former. In this educational model, the student first learns a neutral expert account, thus gains a proper 'understanding', and only then engages with the controversial aspects of biotechnology.

That approach may well discourage interest in the technical aspects, or even perpetuate distrust of science. Moreover, it is misleading to separate the technical from the value-laden aspects. Such a distinction presumes that R&D priorities could be value-free.

What guides biotechnological problem-solving? Who defines the 'expertise' relevant to technological decision-making? How are these aspects portrayed by educational materials?

To explore such questions, each section in this chapter surveys a key issue from the broader debate on agricultural biotechnology. The survey juxtaposes various portrayals of biotechnology, in order to analyse the implicit politics of the educational materials.

The chapter focuses upon state-funded materials which have been widely circulated, especially among secondary-school students. In particular, *Biotechnology for All* (Katz and Satelle 1991) was funded by the European Commission, and sponsored by Britain's Department of Trade and Industry; so was its predecessor booklet (Satelle 1988). *Recent Advances in Plant and Microbial Biotechnology* was issued by Britain's Agricultural and Food Research Council (AFRC 1992); *Biotechnology and You* and *Microbial Friends and Allies* were published by the Biotechnology and Biological Sciences Research Council (BBSRC 1994, 1995). *Biotechnology in Foods and Drinks* was funded by the European Commission and industry (EFB 1994). To ease reading, my main text minimizes references; details are in my articles listed in the References (Levidow 1991, 1995a, 1995b, 1995c; Levidow and Tait 1991, 1992; Levidow *et al.* 1996).

BIOTECHNOLOGY: IMPROVING NATURE?

Issue: what is agricultural biotechnology? How does it extend or change past practices of selective breeding? What potential 'improvements' are pursued – or excluded?

Proponents and critics use similar language to answer those questions: namely, biotechnologists avowedly seek to 'industrialize agriculture', while critics attack biotechnology for seeking 'to convert agriculture into a branch of industry'. Of course, agriculture has been industrialized for a long time, especially through chemical-intensive monoculture. Human labour on the farm now constitutes a small proportion of the money value of crops, especially in western countries. While farmers once improved diverse plant varieties which were still available in the field, they now depend more upon laboratory-based R&D, which has reduced the genetic diversity of the main food crops.

The main issue is whether biotechnological industrialization will alleviate harmful aspects of traditional breeding, or perpetuate them, or even generate new types of harm – and for whose benefit. Also at issue is whether biotechnology simply 'improves' nature. To some extent, those issues have become linked to the novelty of genetic engineering, a technique for selectively transferring genetic material across the species barrier.

Industrialists initially emphasized the unprecedented technical power of genetic engineering, which would enable 'the most dynamic of the great technological revolutions of the 20th century' (e.g. Taverne 1990). In response to public unease, however, government and industry down-played the novelty. 'Genetic engineering' was renamed 'genetic manip-ulation', and later 'genetic modification', evoking a modest, gentle change; the official term became 'genetically modified organism' or GMO (Levidow and Tait 1991). More recently, GMOs have been called 'genetic-ally improved organisms'.

Such terminological shifts were duly imitated by a sequence of school texts. An early version celebrated biotechnology as 'a new industrial revolution' (Satelle 1988). Such provocative language disappeared in a later edition, which reassured readers: 'Biotechnology . . . simply describes the way we use plant and animal cells and microbes to produce substances that are useful to mankind' (Katz and Satelle 1991: 4). Another text emphasized the historical continuity: 'Genetic engineering can be con-sidered a modern, precise form of the selective breeding that has been practised by man for many centuries' (BBSRC 1994: 2).

Biotechnologists portray their work as a natural successor to beer-brewing, yoghurt-making and plant-breeding. 'Biotechnology' is pro-jected back through human history, even though the term itself is relatively recent. According to an industry-sponsored group, 'Biotechnology is the integration of natural sciences and engineering in order to achieve the application of organisms, cells, parts thereof and molecular analogues for products and services. . . . This definition is applicable to both "tradi-tional" and "modern" biotechnology' (EFB 1994: 1). The novel aspects of the technology are linguistically dissolved into ancient practices. With the terminology of traditional/modern (or old/new) biotechnology, the 'new' denotes genetic engineering, yet even the term 'engineering' is projected back through human history. Thus 'the new biotechnology' is symbolically domesticated, as merely extending an evolutionary trend.

Such language downplays the conceptual novelty of biotechnology as well as its technical novelty, for example in crossing the species barrier and in seeking single-gene solutions. In the biotechnological worldview, society's problems arise from inefficient wealth-production, in turn due to genetic deficiencies. When industry genetically modifies plants, for example, it claims to be 'giving nature a little nudge towards greater efficiency'; it gently helps along nature, by correcting the inherited deficiencies which may limit its productivity. This begs the question of what qualities are to be selected, according to what criteria of efficiency, and at what environmental or human cost (see next section).

Some accounts go even further in seeking a natural legitimacy for biotechnology. According to the Monsanto Company, biotechnology is based upon a 'natural science', that is genetic engineering (Monsanto 1984). After all, nature itself recombines genes, which can be 'read' through the universal language of DNA.

Other metaphors animate an educational cartoon series prepared by a plant breeding company. As its narrative tells us, 'The entire alphabet of nature is found in the coded [DNA] strand, but it has only four characters! Billions of years ago, the first coded strand . . . and life appeared'.

'The book of Nature is written in the language of mathematics,' proclaimed Francis Bacon three centuries ago. Now his physico-reductionist worldview is updated with new metaphors, for example of computer codes and industrial efficiency. 'Life' is redefined as the chemical DNA – or rather, as its coded information.

Later in the same cartoon series, a plant generously donates a floppy disk with a copy of the gene for virus resistance, so that other plants may defend themselves. The subsequent text describes biotechnologists genetically modifying plants, by analogy: 'we insert the required program into its DNA, just like you add a program to your computer'.

The cartoon story has an implicit moral: plants have always been genetic engineers, altruistically sharing genes to correct genetic deficiencies. Now humans can follow their benign example; and crop protection depends fundamentally upon fixing the genes.

Even before the advent of computers, molecular biology spoke of reading, copying and editing the genetic code. Software metaphors have become commonplace in the life sciences. Biotechnologists prepare genetic 'cassettes' to ensure that genes are inserted exactly where intended (e.g. AFRC 1992: 9).

Biotechnologists reconceptualize natural history in their own image: life itself is equated with programmed information, encoding a more-or-less efficient productivity. They portray themselves as extending a benign evolution, which confers a legitimate 'natural' status on genetic engineering.

These self-portrayals are not arbitrary or *post hoc*; rather, they extend the 1930s perspectives of molecular biology. This science reconceptualized genetic material as interchangeable, universal coded 'information', which would permit the ultimate human control over life. According to a study of its origins, 'The molecular biological schema purports to describe all organisms as self-assembling, self-maintaining, self-reproducing information-processing machines' (Yoxen 1981: 69; 1983: 34).

Such genetic reductionism also appears in schools materials. In discussing disease resistance in plants, for example, one booklet rightly acknowledges that there is no general-purpose anti-pathogen agent; rather, 'several separate resistance mechanisms are probably induced and affect different types of pathogen'. However, it celebrates the success of bio-technologists who insert single-gene anti-viral mechanisms (AFRC 1992: 6); thus it implies that such measures alone could reliably protect crops.

Another account acknowledges that behavioural variations may be caused by both genetic and environmental differences; on the other hand, it emphasizes only that genetic differences can affect crop yields or disease resistance (BBSRC 1994: 2). These accounts *displace* the fundamental problem of genetically uniform, intensive monoculture which renders crops vulnerable to new pests. They beg the question of why some genetic differences become more important in industrialized agriculture. In sum, biotechnology has been symbolically domesticated by projecting its own reductionist worldview back onto traditional agricultural practices, even onto Nature itself. It emphasizes single-gene deficiencies which must be identified and corrected, within a systemic model of nature as a factory-like bioreactor, while downplaying the systemic causes of agricultural problems. These portrayals of biotechnology are accepted by state-funded educational materials, as surveyed here.

FEEDING THE WORLD?

Issue: will biotechnology help feed the world? Will its products alleviate or aggravate food insecurity?

The agricultural biotechnology industry has portrayed its technical advances as essential for achieving global food security; yet critics have attacked its R&D priorities for solving commercial problems rather than people's problems.

According to Jerry Calder (1991), President of the USA's Industrial Biotechnology Association, we must correct genetic deficiencies in order to secure and expand the food supply. Our society has temporarily proven Malthus wrong, insists Calder, because 'the American farmer has adopted science and technology as rapidly as it has become available, allowing farm production to outpace population growth'. (Malthus had predicted that an exponentially increasing population would outstrip an arith-metically increasing food supply.) Thanks to higher-yielding varieties, 'our existence is now dependent upon fewer than 20 species of plants; we must use all available resources to assure that [those] species are genetic-ally fit to survive under the wide range of environmental extremes' (Calder 1991: 71).

Industrialized agriculture has led to a genetic uniformity which makes crops more vulnerable to the vicissitudes of nature, yet biotechnologists respond by attempting to fix the genes. Pleading for genetic 'improve-ments' of crops, they extend familiar neo-Malthusian arguments: agricultural yield must keep pace with the Third World's growing population in order to avert more famines. According to Britain's single largest seeds merchant, ICI Seeds, 'biotechnology will be the most reliable and environmentally acceptable way to secure the world's food supplies'; it can provide essential tools for 'feeding the world' (cited in Levidow 1991; Levidow and Tait, 1991).

A school textbook conveys a similar account of the problem – and solution:

> In a world where the population is growing by millions every year, feeding everybody is a problem which is becoming more and more difficult to solve. With the aid of biotechnology, scientists can produce new strains of plants where once there would have been little hope of a successful harvest.
>
> (Katz and Satelle 1991: 12)

In a similar vein, a Monsanto advertisement depicts maize growing in the desert, with the headline: 'Will it take a miracle to solve the world's hunger problem?' As the text explains: 'thanks to the science of biotechnology, in the future, it won't take a miracle'. Through this 'natural science', working 'in partnership with nature', biotechnology will design crops to grow in inhospitable climates, the advertisement suggests.

Few biotechnologists make such ambitious claims for plausible products; little (if any) commercial R&D has such priority. Biotechnology proponents nevertheless attribute world hunger to genetic deficiencies which can be corrected through 'natural means', that is by inserting the required genes. This diagnosis complements political claims that 'overpopulation' and 'inefficient' agriculture cause world hunger (e.g. World Bank 1992).

The causes in capital-intensive modernization itself have been ignored. Recent decades have seen a systematic appropriation of Third World land and resources for producing cash-crop exports. Given this type of 'efficiency', innovations have often driven down prices or substituted cheaper products, thus eliminating entire sectors of farmers. In our profit-driven world, greater productivity or flexibility often means more insecurity, poverty and dispossession.

The Green Revolution is a prime example, with its 'high-yielding' varieties of grain. Or rather, these were high-response varieties, whose higher yield depended upon irrigation, machinery and chemical inputs. To cover the necessary investments, Indian farmers took on a substantial debt burden; many lost their land from subsequent crop failures, and/or from inability to sustain the necessary loans. Moreover, the R&D emphasized rice and especially wheat varieties, whose increased cultivation displaced oilseeds and pulses, the prime source of protein for many Indians. Although the Green Revolution generally increased food production, it did so in ways which increased crops' vulnerability to pests, exhausted the soil, made yields less reliable, and aggravated food insecurity; meanwhile it intensified people's dependence upon both purchased inputs and/or government aid.

The biotechnology industry now claims to develop new plant varieties not requiring great capital investment by farmers. Even if this is true, the single-gene 'improvements' may still leave new varieties – and farmers – vulnerable to the same agronomic problems which struck the Green Revolution. Even if genetically modified varieties do increase food production, this does not necessarily enhance food security. World hunger has political-economic causes which remain to be overcome, and which may be aggravated by the main products of commercial biotechnology.

The pretence of 'feeding the world' is already belied by the R&D priorities of the biotechnology industry. Its own house journal, *Agro-Industry Hi-Tech*, has a revealing subtitle: *International Journal for Food, Chemicals, Pharmaceuticals, Cosmetics as Linked to Agriculture Through Advanced Technology.* This subtitle expresses the priority of making biological materials more flexible and interchangeable, convenient for obtaining the greatest return on investment.

The journal also emphasizes the political context of reduced farm subsidies, which will make productivity less important in the future: 'Agriculture is bound to go for more [high] value-added products, better adapted to demand from downstream industry and the consumer'. It is hence going irresistibly towards a global system where contents matter more than quantities. Indeed, 'high value-added' became an explicit R&D criterion back in the 1980s, when genetically modified organisms (GMOs) were developed for manufacturing valuable substances on an industrial scale. ICI developed a microbe to transform natural gas (or waste products) into single-cell protein, called 'Pruteen' for marketing purposes. However, its development was halted:

> This [Pruteen] was an outstanding technical achievement, but with soya and oil prices turning against us, it was not a commercial success. . . . More than anything else, this focused our biotechnological attention on higher added-value products at the speciality-end of the chemical business.
>
> (Dart 1988: 5)

Several years later, a school textbook was still expressing hope that single-cell protein could be 'used for animal feed', or even 'could be a low-technology solution to some of the food shortage problems' in developing countries (Katz and Satelle 1991: 15). This starry-eyed, humanitarian account of biotechnology ignores the commercial pressures which had already diverted R&D investment away from 'low value-added' products.

Its account also ignores the likely scenario that single-cell protein would undermine Third World exports of soybeans as animal feed.

If the real priorities are 'high value-added' products, then what defines 'value'? According to a US industrialist, 'value-added genetics determines the processability, nutrition, convenience and quality of our raw materials and food products' (Lawrence 1988: 32). Or rather, market competition directs the strategic choice of genes to be 'valued'. And 'value added' often means value lost for some people, by imposing an industrial-type efficiency.

Even before biotechnology, food products were becoming mere raw materials, whose potential suppliers had been thrown into greater competition with each other. That dynamic is now being extended: 'Biotechnology makes food production more and more like an assembly industry. Crops as such are no longer agricultural commodities, but their molecular components increasingly are ... Interchangeability of crops also means interchangeability of producers' (Hobbelink 1991: 95; compare with Goodman and Redclift 1991).

Some biotechnology companies are developing substitutes for 'high-value' crops or materials hitherto imported from Third World countries. If technically successful, such new products would undermine the livelihoods of entire communities, just as European sugar beet and high-fructose corn syrup devastated sugar-cane production elsewhere. Oilseed rape has been genetically modified for an altered oil content, so that it may substitute for tropic oils, for example from coconut and palm trees (Hobbelink 1991: 93; Walgate 1990: 57; Panos 1993: 12–14). Such oilseed rape is being developed by several companies – e.g. Zeneca (formerly ICI Seeds) – which had promised that biotechnology would help 'feed the world'.

Problems of import-substitution are at least mentioned by an industry-sponsored brochure (EFB 1994: 3). The problem is not even acknowledged by any of the schools materials, yet these imply that biotechnology will enhance food security. One account mentions that lipases are studied for 'their potential for upgrading low-value oils such as palm oil to produce high-value products such as cocoa butter'; but it remains silent about who may lose from these substitutions (AFRC 1992: 14; cf. Hobbelink 1991: 85–6).

If biotechnology products can undermine people's economic security, even their food security, then how are such innovations justified as progress? That question has been answered by an industry-wide lobby group, in which Zeneca plays a leading role: 'Let there be no illusions: as with any innovative technology, biotechnology will change economic and competitive conditions in the market. Indeed, economic renewal through innovation is the motor force of democratic societies' (Senior Advisory Group on Biotechnology (SAGB) 1990: 15).

As the industry acknowledges, 'value-added genetics' does not simply respond to new 'competitive conditions', but also intensifies them. Apparently our consolation is that such insecurity is the price to be paid for renewing 'democratic societies'. In this way, a disruptive force is legitimized as progress; indeed, any demand for social accountability is cast as a threat to democracy.

At stake here is the profit-seeking prerogative of biotechnology R&D. This is graphically celebrated in a British government promotional handbook, which portrays the DNA double-helix as a money tree sprouting £5 banknotes (Department of Trade and Industry/Laboratory of the Government Chemist (DTI/LGC) 1991: 26). Of course, biotechnology has no guaranteed profits, despite enormous state subsidies for its R&D; for 1994–8, the European Union allocated 1.5 billion ecus (>£1 billion) to the life sciences, with at least one-third for agricultural biotechnology.

In sum, agricultural biotechnology is celebrated as a genetic fix for feeding the world by attributing present insecurities to the genetic deficiencies of crops. State-funded schools materials collude with such portrayals, which in turn legitimize state subsidy for biotechnology. These materials exclude alternative accounts which attribute food insecurity to misguided types of efficiency, for example to genetic uniformity, substitutions and interchangeability of products.

GREENING PEST CONTROL?

Issue: does biotechnology offer environment-friendly products? How might it affect options for pest control, for example for reducing agrichemical usage? What motives drive R&D for the genetic modification of herbicide-resistant crops and insecticidal products?

Herbicide-resistant crops

Even before their commercial use, herbicide-resistant crops have been celebrated for helping farmers to reduce herbicide usage – and attacked for perpetuating dependence upon herbicides. Of all the genetically modified organisms (GMOs) recently released in field trials, approximately half had an inserted gene for herbicide resistance. The herbicide vendor often has a close link with the seeds company, or even has become its owner. As some companies have acknowledged, their main purpose is to perpetuate or increase sales of the herbicide to which the crop has been made resistant.

Biotechnologists portray herbicide-resistant crops as relatively 'clean' products. According to ICI Seeds, herbicide-resistant crops will reduce dependence upon chemical inputs, by reducing quantities of their use. Such crops will offer greater choice to farmers, who can thereby defer herbicide applications until after the crop seedlings have sprouted (e.g. Bartle 1991).

However, this R&D agenda has been denounced for perpetuating dependence upon chemical herbicides, regardless of whether quantities are reduced (Biotechnology Working Group (BWG) 1990). Ecologists remind us that some herbicides have already weakened the crop's natural defences against disease and so necessitated additional chemical treatments, such as fungicides; herbicide-resistant crops may repeat this problem (Pimentel 1987). New herbicide-resistant weeds could result, either by inadvertent spread of the herbicide-resistance genes to weedy relatives, or by sheer selection pressure from the herbicide sprays. Environmentalists have warned against such scenarios of a 'genetic treadmill', by analogy to the chemical 'pesticide treadmill' of pesticide-resistant pests.

These issues came to a head when the European Commission received a proposal to grant market approval for a herbicide-tolerant oilseed rape in 1994. In response, member states disagreed over the breadth of safety regulation. Some regulators criticized the company's risk assessment for ignoring the herbicide implications; they emphasized the prospect that inadvertent spread of the inserted gene could generate herbicide-resistant weeds and so preclude some herbicide options or crop rotations. Other regulators argued that such effects lie outside the safety regulation of GMOs. The latter stance won, in effect, when EU member states resorted to voting on the market approval (Levidow *et al.* 1996).

By default the regulatory procedure accepted the agricultural strategy of biotechnology R&D. Its biotechnological solution defines the weed-control problem as crop vulnerability to herbicides, rather than dependence on herbicides.

Despite the long-standing controversy about herbicide-resistant crops, and their prominence in biotechnology R&D, their very existence has been ignored by schools texts surveyed here (except see next section). They are at least mentioned by an industry-sponsored brochure, which invents a benign environmental motive for the R&D investment: 'To lower the burden of herbicides in the environment, plants are being developed with resistance to specific herbicides' (EFB 1994: 2). There is no basis for attributing that motive to companies, and little basis for claims about how such products would affect herbicide usage in practice.

Insect-resistant products

Though insecticidal GMOs are not yet on the market, they have been celebrated as benign substitutes for chemicals – or criticized as environmental threats. These new organisms are developed by transferring a toxin gene from a microbe to another organism which will persist longer and/or target the pest more effectively. Some R&D even combines genes

111

for different toxins in the same microbe, so that it can kill a broader range of insect pests.

What problem is this solving? Natural microbial pesticides occupy only about 1 per cent of the pesticide market. The small share is due to their lack of environmental persistence, narrow host range, limited virulence, and high production costs. One specialist laments that a traditional microbial pesticide 'is like a rifle shot rather than a shotgun shot into a pest group'.

Those 'rifle' features, which are an ecological attribute of natural biopesticides, also make them unattractive economically to companies, regardless of whether the products would benefit farmers. The biotechnological solution is a genetic redesign to make the biopesticide less specific, more persistent and/or more deadly. Such research seeks to overcome the economic limitations of traditional biopesticides.

Biopesticide R&D exemplifies 'value-added genetics', that is the search for genes which can enhance the market value of products, even if an effective product already exists. In designing such products, the genetic solution predefines the problem as a genetic deficiency to be corrected. The solution displaces (or hides) the fundamental problem of intensive monocultural methods, which generate the ideal habitat for pest epidemics.

These R&D priorities are given a green gloss. According to one industrialist, such research attempts 'to do better than mother nature in designing improved, more efficacious toxins'. Another leading company in biopesticides, Novo Nordisk, portrays their new biopesticides with the visual metaphor of a green bow-and-arrow, which suggests a benign precision: 'Fighting for a better world, naturally'.

For most genetically modified biopesticides, the toxin genes come from a traditional biopesticide, Bt. After decades of spraying Bt on crops, its heavy usage has generated selection pressure for Bt-resistant insects. If such resistance undermines the effectiveness of the traditional biopesticide, then farmers will lose a relatively safe alternative to chemicals.

When biotechnologists first inserted Bt-toxin genes into prospective products in the 1980s, environmentalists warned that such products would intensify selection pressure for Bt-resistant insects. They warned that farmers would face a 'genetic treadmill', with increased dependence upon a series of genetic or chemical solutions. As critics then argued, this innovation was designed to solve problems of intensive monoculture – indeed, to sustain 'efficient' cultivation methods which happen to enhance opportunities for plant pests.

These issues recently came to a head in the European Union. In 1995 Ciba-Geigy requested EU-wide market approval of a Bt-toxin maize. In response, member states disagreed over the breadth of safety regulation. Some regulators emphasized the prospect that the product could generate

Bt-resistant insects, and thus intensify dependence upon chemical insect-icides; others denied that the safety regulation encompasses this scenario. In any case, regulators would have practical difficulty in preventing pest resistance – short of simply banning the product.

In the state-funded materials surveyed here, biopesticidal products are simply praised for solving pest problems. An early text depicted a 'supercrop' which has been genetically modified for resistance to both insect attack and high doses of herbicide: 'this insect could be eating its way to death' (Satelle 1988: 31). One text rightly describes Bt as a 'natural pest control agent' but mentions no genetically modified versions (BBSRC 1995). Another simply mentions that a Bt gene 'confers resistance to insect predators without the use of insecticides' (EFB 1994: 2). No text acknow-ledges the resistance problem, despite all the public and scientific debate. (Technical references for this section may be found in Levidow 1995a, 1995b.)

MAKING COWS MORE EFFICIENT?

Issue: what does biotechnology mean for the treatment and welfare of farm animals? What genetic or hormonal alterations are warranted?

A sharp controversy hit the very first product of agricultural biotech-nology, BST, a hormone supplement which increases milk yields in dairy cattle. The opposition campaign has united animal welfare groups, small-scale farmers and consumer groups. The product has become a public-relations disaster for the biotechnology industry, as well as a commercial disaster in the European Union, where its use has been provisionally banned.

Although not itself a GMO, the hormone is mass-produced by micro-organisms which have been genetically modified with a bovine gene. The industry, perhaps defensively, calls the product by its more technical term, bovine somatotrophin (BST). According to the agrochemical company, Monsanto, BST is a natural protein supplement which enhances the cow's efficiency.

Its opponents call the product 'bovine growth hormone' (BGH), thereby emphasizing its interference with metabolic processes. According to them, Monsanto is pushing drugs which force cows to work harder on the factory farm, by producing more milk; it is a chemical pollutant which con-taminates an otherwise 'pure' product. Each side appeals to the 'natural' status of their own social values; either BST enhances a natural efficiency, or BGH transgresses a natural purity.

BST was already a problem, long before it was turned into a commodity. Dairy cattle have been selectively bred for high 'natural' BST levels; the resulting supercows have greater susceptibility to disease, (e.g. mastitis), which is then treated with antibiotics (M. Hansen 1990: 9). BST merchants insist, however, that such problems can be avoided if BST supplements are carefully managed.

During the early 1990s the European Union deferred any decision on market approval for BST. Its scientific advisory committee had recommended approval, on grounds that it would be safe for dairy cattle if used as directed by the manufacturer's instructions, for example by carefully controlling dosage and monitoring health effects. In developing BST, the manufacturers had presumed that such controls could be reliably extended from the laboratory to real-life factory farming, despite commercial pressures to maximize milk production and to minimize costs.

Meanwhile the European Commission established a Group of Ethical Advisers to consider such issues. Its official rationale was that addressing the ethical challenges of biotechnology would facilitate public acceptance of its benefits. In explaining the Group's role, a member of the European Parliament argued that we must accept the 'new mental images' of biotechnology, which tend to upset our traditional concepts of nature and human identity.

The Group eventually issued its advice on 'performance-enhancers' in agriculture. It advised 'that the use of BST to increase lactation in cows is ethically unobjectionable, and safe for both human and animals, provided that the following measures are adopted'; the measures included a cost-benefit analysis of 'animal discomfort', and labelling of BST-treated milk. Thus the Group provided 'ethical' legitimacy for the socio-economic assumptions of scientific experts, for example in trusting dairy farmers to observe elaborate safeguards, and in extending models of industrial efficiency to animals.

In 1993 the EC finally decided to prohibit the European sale or use of BST – mainly on grounds that increased milk surpluses would contradict the agreed policy of reducing agricultural subsidies. In effect, EC policy still accepted the expert advice on animal welfare and its assumptions about farming practices.

The BST controversy is simply avoided in the state-funded materials surveyed here. According to one booklet, 'cows receiving extra BST (and more food) can produce much more milk' (Katz and Satelle 1991: 16). That example appears under the heading, 'Healthier Animals', though the text does not explain how BST makes cows healthier.

According to the director of Pharmaceutical Proteins Ltd, 'The mammary gland is a very good factory. Our sheep are furry little factories walking around in fields and they do a superb job' (quoted in Shiva 1995: 273). A brochure emphasizes the production of pharmaceutical proteins from genetically modified sheep. It also asks the reader, 'Is it acceptable to genetically engineer cows to produce milk with improved nutritional quality for human consumption?' (BBSRC, 1994: 3). Although this ethical question is worth posing, it begs the question as to whose problem – if it exists – such cows would be solving. In general, the educational texts emphasize benefits for animal or human health, even imaginary benefits, while ignoring the BST controversy, as well as the attempt at turning animals into more efficient factories. (For detailed references on this topic, see Levidow 1995c.)

BIOTECHNOLOGY EDUCATION: WHAT ALTERNATIVES?

State-funded materials for biotechnology education, as surveyed here, are hardly neutral. Like the R&D agenda itself, these materials accept the dominant biotechnological model of industrializing agriculture, with its metaphors of computer codes and industrial efficiency. In the guise of providing technical explanations, they celebrate putative benefits from solving problems which are attributed to genetic deficiencies. They exclude alternative diagnoses of our problems, for example tendencies towards genetic uniformity, towards an interchangeability of organic materials, and towards a cost-cutting efficiency.

The R&D agenda is therefore protected from scrutiny. Biotechnological knowledge-production is accepted as politically neutral, as a matter for experts in identifying and correcting genetic deficiencies. Value-laden issues are acknowledged only in the margins, for example for anticipating the socio-economic 'impacts', or drawing the proper ethical 'limits' for potential applications.

State-funded materials have an implicit politics by taking for granted a particular model of nature and society. They appeal to a general societal interest in solving problems which in fact arise from profit-driven, intensive monoculture. Their partisan role lies in accepting such models, as if they were not 'political' issues.

These materials lend legitimacy to the more extreme claims by the biotechnology industry itself, such as in advertisements promising benefits for the common good. Together, such portrayals serve to narrow the range of issues for public debate.

To play a more democratic role, biotechnology education would have to accommodate the wider public debate on the broad causes of our socio-agronomic problems, and on alternative problem-setting agendas. For example, we could learn much from the so-called 'old biotechnology'. In some traditional societies, diverse crops have been cultivated symbiotically in a farming system, rather than branding them as dangerous invaders to be exterminated. Public-interest groups now help plant breeders to reorient their research on farmers' terms, thus putting new choices of biodiversity under farmers' control (Hobbelink 1991: 146; Perlas and Hobbelink 1995).

Even in western countries, agronomists and farmers are developing less intensive methods. They learn to use local resources as inputs, and avoid the agricultural designs which attract pests. Some have begun to obtain government funding for such methods, and have demonstrated their economic viability (National Research Council (NRC) 1989).

Regardless of the particular alternative, its realization depends upon a social network linking research to agricultural practices. This may require state subsidy, which so far has overwhelmingly funded the search for a 'genetic fix', as the most relevant expertise for problem-solving. Critics have challenged the prevalent R&D priorities as anti-democratic, as foreclosing potential futures for agriculture and society. They have counter-posed broader accounts of the relevant expertise, thus opening up prospects for democratic participation.

In this context, biotechnology education faces political choices, though these are hardly acknowledged as such. Either it can promote the genetic-reductionist account of problem-setting which dominates biotechnology R&D. Or, alternatively, it can strengthen people's capacity to engage in the wider public debate – as regards what features of 'nature' we should value, what agriculture and social order we should promote, and for whose benefit.

ACKNOWLEDGEMENTS

This chapter arises from two related studies, both funded by the UK Economic and Social Research Council: 'Regulating the Risks of Bio-technology', 1989–91, project number R000 23 1611; and 'From Precautionary to Risk-Based Regulation: the Case of GMO Releases', during 1995–6, project number L211 25 2032.

Part III

SCIENCE FOR ALL?

INTRODUCTION

Previous chapters have touched on the tensions between the role of science education in the training of professionals and the need to provide a coherent and lasting school experience of science for all. Part III charts the unsteady progress that has been made to providing science curricula that satisfy both requirements.

Peter Fensham's view (Chapter 9) is that much of the traditional curriculum reform has been geared specifically towards the needs of those who will be induced into scientific disciplines. There is currently renewed interest in curricula that promote science literacy but Fensham identifies some of the barriers and difficulties that are encountered, as well as describing some promising areas of development and proposing strategies for success.

Edgar Jenkins (Chapter 10) emphasizes the point that concerns with the school curricula are long-standing and universal. He reveals the full depth and range of criticisms that are currently levelled at science. Science's traditional tendency to make extravagant claims for itself – for example in relation to the levels of certainty of scientific knowledge or the dependence of economic prosperity on a scientifically literate society, render it vulnerable to continued scepticism. He too recommends a change of emphasis in the science curriculum – one which provides an opportunity for a functional public understanding of science. He argues for science teaching that portrays science as problematic, where objectivity and certainty are not taken for granted – a curriculum that provides a platform for action, self-knowledge and social responsibility.

Joan Solomon (Chapter 11) describes the idea of scientific culture within a European perspective. Culture, rather than the notion of scientific literacy or PUS, provides greater insight into what is significant in people's lives. This can lead to a broader and more democratic basis for understanding science and narrowing the divide between formal and informal science learning.

117

The notion of scientific culture raises the issue of what uses people make of the science they learn. Jeff Thomas (Chapter 12) suggests that the relation between raised levels of scientific literacy and more informed decision-making is too simplistic. He reviews surveys of attitudes to science and draws on his own experience and research in chairing an Open University course dealing with current scientific issues.

9

SCHOOL SCIENCE AND ITS PROBLEMS WITH SCIENTIFIC LITERACY

Peter Fensham

From 1983 to the present day, Science for All, or a variant of it, has been officially espoused as the intention for school Science in country after country. The Ministers of Education in the Asia Region of Unesco (from Pakistan and India to Japan and New Zealand and a dozen countries in between) determined that this goal was an urgent priority for their educational systems (Unesco 1983). In the same year the National Science Foundation (1983) was presented with a high-level report that called for Science for All Americans. In 1984 in Canada, Science for Every Student appeared, and soon after the Royal Society (Bodmer 1985) in Britain argued persuasively that Science is for Everybody.

The substance of all these reports is very similar; they can be summarized by the set of goals for school Science that the report of the Science Council of Canada (1984) recommended following the most searching of these reviews.

A science education appropriate to individual needs and designed to enable students to:

- participate fully in a technological society as informed citizens
- pursue further studies in science and technology
- enter the world of work
- develop intellectually and morally.

The traditional role of school Science is present in the second of these goals, but only as part of it since it (like the other three) is concerned with all students, not just the small minority (less than 20 per cent of any age cohort) who will take up science-based careers of any sort.

With such expert and official agreement about the need for school Science to contribute to the scientific and technological literacy of all future citizens, one would expect to find by now that new curricula consistent with these goals would be in place and that appropriate pedagogies and assessment procedures would be practised in many classrooms. In fact, remarkably slow progress has been made; in a number of countries, promising initiatives in the later 1980s now seem less likely to be implemented or to have been stifled.

In this chapter some of the factors that make it so difficult for school Science to contribute to general scientific literacy are considered. To do this a brief account is provided of school Science that predated these goals, and second, the circumstances in which these new goals were set.

THE LEGACY OF THE 1960s

In the 1960s and early 1970s many countries reconstituted the curriculum for Science in their schools. The models for these changes were a number of curriculum projects established by the National Science Foundation in the USA and in Britain by the Nuffield Foundation. In both cases these initiatives were supported by hitherto unheard-of amounts of funding. They were a response to well-justified claims that school Science was hopelessly out-of-date due to the neglect of its curriculum during the world depression, the Second World War and its aftermath.

The priority for these reforms was clear when the first projects to be established were all concerned with Science at the upper levels of second-ary schooling which, in the 1960s, involved only that small minority of each age cohort who were aiming for university studies in science-based courses. With leadership and involvement from enthusiastic academic scientists, experienced science teachers with strong scientific backgrounds developed materials for chemistry, physics and biology. Bringing school Science up to date turned out to be presenting abstract concepts that are of basic importance in each science as the primary content of importance for their study in school. It did not mean new topics that reflected the many advances, like polymers, semiconductivity and biosynthesis, that had been made in these sciences in the previous thirty years.

This change in content discarded two social dimensions of Science – the applications of science in society and the individual and co-operative processes in the scientific community that leads to these abstract concepts. As a consequence there was no basis in school Science on which to develop a critique of the role Science plays in society or an appreciation of its strengths and limitations (Fensham 1973). The change did, however, mean that school Science in the years immediately before students moved into its study at university was coherent with, and a logical preparation for such further studies.

Other projects followed that took up the issue of Science at the lower levels of schooling. Their direction and character were, however, very much influenced by the conception of school Science as the beginnings of an induction into Science that was to be completed by studies of the disciplines in higher education. Although a few projects which originated in the USA did develop materials that could enable school Science to serve other purposes, such as an understanding of Technology (Engineering Concepts Curriculum Project) and creativity about the natural world (Environmental Studies Project), nowhere were these adopted as the mainstream curriculum. By the mid-1970s the legacy of these exciting reforms was well established as the curriculum of what school Science should be in most of the industrialized countries and a number of developing ones.

For the lower secondary years, there was a belief that an introduction to these specialized languages, models and processes of the sciences was good for everyone, paving the way for the accelerated treatment of this conceptual approach in the upper secondary years. For the primary years, where Science had not hitherto had a significant place, the most commonly encouraged content for learning was the so-called 'processes of science' like classifying, measuring, controlling variables, and so on, practical and intellectual procedures that stemmed from a positivist and utilitarian view of what scientists do.

Roberts (1982) identified seven emphases or purposes that curriculum materials for school Science over time had, or could have served. The curriculum legacy just described had given clear priority to three of these emphases:

1 *Solid Foundation* knowledge that prepared for the scientific topics that came in the succeeding years of schooling
2 *Correct Explanation* a representation at the school level of a topic of its current description in Science
3 *Scientific Skill Development* practice in the laboratory of some standard scientific procedures involving technical equipment.

The other four were discarded or quite under-used as sources for content or pedagogy: *The Nature of Science* (philosophical and historical aspects of Science) and *Self as Explainer* (active involvement of the students in scientific reasoning) are interesting among these discards because a number of the scientist architects of the 1960s reforms, like Zacharias and Rogers in physics, Schwab in biology, Halliwell and Campbell in chemistry and Bruner had argued that both of these were important. *Everyday Coping* (local and wider applications of science) was eliminated to make room for the new conceptual content and *Science, Technology Decisions* (being informed and equipped to make informed judgements about socio-scientific issues) was not itself considered an issue for school Science in 1960.

UNPREDICTED SOCIAL CHANGES

During the 1960s and 1970s a number of changes occurred in the industrialized societies that were not apparent when the definition of school Science that this curriculum legacy represented was laid down in the late

1950s. The nuclear threat of the Cold War following the Cuban missile crisis in 1962, and the increasing recognition of the serious damage that unbridled technology causes in the biosphere, regularly gave Science a bad image in the media.

The rebuilding of the totally devastated German and Japanese industries enabled these countries to incorporate the latest technologies, and hence to threaten economically the traditional means of production in other countries that had not had their industries destroyed. The new technologies did away with many of the less skilled workers, and required different skills from those who remained. From the middle of the 1970s higher levels of unemployment than had been known since the 1930s became a chronic feature in many societies. In response to these pressures, students were encouraged or required to stay for more and more schooling, and secondary education began to change from an elite to a mass phenomenon.

Two other social movements highlighted other inadequacies in school Science. The women's movement raised questions about the participation of girls in schooling and about their access to certain professions and occupations after school. These questions of access focused attention on the participation of girls in the physical sciences which, everywhere, had become gateway subjects biased in favour of boys. The second societal change stemmed from the growth of multi-culturalism as immigration brought in many new citizens with a variety of new ethnic backgrounds. The participation of their children in the education system was of great importance to these immigrants' social mobility, and once again they were often disadvantaged by the elite character that Science had in the curriculum.

It was thus not surprising that evaluators of the new science curricula repeatedly found that these were not being implemented in the manner that was intended, and that a decreasing proportion of the student body was being attracted to, and was benefiting from their school Science. Whatever the curriculum achieved for those who went on to further science-related studies, it was not enthusing the great bulk of students, nor providing them with a scientific basis to participate with confidence in societies that were increasingly influenced by science and technology. It was the recognition of these failures that prompted the reviews and reports referred to at the beginning of this chapter with their urgent calls for alternative approaches to school Science.

SEARCH FOR ALTERNATIVES

The difficulties in making school Science more meaningful for all students as future citizens are not due to a lack of alternative approaches to the induction and preparatory ones that I have described as the legacy from the 1960s. Indeed, the 1980s proved to be an extremely fruitful period, both in terms of research into the problems of better and more widespread science learning, and of the development of ideas and novel materials for school Science. Rather, the difficulties lie in the hegemony of school systems and Science's role in them, in the place of choice of Science in senior secondary schooling. These reflect the conceptions of school Science that prevail in educational systems and are reinforced by the attitudes and behaviour of some key players in the school Science scene. Academic scientists, science teachers and science educators are the main groups of players, with the first group usually maintaining the legacy and the third group contesting it, while the members of the second group are divided between the two positions.

How these structural, corporate and personal features of this curriculum scene act as barriers to Science for All will become apparent as the development of some of these alternatives is described.

UNCOVERING ALTERNATIVES

With the considerable resources that the national reviews once again released for school Science, a number of projects and research studies began in many countries. These processes were greatly assisted by the fact that science education by the early 1980s had become an established and active field of scholarly research. This meant that the projects in the 1980s had a much sounder base for their development than the ideas from general psychological learning theory that had been almost the only theoretical underpinning for learning science in the 1960s.

Many of the new projects did not in the first instance set out to develop materials as the earlier ones had all done. The *Learning in Science Project* in New Zealand spent most of its first phase exploring children's conceptions or understanding of a wide range of natural phenomena and science concepts. Among these were the widely and strongly held ideas that motion is associated with the force *in* the moving body, that things get lighter when they burn, and that what *Life* or *Animal* mean is often quite different from their sense in biology. The shift of focus that Osborne and Freyberg (1985) achieved in this project from the teacher and teaching to the learner and learning reverberated around the world in a quite remarkable fashion. A better understanding of the needs and character-istics of young science learners and how they conceived of learning science became recognized as precursor conditions for the sensible development of new materials and new curricula. The *Secondary Science Curriculum Review* in England and Wales brought groups of teachers together to share their experience of the problems of teaching Science to the demo-graphically different school populations of the 1980s.

Some of the projects focused on the knowledge content that could make

Science more relevant to students in the different stages of schooling. Others concentrated on how science learning could be a deeper, more active process than the shallow short-term learning of unconnected facts, concepts and algorithmic rules that school Science was for so many. This sense of 'active learning' was quite different from the emphasis on laboratory activity that many of the 1960s projects had advocated. Now 'active' referred to the learners being active in mind, personally constructing and reconstructing meaning from their experiences of phenomena in the laboratory, and from their teacher's inputs.

Yet another area of exploration related to the purposes for Science at different stages of schooling and the aspects of Science that could contribute most effectively to these different purposes. Roberts' (1982) work on broad categories of purpose has already been mentioned. Aikenhead (1986) and Solomon (1988) spelt out how the relationships between science, technology and society could be related to school Science. Hodson (1988) did a parallel job for the philosophy of science, and Fensham and May (1979) provided an epistemology for a science education that set out to make students environmentally aware and responsible.

A number of projects did produce materials, many of which claimed a place within Science-Technology-Society (STS), a slogan that became shorthand for moves to extend school Science to purposes like Roberts' *Nature of Science*, *Everyday Coping* and *Science, Technology Decisions* and to *Science in Applications* and *Science in Making*, two other categories of purpose that are needed to cover some of the new materials from the 1980s.

Salters Chemistry and *Salters Science*, two British projects based at York, set as a guiding principle that the science concepts (required for course approval in England and Wales in the mid-1980s) would be introduced only when the need for them could be rooted in material and phenomena familiar to 13–16 year olds from their own experiences or from television and books (N. Smith 1988). This principle called for radical new foci and reordering of traditional content in school Science. It can be contrasted with the earlier and very popular *Science and Technology in Society (SATIS)* project, which produces short modules about applications of science that can be added, if a teacher wishes, to topics in the existing science curriculum.

In the Netherlands, the *PLON Physics* project evolved materials slowly through the 1980s, learning from the classroom trials of one unit the aspects to strengthen and delete in subsequent units (Eijkelhof and Kortland 1988). One of these, 'Ionizing Radiation', included some topics and concepts in pure physics such as the characteristics and measurements of short-wave forms of electromagnetic radiation that are not part of traditional school physics in many countries. While academic physicists are attracted to this advanced physics in the PLON materials they are not, however, comfortable with the biology that is included to make sense of the interactions between these radiations and human beings, or with the socio-scientific concepts like 'radiation damage' and 'social risk' that this unit introduces as society's ways of quantifying and regulating such phenomena.

These selections of STS materials and a number of others from Germany, USA, Australia and Canada are examples of *Concepts in Contexts* – an approach to curriculum that is strongly supported by research on how students learn and are attracted to learn science. It uses familiar and motivating contexts from the students' world outside school to provide meaning and interconnectedness for the science concepts, and the concepts, in turn, provide the students with powerful new insights of the contexts (Lijnse 1990).

While the materials mentioned so far do not avoid 'decision-making' about socio-scientific issues, they do not emphasize it. This educational objective for school Science is, however, quite prominent in the rhetoric of national reports, for example 'the scientific knowledge necessary to fulfill civic responsiblities' (National Science Foundation 1983: 44), and of politicians, 'to grapple with environmental issues' (Gillian Shephard, UK Secretary of State for Education, February 1995). *Chemicals in Public Places* (Thier and Hill 1988) and *Logical Reasoning in Science and Technology* (Aikenhead 1991) are two examples of curriculum materials that have made such decision-making a quite explicit learning outcome.

The issue of girls and Science led on to comparative studies of the interests of boys and girls. Smail (1987), for example, found an interest in nurturing more strongly but not exclusively in girls. However, a number of studies found that the differences in interest of topics for study were less than had been thought. In many countries there are differences in participation and in achievement in the physical sciences in senior secondary schooling. These may be more due, in that attenuated remainder of the original cohort, to the subgroup of boys who, for extrinsic and intrinsic reasons choose to continue with these subjects, than evidence that boys as a whole are more interested in them than girls.

'COMETS: *career orientated modules to explore technology and science*' (W. Smith 1987), *Girls into Science and Technology* (Kelly *et al.* 1984) and *Chemistry from Issues* (J. M. Harding and Donaldson 1986) are examples of materials that were developed to incorporate in various ways the nurturing interest. It may be reasonable to include as also expressing this interest the many materials that have been developed with an environmental concern. Together they would then fall in yet another purpose for school Science, namely *Science for Nurturing*, in which care for people, society or the environment is explicitly present.

There is thus no shortage of alternatives to meet the official calls for Science for All: new purposes for school Science have been spelt out, and new content and new pedagogies devised and invented to serve them. As yet, however, there has been very little decisive will at the educational system level.

CONTRADICTIONS IN INTENTIONS

In discussing why it is so difficult for school Science to make serious contributions to general scientific literacy, I will draw on a number of specific examples from the debates and efforts that have occurred in Australia (and especially in the State of Victoria). I do this partly because of my knowledge of these scenes, and because there are now enough similar reports from other countries that suggest these are, indeed, examples of factors and conditions that have very widespread currency.

Education systems in general are well known for their in-built properties of benefiting the children of rich and well-educated parents more than disadvantaged children from poor backgrounds. Despite repeated attempts to compensate disadvantage, the basic hegemonic effects of these systems and their curriculum of schooling are rarely disturbed (see Bourdieu and Passeron 1973; Lundgren 1981; Connell *et al.* 1982).

Earlier in the twentieth century Science (with advanced mathematics as a concomitant partner) began to take over the hegemonic role that the classical languages had played for so long. This accelerated with the coherence the 1960s reforms brought about between the content of the science disciplines in schooling and their counterpart parent disciplines in the universities. The study of the sciences, particularly the physical sciences, became the most powerful factor in sustaining the differentiating function of schooling (see Fensham 1980; Scriven 1987).

Science (plus mathematics) was well placed to assume this mantle. Its history in schooling is quite different from that of mathematics itself. Until very recently – the 1960s – it had no place in primary schooling, whereas elementary mathematics has always had a central and expected place from the earliest levels of schooling. David Layton (1973) described the failure of an attempt in the middle of the nineteenth century to introduce Science in the primary schooling of rural children before it was established in elite schooling in England. In the USA a similar suggestion from the philosopher, Spencer, failed, and it was late in the nineteenth century when Science began to appear in the US upper secondary years as part of the selection process for university entrance.

Parents, secondary teachers, school authorities, employers and society quite generally expect pupils to learn elementary mathematics. No such consensus exists about an elementary science. The current press for it comes much more from the compelling logic confronting educational and societal leaders, that it would be irresponsible in late-twentieth-century technological society if Science was not part of all levels of schooling.

So Science entered the school curriculum in the form of senior secondary subjects associated with the separate disciplines of science in the universities. Indeed, until as late as the 1970s it was not uncommon to find subjects for botany, zoology and physiology in the school curriculum, rather than biology. The combination of their content to form a single subject was made possible by the shifts in emphasis in universities from the whole organism to the micro-biological level of cells, biochemicals and genes and to the macro-level of ecology and hence to the reorganization in the 1960s of first-year teaching in universities to a common year of biology.

A number of university courses that led to prestigious and financially rewarding professions like medicine, engineering, dentistry, veterinary science, and to a lesser extent science itself, expected or required entering students to have high achievement in the physical sciences (with mathematics) at school. Many of these professional fields also involve biological sciences, but if science faculties in the universities, and even biological science departments themselves, have to choose between the physical sciences and biology as a prerequisite study, they usually choose the former. This purchasing power of the physical sciences for university entry is further strengthened by the fact that, in many countries, students with high achievement in these subjects are also looked on favourably for highly selective courses like law and economics, that have little need of specific prerequisite knowledge.

The expansion of higher education everywhere since the 1960s has done nothing to lessen the discriminating power of these science subjects. Rather, it has served to heighten the competition (fundamental to hegemony) to get into the exclusive courses at the higher-status universities that lead to the greatest social rewards. Universities increasingly draw their status from the research success of their scientific and technological academics, and the academic quality of their entering students. Identification of its name and content with a university discipline that is recognized as important is a major factor for gaining status. It is not, however, a sufficient condition as the differential status between school chemistry/ physics and biology indicates. With status comes constraint and chemistry and physics were more constrained to include only preparatory content in the 1960s than was biology, into which more frontier topics were allowed (Fensham 1980).

When Araos (1995) asked secondary school teachers in Victoria to list the subjects in the final years of schooling in order of academic status and difficulty, physics, chemistry and advanced mathematics invariably occupied the top positions, followed usually by literature and economics. At the low status end were found the interdisciplinary subjects like home economics, physical education, environmental studies and the integrated forms of science that have been developed and adopted in the last few years in some systems. By academic status teachers mean quite simply the purchasing power that a subject has, *vis-à-vis* university selection. To maintain their own reputation, schools tend to encourage only students with high achievements in middle-school mathematics and science (separate or combined) to undertake the 'difficult' physical sciences. Lesser achieving students will be discouraged from taking these subjects or encouraged to study the 'less demanding' interdisciplinary science subjects if these are available. It is this sort of hegemonic pattern that leads teachers to the contradictions of agreeing that environmental science ought to have a very high priority but not insisting on it being in the school's curriculum, or if it is, ascribing only the weakest students to it.

Van Berkel (1995) in a study of the structure of school chemistry has been concerned with a subject's maintenance of status as well as gaining it. One of the conditions his international set of respondents emphasized is demarcation. Three demarcations are reported – from common everyday thinking about substances, from technological applications and from treatment in other sciences. The problem with many of the alternative approaches to Science for All outlined above is that they deliberately set out to blur these demarcations. Van Berkel's three correspond almost directly with Society, Technology and Science – the STS movement's favoured bases for scientific literacy. If school science is to be about real-world situations and issues they will inevitably involve content from a number of sciences. Furthermore, these situations also involve technological or science knowledge for 'practical action' (D. Layton 1991), that is as much of society's making as it is of the academic scientific community.

CHOICE IN THE CURRICULUM

In many western countries there has been recognition since the early 1980s that the existence of choice in the upper secondary years means for school Science that girls preferentially choose biology compared with physics. This choice (as has been indicated above) restricts their choice of courses of study in higher education and hence their science-based career options (see J. M. Harding 1983; Kelly 1981; Parker 1986). Furthermore, for a career like primary school teaching, which is not usually thought of as a science-based one, there is evidence that studies in biology at school do not give many of these teachers confidence about Science or its elementary teaching. The physics and chemistry that they have not studied seem to have more influence on this aspect of their self-esteem (Speedy *et al.* 1989).

Although a number of countries have acted to disallow this choice and reorganized Science in their curriculum so that it is accessible in schooling in more gender-inclusive ways, most western countries have continued to allow subject choice within the senior sciences. They seem now to think of choice in this way being an important feature, because it is a cherished value in society more generally. Or perhaps it is simply a relic in upper-secondary schooling that made sense in the 1960s when only a small minority of an age cohort made these choices with very clear intentions of their university studies. Now, with mass secondary education and many students unclear of their future, these choices in the curriculum in reality act, for both girls and boys, as a major instrument of hegemony.

Thailand was the first country to record, for the large school system in the Bangkok area, equal and substantial participation in physics for both boys and girls, and more significantly equal learning achievements (Fensham 1986). Furthermore, apart from the role models that a larger percentage of women physics teachers presented, there were no particularly gender-inclusive aspects in the Thai physics curriculum. The decisive factor was the removal of the choice of individual subjects that was an obvious feature of the problem in the west, and replacing it with what was, in effect, the choice of a course of study.

Early in the 1980s schooling beyond the ninth grade (age 14–15) in Thailand began to be conceived of as vocational for all students. Students who entered academic high schools were aiming for professions requiring university education. Other students seeking careers involving specialized technologies entered schools that focused on equipping them with the relevant knowledge and skills. A specific Science curriculum was designed for each of these types of senior secondary school. In the academic schools, students chose between a science stream and a humanities stream. In the science stream they studied all three of biology, chemistry and physics in each of tenth, eleventh and twelfth grades. In the humanities stream they studied biological science and physical science for at least two of these years. Without the option of no science at all (or of just biology) and the science stream leading to a wider range of further studies, it is not surprising that as many of the able girls chose the science stream as did the boys.

Rethinking how choice should exist in the curriculum of schooling when the upper-secondary years are now a mass phenomenon in many countries may, in fact, prove to be a major breakthrough in the search for scientific and technological literacy.

CONCEPTIONS OF SCHOOL SCIENCE

I have argued in this chapter that the dominant conception of school Science in the 1960s reforms and in the curriculum legacy that still prevails in most countries is one of induction into the scientific disciplines – a process that can at best be achieved only to a limited extent in schooling. The fact that so few science teachers, even with a tertiary degree in Science, think of themselves as scientists testifies to the extended nature of this induction process.

As part of a national review of mathematics and science teacher education in Australia, Speedy *et al.* (1989) asked the staff in the science departments of universities and institutes of technology – the two types of tertiary institutions involved – what image of a graduate scientist determined their curriculum. A future secondary teacher spends three years in science studies and one year in education.

The replies from the institutes were readily forthcoming as 'an applied chemist or an applied physicist, etc.', usually to fit specific niches in the Australian industrial scene. These institutes have evolved since the 1960s from senior technical colleges with close links to industry to degree-granting bodies, rather like polytechnics in a number of other countries. The staff in the universities, the origins of which will be familiar, have long been very explicit about their research role. At first they suggested that the question was meaningless because a chemistry (physics, etc.) course was simply self-defining, but discussion of the content included in the various years soon led to the answer, 'an academic research chemist, physicist, etc.'. Since only the university staff exert a large influence on school Science, it is thus not surprising that induction into this long process, stretching from school through a degree to a PhD, remains the dominant conception for school Science.

Science, Technology and Society (STS) – with the addition of Personal Development (PD) – was adopted in the mid-1980s as the official curriculum framework of school Science for seventh to tenth grades (ages 12–13 to 15–16) in Victoria (Malcolm 1987). The prevailing high degree of school-based curriculum development and the strangeness of these ways of conceiving of school Science meant that Chan (1993), for her studies a few years later, could find only a handful of teachers who claimed strong identification with this STS-PD approach to Science. When a brave attempt was made to extend the STS alternative conception to the final two years in Victoria, Fensham and Corrigan (1994) found that even the more innovative teachers had reinterpreted the STS use of contexts into pedagogical procedures that enabled them to teach the traditional concepts more effectively, rather than to see them as opportunities for new content and learning outcomes.

When some of the alternative conceptions of school Science were included in draft proposals for a possible national curriculum for first to tenth grades (ages 5–6 to 15–16) in Australia in 1993, they were strongly attacked by a number of leading academic scientists, and by their spokespersons in the professional institutes of chemistry and physics. 'Subjective revisionism', 'a mess shrouded under the mantles of feminism and aboriginal culture', 'hand waving descriptions of natural phenomena', 'the impact of science and technology on society is simply not science', 'a takeover of true scientific teaching by a socially motivated, pseudo-scientific approach' and 'undermines the Western scientific tradition' are but some of the scornful or angry epithets that were heaped in a number of reports in the mass media on what was, in fact, a very compromised version of what some science educators and teachers had hoped for when this project began in 1989. Paul Davies, the 1995 Templeton Prize-winner for his own very popular but highly speculative writings on the religious meaning of modern physics, was a leading member of one of these groups of hard-liners. At one point in his group's article they did seem to acknowledge that schools should cater for the majority who need some acquaintance with scientific ideas without advanced mathematical skills. They immediately, however, go on to confirm their need to maintain the *Solid Foundation* purpose for school Science that marks the induction conception: 'one cannot start teaching real science in grades 11 and 12 (ages 16–18) – students simply would not be able to cope without prior grounding'.

A comparative analysis of science curriculum developments in Australia, England and Wales, New Zealand, and Canada from 1985 to 1995 (Fensham 1995a) has revealed that educational bureaucrats have played quite decisive roles in preventing or delaying the adoption of alternative conceptions of school Science. Very often these persons have been innovative in their own other areas of the school curriculum but, for Science, they prove to be identified with the induction conception. Whether this is because they view Science (like the primary teacher students above) in terms of what they did not study when they were at school or because they assess where the power lies between the advocacy groups proposing what school Science should be will require more detailed case studies to reveal (see Blades 1994; Hart 1995).

THE POWER PLAYERS

The difficulties that schools face in teaching scientific literacy discussed so far arise from relative power plays between different advocacy groups, or between individuals who can call on institutional or other supports for their case. In this last section of the chapter the positions and powers of the three main groups are described.

Academic scientists

The most powerful and persistent of these groups is to be found among academic scientists. Traditionally academic scientists and their acolytes among the science teaching ranks have completely controlled what counted as school Science (see e.g. Fawns 1987; D. Layton 1984). In general they welcomed the reforms of the 1960s and some of them played leadership roles. As has been indicated, these changes to a conceptual content for school Science meant that students entering universities to

131

study the sciences were prepared at school and selected in terms of the same type of content as university Science.

Since then, a few scientists (see e.g. Gillespie 1976 in Canada; Bucat and Cole 1988 in Australia) have been concerned about entering students' lack of experience with many of the phenomena they seem able to define and handle in conceptual and algorithmic terms. However, the main complaints from academic scientists about school Science stem from quantitative features of the current scene. Not enough of the high-school achievers are taking science subjects at school and too few of those who do are choosing science courses in higher education. This leads to students with weak backgrounds in physical sciences and mathematics entering science courses to the dismay of the academics who have to teach them. This has not led many academic scientists to question the appropriateness of the curricula of the legacy type. For example, there is currently a particularly widespread concern about the shortage of students interested in physics, but academic physicists often continue to be the main opponents of any attempts to introduce alternative approaches to school Science and to school physics itself that could make this subject more appealing (see Rowell and Gaskell 1986; Hart 1995; Fensham 1995b).

Another case of this support of the legacy-type content is typified by the concern that has been expressed by some academic scientists in England at the various suggestions to widen the number of subjects to be studied for the A Level examinations that precede university entry. This could be to the advantage of science students being able to be more broadly educated, but it would be at the expense of them studying proportionately less of the traditional content of the prerequisite physical sciences and mathematics. An even more radical move for many countries would be general acceptance by the universities that, at least for some able students from school, studies in physics and chemistry could begin from scratch at university (as is now commonly the case with the biological or earth sciences). This approach has been tried in some universities with considerable success, provided the mathematical base of the students is strong.

Although some scientists were part of the reviews in the 1980s (referred to on pp. 123–6) that recommended that new approaches be developed, the academic scientists in general have been relatively uninvolved in, or negative about the development of the alternatives being suggested. When these alternatives are at the point when they might be implemented, there has usually been strong opposition from leading scientists, especially if changes are suggested to Science in the final years of schooling. They have, of course, much to lose in these changes, namely the narrow, but concentrated, conceptual preparedness of their first-year students in the physical sciences. They may, however, gain a much broader base of able students interested in further studies in Science, and overall, future citizens who are more able to differentiate those programmes of scientific work that are in the long-term interests of society and hence be a base of support for them. At the moment most academic scientists seem to have chosen to stay with the preparedness potential they see in the curricula of the narrow conceptual legacy (if only more of their students had succeeded in it) and they fight hard to retain it.

From the collection of quotes above it is evident that academic scientists are vehemently against the suggestions that school Science should acknowledge that the subjective, the irrational, or social construction play a part in Science. Although, in their own circles, and, as Marton *et al.* (1994) found among Nobel laureates, features such as the subjectivity of much scientific work, the role of intuition in it, and the importance of the various disciplinary communities, are accepted and often shared, they are not to be shared with neonate science students or with non-science audiences. It is as if this would undermine an authority about their scientific knowledge that these academics need to keep and, indeed, are responsible for guarding. Bingle and Gaskell (1994) have discussed how this power and authority of Science is threatened by the complexity of real-life environmental situations for which a total scientific analysis is impossible.

School science teachers

Although a growing number of science teachers are now regularly confronted by the open boredom of their students (Baird *et al.* 1991) and their inability or unwillingness to learn school Science, the general response of science teachers to the new approaches has been conservative and unenthusiastic. In England and Wales relatively few science teachers participated in the curriculum innovations made possible by the substantial funds in the Technical and Vocational Educational Initiative (TVEI) programme. In Canada and Sweden, subject groups of teachers have used their union affiliations and other means to resist changes to their science curricula. In Australia, science teachers were found to be very inarticulate about why students should study Science compared with the way other teachers argued for their subjects. They were more inclined to rest with the strength of position the eliteness of their subjects gave them than to be concerned with the mass of students' education in Science.

Reference has already been made to the socialization that most of today's science teachers have been through in their own education in Science. Few of them experienced the very different more concrete and social curricula that existed before the legacy of the 1960s took over. They have all been socialized in its induction approach in their schooling and in their university studies in Science. Furthermore, at school they were among its most successful students in that they continued in tertiary scientific studies for a long way, albeit not far enough to feel like scientists. It is no wonder so many of them also have a stake in its maintenance and a reluctance to teach students whose academic interests are so different from their own. There are, however, growing reports in a number of countries of groups of science teachers who are working together to use as much of these alternatives as their formal curriculum will allow.

The formal professional associations of science teachers and their umbrella organization, International Council of Associations for Science Education (ICASE), have generally been more progressive and open to the exploration of alternative approaches. A number of these bodies have provided status, publicity and, in some cases, financial support, for developing or distributing material that embody these options. There are a growing number of reports of teachers in many countries working together on alternative approaches and, indeed, using them in their classrooms.

Academic science educators

One of the lasting and more interesting outcomes of the 1960s projects has been the emergence of a second group of academics with interests in the nature of school Science. Many of the outstanding teachers who were recruited as writers and team members of these projects did not return to their classrooms when the projects ended. Rather, they took up positions in the expanding higher education scene as teacher educators. Informed by the extensive and intensive experience in the large-scale projects, they shared not only their own experience of teaching, but also the range of approaches and ideas that had been learnt about in the project. They also had many questions about science teaching that needed answers; quite quickly science education became established as a field of lively research and scholarly discourse that could inform and influence school Science.

With the renewal of official interest and support for school Science in the 1980s, a number of these science educators became very active in promoting and developing the alternative approaches that have been outlined earlier. With the responsibilities and opportunities they have in the pre-service and in-service education of science teachers, they are well placed to explain the new conceptions of school Science and to contribute to teachers' ability to accept and act on them in their teaching (see Fensham et al. 1994; Solomon and Aikenhead 1994). Accounts are also now appearing of the way in which these science educators have also played important roles in the debates and decision-making about whether the new approaches will be implemented (see for instance several papers in the theme issue on Policy and Science Education, International Journal of Science Education 17(4) 1995).

The role played by science educators in the proposed changes has, however, been much more ambiguous than has so far been suggested. This stems from the results of what is their most successful area of research since the mid-1980s, and from the limitations that their positions in higher education impose.

The shift of focus from teaching to learning and some easy-to-use methodologies (see R. T. White and Gunstone 1993) unleashed what has become a flood of more than 3,000 research studies of students, alternative conceptions of natural phenomena and of basic scientific conceptions (Pfundt and Duit 1994). Almost all of these studies have been of science concepts and topics associated with the legacy Science curriculum, for the obvious reason that this was what students were supposed to be learning in school. The research has been fruitful in laying bare the extent of the problem of poor science learning and in leading to the invention of many new pedagogies that have been shown to enhance this learning. These findings together provide a very solid research base for the renewal and resurrection of the legacy curriculum and the induction conception of school Science. 'Things are bad but we now know how to do it better' is one reasonable interpretation of this decade of research, whether this is what these science educators with their curriculum hats intend or not. If any of us had bothered to conduct the same sort of research into students' conceptions of socio-scientific issues (like the historical nature of science) or of technological and environmental concepts (like 'social risk', 'product shelf life' and 'radiation damage', etc.) we would, I am sure, have found a similarly amazing range of alternative views and misinformation, and of useful pedagogies. A parallel research base to support the social constructivist and STS alternative approaches would then exist, and the reforming science educators' hands would have been much stronger.

In a number of countries science educators are discipline-based and their positions are located in the respective science departments. They are thus dependent on academic scientists for their institutional support. Not surprisingly, their research interests and professional activities have tended to relate to the concerns they can share with their scientist colleagues about the quality of students' conceptual learning. These science educators thus do not have a strong research base to promote other purposes for school Science, that would, in any case, be opposed by their colleagues.

In other countries, science educators are located among other educators. It is usually these who have taken up the cause of alternatives and who promote Science for All. They have been instrumental in providing research bases for the extent of the problem and for supporting many of the ideas, sufficiently so that they have become viable options in a number of countries for the primary years and for the earlier secondary years. It is at the upper-secondary level that their influence is, as yet, not very substantial in practice.

Perhaps the most promising approach for these later levels of schooling will be one in which both academic scientists and science educators can be seen to be supportive of the ideas that the science teacher associations are putting forward. Continuing the science education in the upper-secondary years of the majority of students who do not wish to proceed to science-based tertiary studies is seen as desirable by all three groups of power players. Furthermore, when it is clear that the goal is about Science for the 'non-Science' students and that the preparatory role does not apply, there is evidence that the academic scientists are much more ready to encourage the range of ideas that have been so well developed in the case for STS school Science. Thailand (as has been described) achieved this goal in the 1980s, and Israel and the Netherlands have now embarked upon establishing an appropriate finale to school Science for this large group of students. When enough good examples of what these studies can be are available, other countries may find that they too can move forward towards the scientific literacy they have affirmed but done so far so little to achieve.

10

TOWARDS A FUNCTIONAL PUBLIC UNDERSTANDING OF SCIENCE

Edgar Jenkins

Why should pupils at school study science? What is school science *for*? Seemingly, the questions have little point since the answers are straightforward and self-evident. Young people are growing up in a world which is increasingly shaped and controlled by science and technology, and innovation in these fields underpins not only economic prosperity but also the many social and other changes which will affect them in ways that in some cases cannot yet even be imagined. Science and technology are among the great imaginative and cultural achievements of the human race and the ability to function effectively as a citizen in the modern world seems to demand some scientific knowledge allied with an insight into the nature of the scientific endeavour.

However, as so often in education, neither the questions nor the answers are as simple as they may initially appear. The history of school science education is marked by debate and controversy about the rationale and practice of teaching science to young people, and the claims made for science in education show a marked dependence on time and context. Such claims are also contingent upon the answers to several other questions, notably, what kind of science are the pupils to be taught and what use might they reasonably be expected to make in their adult lives of what they have learned?

Two general responses can, however, be made. The first is that a distinction has frequently been drawn between scientific knowledge and some understanding of what it means to engage in scientific activity. When the British Association for the Advancement of Science (BAAS) produced a seminal report in 1868 on *The Best Means of Promoting Scientific Education in Schools*, a sharp distinction was made between scientific *information* and scientific *training*, that is between general 'literary acquaintance with scientific facts and the knowledge of scientific method that may be gained by studying the facts at first hand under the guidance of a competent teacher' (BAAS 1868: xxxiv). The language and the assumptions about learning and teaching which underpin this distinction have, of course, undergone many changes since the mid-nineteenth century. In recent times, it is 'process' which has been contrasted with scientific 'content', the former frequently being elaborated in terms of allegedly distinct 'skills' (or even 'process skills') such as 'observing' or 'hypothesizing'. Such a characterization allows at least one author to identify with particular clarity and confidence 'what it takes to be good at science', namely 'communicating and interpreting, observing, planning investigations, investigating and making', together with such basic skills as the ability 'to follow instructions for doing experiments' (Coles 1989: 4–5).

The relative emphasis to be placed on 'scientific methodology' and scientific content has also changed over time. For Henry Armstrong in the early years of the twentieth century, the teaching of scientific method was of paramount importance (Armstrong 1903). During the curriculum development era of the 1960s, when the rhetoric referred to 'finding out' and 'learning by discovery', pupils were encouraged to 'think like scientists' or 'behave like a scientist for a day'. In 1985, official policy for school science education in England and Wales advised that 'Each of us needs to bring a scientific approach to bear on the practical, social, economic and political issues of modern life' (DES 1985: para. 7). This same commitment to giving pupils some insight into scientific activity is evident in the various versions of the science component of the National Curriculum introduced following the passage of the Education Reform Act 1988, most obviously in the first of the four Attainment Targets in the 1991 Order, Scientific Investigation. It is perhaps not surprising that it was this Attainment Target which caused teachers, and secondary science teachers in particular, especial difficulty, since it enacted in statute for pedagogic and assessment purposes, an activity which is creative, complex, contingent and collaborative and about the nature of which scholars cannot reach agreement.

The second general response is that contemporary justifications for teaching science at school are commonly cast in terms of 'scientific literacy for all'. A recommendation of a Select Committee of the House of Commons that 'scientific and technological literacy should be the key aim' of schooling in England and Wales (House of Commons 1995b: para. 89) mirrors views already expressed in many other countries. For example, *Project 2061*, initiated by the American Association for the Advancement of Science, aims to make all students literate in science, mathematics and technology by the time they graduate from high school (AAAS 1993). At an intergovernmental level, the Unesco *Project 2000+* seeks to establish, by the year 2000, appropriate structures to foster such literacy for all, in all countries of the world (Unesco 1994).

Beyond formal systems of schooling, concern to promote scientific literacy and the public understanding of science underpins a world-wide interest in 'hands-on' and interactive science centres and museums, complemented by a significant investment in science education by the broadcast and print media. Different perspectives are represented by initiatives such as the science 'Olympiads' and other, more local or national competitions; the 'science shops' developed in the Netherlands; the 'consensus conferences' held in the Netherlands and Denmark and, more recently, in the UK; the Science for Citizens Programme from 1977 to 1981 and the Ethics and Values in Science and Technology Programme in the USA; the Kerala People's Science Movement in India and the Living Space Science programme in Brazil (for an overview of some of these developments, see Jenkins 1996). Overall, it is clear that more people than at any time in history are engaged in some way with science education, although the quality, nature and form of provision differ greatly from one country to another. Ironically, this high level of global activity comes at a time when the notions of scientific literacy and of scientific method have been dismissed as 'myths' (Bauer 1992; Shamos 1995), and the assumptions underlying recent science curriculum reform have been challenged on educational, political, economic, industrial, social and philosophical grounds (Chapman 1991).

SOME ISSUES AND TENSIONS

Despite the world-wide commitment to the promotion of scientific literacy, it is clear that concern about science education, especially that provided by formal educational systems, remains widespread. Quantitative estimates of scientific literacy, based principally upon measured understandings of scientific knowledge and, to a lesser extent, of scientific procedures, have produced results widely regarded as disappointing. Jon Miller (1983) concluded on the basis of a test administered to a sample of 1,635 adults in the USA that the overwhelming majority of the American adult population is scientifically illiterate and subsequent studies in many countries have commonly revealed only modest proportions of correct responses to such true/false statements as 'The centre of the earth is very hot', 'All radioactivity is man-made' and 'It is the father's gene that determines the gender of a child'. As an example, 85 per cent, 72 per cent and 75 per cent respectively of adults in Greece, France and Spain believed in 1992 that antibiotics killed viruses as well as bacteria, a finding of some significance for health education (National Science Board 1993). The relationship between percentage responses of this kind and formal education in science is unclear and any improvement in this measure of scientific literacy is likely to be difficult to disentangle from the more general effects and consequences of extended schooling. It is also worth asking whether, in studies of this kind, scientific literacy is being measured by reference to what the scientific community believes should be widely known and appreciated rather than to the scientific knowledge and understanding that adults themselves believe to be of significance in addressing their

139

everyday concerns. The potential here for mismatch is considerable and has been well captured by Ziman in his reference to 'the interests of those who are already inside science, and the motives of those whom they would wish to draw in' (Ziman 1984). The phrase 'draw in' is, of course, significant since it hints at the concern about scientific literacy as perceived by the scientific community.

There is also concern about the seeming unpopularity of the sciences, especially the physical sciences, as subjects for advanced study by young people. Although by no means universal, the phenomenon is common to a number of industrialized countries. In England and Wales, the numbers of 15 year olds passing GCSE and 17 year olds passing A Levels in mathematics and science decreased significantly from 1980 to 1994. The major reason for this decline is demographic, a trend which, from 1994, has begun to reverse. In contrast, the proportion of the age group passing these examinations in science or mathematics has risen steadily, although the increased proportion at age 15 has not translated into a correspondingly rapid growth at 17. The pattern is complicated by the growth of so-called 'mixed' A Levels. In 1993, around 41 per cent of those with a pass in science or mathematics at A Level had specialized in these subjects, with the remaining 59 per cent also passing in arts or social science subjects. Within higher education, there has been a substantial increase since 1980 in the numbers of students reading all subjects at first degree level, although, since 1988, science and engineering graduates have constituted a declining share of the overall graduating total (Department for Education (DfE) 1994). The several factors underlying these trends are difficult to disentangle and it is by no means clear what weight should be attached to any one of them.

These essentially educational concerns are indicative of a number of wider issues. Arguably the most politically and rhetorically important of these issues is the relationship between science education and economic productivity. For the industrialized countries such as the UK and the USA, investment in scientific education is seen as a key element in enabling their economies to compete more successfully with those of the prosperous countries of the Pacific Rim. For the developing world, scientific education underpins the industrialization and improvement in agricultural practice, health care and sanitation needed to sustain economic development. Economic arguments have become more prominent in the advocacy of greater scientific and technological literacy, such presentation frequently forming part of a more general political commitment to instrumentalism and vocationalism in education. The fact that, at a detailed level, the relationships between scientific literacy and economic prosperity are poorly understood has proved no bar to the making of some grand claims.

The presumed link between science education and industrial development or economic prosperity has led, however, to some significant challenges to the scientific endeavour in the modern world. More is involved here than the anti-science sentiments associated with environmental and human tragedies such as those associated with Chernobyl, Three Mile Island, thalidomide or Bhopal. For some in the developing world, western science and technology are regarded as a form of imperialism with all that this entails. For example, a conference on the 'Crisis in Modern Science', held in 1986 and attended by 140 scientists, journalists, grassroots activists and academics from countries as diverse as India, Argentina, the USA, Japan, Hong Kong and Thailand declared that 'science education in the Third World is a colonial legacy rooted in the Western system of education and has no relevance to our societies'. The alternative offered, the evolution of a Third World science and technology which 'relies upon indigenous categories, idioms and traditions in all spheres of thought and action', places the social responsibility of scientists and the political issues surrounding science, including environmental and ecological concerns, at the centre of science education, emphasizes the importance of indigenous medicine, shelter, food, industry and transport, and argues for the application of science to improve the livelihood of all (Third World Network 1986). Clearly, there are resonances here with the Science, Technology and Society (STS) movement which commands some support in many parts of the world (Solomon and Aikenhead 1994).

In the developing world, this essentially political agenda owes something to the notion of ethnoscience which, at least in part, can be regarded as a set of indigenous and local responses to the universality and domination of modern technoscience. Pomeroy, among others, has explored the implications for science education of revaluing local knowledge systems in understanding the natural world (Pomeroy 1996) and she contrasts the position of the 'universalists' with that of others who have been categorized as 'robust multiculturalists' (M. R. Matthews 1994). She is surely correct in her assertion that such a simple contrast oversimplifies and diminishes the complexity of the issues involved, the importance of which is clearly not confined to the developing world.

The political challenge to science implicit in ethnoscience has something in common with the critiques of the scientific endeavour offered by a number of feminist scholars working principally, but not exclusively, in the developed world. This is because, in each case, science education is to be revised or reformed as a means of redressing some social, economic, or other injustices and imbalances associated with science itself. However, the challenge is also epistemological, some radical feminist scholars arguing, for example, that the construction of science itself, including the notion of objectivity, is intrinsically masculine and, therefore, open to contrary and feminine interpretations. Feminist positions on science are, of course, far from unified as the writings of, for example, Sandra Harding (1986), Nye (1990) and Koertige (1981) make clear.

141

The claims of those working within the so-called 'strong' school of the sociology of science have provided a further epistemological challenge to science by questioning the genesis of scientific knowledge, and, therefore, its nature and the confidence that can, and should, be placed in it. The 'social constructivist' stance of scholars like Woolgar and Latour has produced both polemical (e.g. Gross and Levitt 1995) and defensive responses (e.g. Allaby 1995) on behalf of science, some of which have been related to school science education (e.g. M. R. Matthews 1995).

No response, however, has yet been as heated as that to Appleyard's book, *Understanding the Present: Science and the Soul of Modern Man* (Appleyard 1992), which addressed the dangers he saw as arising from the triumph of science as an activity which can 'say nothing about the meaning, purpose and significance of our own lives'. For Appleyard, science is 'spiritually corrosive, burning away ancient authorities and traditions' and it presents the world with 'the trick' of beginning by 'saying that it can answer only *this* kind of question' and ending by 'claiming that *these* are the only questions that can be asked' (Appleyard 1992: 9 and 248, original emphases). For some of his critics, Appleyard had launched not simply an assault upon institutionalized science but a 'New Ignorance Movement'. Clearly, as the end of the twentieth century draws nigh, the cultivators of science, to borrow a term used in the founding constitution of the British Association for the Advancement of Science in 1831, feel themselves not merely misunderstood or misrepresented but challenged and threatened (see Midgley, Chapter 3 in this volume).

The long-term significance of some of these contemporary criticisms of science is not clear. If they are more than a manifestation of *fin-de-siècle* sentiments, the consequences for the future of science and technology, and for society, could be profound. Holton's warning is of some importance:

> the record from Ancient Greece to fascist Germany and Stalin's USSR to our day shows that movements to delegitimate conventional science are ever present and ready to put themselves at the service of other forces that wish to bend the course of civilisation their way – for example, by the glorification of populism, folk belief, and violence, by mystification, and by an ideology that arouses rabid ethnic and nationalistic passions.
>
> (Holton 1993: 184)

It is evident that the questions posed at the beginning of this chapter can never command single, unequivocal and universally acceptable answers and that no single science curriculum could meet the entire range of implied objectives. Those with an interest in the school science curriculum, or, more widely, in science education, are simply too numerous and too diverse in their primary concerns. In addition, some of these concerns are almost certainly mutually incompatible. The preceding paragraphs also confirm that, despite a massive investment in formal (and increasingly in informal) science education, widespread scientific literacy remains an elusive goal. There appears, therefore, to be something of a gap between what has been achieved and the aspirations of those who might be described as science educators.

Several explanations might be offered to account for this gap. It is difficult to avoid the impression that science education has often been loaded with responsibilities that it cannot realistically hope to meet. In addition, school science education, despite large-scale investment in curriculum reform, seems rarely to allow pupils to engage with science in ways that resonate with their own concerns and priorities and encourage them to ask questions about aspects of the contemporary scientific endeavour. Central to this interrogation is the picture of that endeavour presented by much formal and informal science education. To a large degree, the picture seems obsolete. Ravetz's influential book *Scientific Knowledge and its Social Problems* was prompted by the 'rapid social changes in the character of the social activity of disciplined inquiry into the natural world and the consequent changes in its understanding of itself' (Ravetz 1971: 1). Twenty years later, Hurd, writing from the perspective of the USA, claimed that 'the ethos of science has changed.... 58% of all research scientists are located in industry; science and technology have become an integrated system, and research is now more social rather than theory driven' (Hurd 1990: 413). Gibbons and his colleagues have referred to the 'new production of knowledge', based upon a new dynamic between science and research and supplementing that which has hitherto prevailed (Gibbons *et al.* 1994). Much of science education, at all levels, has yet to respond adequately to the emergence of technoscience or 'postmodern' science and all that this implies for the traditional portrayal of science as the disinterested pursuit of objective truth.

Perhaps, however, the gap is reflective of a series of ill-founded or exaggerated concerns about, for example, a potential shortage of qualified scientific personnel, declining economic prosperity or standards in schools, all of which can seemingly and conveniently be addressed by supporting calls for more and better science education encompassed by the slogan 'scientific literacy'. Shamos, for example, referring to the series of 'crises' which marked science education in the USA in the 1980s, has described these as 'a false alarm' (Shamos 1988), echoing sentiments which Chapman has expressed in relation to science education in the UK during the same period (Chapman 1991). Shamos, it should be noted, goes further and argues that 'universal scientific literacy is a futile goal' and one that should be abandoned in favour of science education programmes which define scientific literacy in terms that are both functional and attainable (Shamos 1995).

A FUNCTIONAL PUBLIC UNDERSTANDING
OF SCIENCE

A public understanding of science which claims to be functional relates, in integral and intimate ways, knowledge and understanding of science to the context of usage and action. For John Dewey, this is essentially what understanding was about.

> Understanding has to be in terms of how things work and how to do things. Understanding, by its very nature, is related to action: just as information, by its very nature, is isolated from action.
>
> (Dewey 1946: 49)

However, this Deweyian perspective upon the relationship between knowledge and action is not commonly reflected in school science teaching. Conventionally, the emphasis in school science education is on universal and decontextualized knowledge, and on 'an individually centred analytical approach to tools of thought [which stress] reasoning and learning, with information considered on its own ground, extracted from practical use' (Rogoff 1990: 191). The 'applications' of scientific principles may, of course, be frequently acknowledged or described. However, this is unlikely to be done in ways that expose the complexity of what is involved in the notion of application or which challenge the widely held assumption that 'application' is a routine and unproblematic act, and, therefore, subordinate to, and less creative than, research leading to the establishment of scientific principles.

Insights into application and knowledge within the context of action are available from a number of different scholarly literatures. Studies in the history, philosophy and sociology of technology (e.g. Vincenti 1982; Staudenmaeir 1985; E. Layton 1987) confirm that before scientific concepts can be used in a technological context, 'they must be appropriated and restructured according to the specific demands of the design problem at hand' (Staudenmaier 1985: 102). As two simple examples, detailed knowledge of the properties of radio waves is insufficient to allow the construction of a radio, and close familiarity with the mathematics of Maxwell's electromagnetic theory cannot lead in any direct way to the design of an effective linear induction motor. Likewise, in the field of psychology, studies of 'everyday understanding' (e.g. Lave 1988; Semin and Gergen 1990) confirm that thinking is intimately interwoven with the context of the problem to be solved. From this perspective, it makes no sense to try to distinguish 'theory' from 'practice', since problems are defined by answers at the same time as answers are being constructed during the shaping of the problems. Of most immediate relevance in the present context, however, is the literature relating to the meanings and social uses which science has for members of the adult public who are not themselves professional scientists. At a younger age, it is, of course, these adults who form the bulk of the school population and what is at issue here is the potential of science to engage in meaningful ways with the daily lives of ordinary people in a variety of contexts, including their homes, environment and places of work or recreation.

Typically, therefore, this literature explores such issues as those associated with parents bringing up children born with Down's syndrome, local councillors considering how best to deal with waste disposal or other environmental problems (D. Layton *et al.* 1993), workers and their families living near to a nuclear facility (Macgill and Funtowicz 1988), farmers in Britain responding to the local consequences of the Chernobyl explosion (Wynne 1991) and scientific expertise in the context of litigation, complaint or protest (Yearley 1989). Unlike questionnaire-based approaches to the measurement of scientific literacy, the research commonly relies on interview and other in-depth techniques for data collection. The work that has been done, in a variety of contexts, sustains a number of conclusions about the ways in which science is represented, understood and used by lay adults, and about the articulation of science with practical action. Some of these conclusions are not readily reconcilable with the image of science presented by formal schooling.

Formal science education commonly portrays science as coherent, objective, unproblematic, and clearly distinguishable from non-scientific activities. However, beyond the controlled world of laboratory science, the perception and the reality are very different. Expert judgements are often in conflict, as in forensic, disaster diagnosis and risk analysis contexts, so that the ability to judge the quality of the evidence offered by conflicting parties becomes important, sometimes critically so. In addition, expert advice comes to be challenged on a number of different grounds, as, for example, in the controversy about the use of lead in petrol. In this controversy, technical questions could not be answered despite the vast quantities of technical data available and each party to the dispute accused the other of bias in the selection of data to support the case it wished to make. Ultimately, policy issues of this kind cannot be resolved simply on technical grounds (Collingridge and Reeve 1986). Similar problems arise when lay adults engage with questions that have, or seem to have, a scientific dimension, questions such as what constitutes a safe level of noise in the workplace or in a domestic dwelling close to a proposed extension to an airport runway, how soon sheep or cattle can be allowed to return safely to graze on land contaminated by radioactive fall-out, whether living under high-voltage power lines is hazardous to health, or whether there is a link between the incidence of leukaemia and proximity to a nuclear facility. The last of these examples may be used to further illustrate the uncertainties and value-laden qualities of the data available for the public to evaluate in circumstances such as these. A radiobiological estimate of the number of cases of leukaemia which it was calculated could have been caused by accidental and planned discharges from the Sellafield nuclear reprocessing plant in the north-west of England over a period of almost twenty years depended on a series of assumptions all of which were open to challenge. Likewise, an epidemiological estimate of the number of cases of leukaemia among the local child population, over the same period, was both time-sensitive and afflicted by arbitrary decisions about, for example, whether death or diagnosis constituted a case (Macgill 1987). The general position has been described by Ziman (1991). Reviewing a programme of ten research projects concerned with the public understanding of science, he commented:

> the most important finding of the research programme is that 'science' is not a well-bounded, coherent thing, capable of being more or less 'understood' . . . [It] is not a sharply-defined and special type of knowledge, which only starts to be misrepresented and misunderstood outside well-defined boundaries by people who simply do not know any better. . . . In this programme of research, we have seen many everyday questions that cannot be addressed properly, let alone answered, simply in terms of a shortfall in potential understanding.
>
> (Ziman 1991: 100–1)

Adult members of the public do not encounter basic scientific knowledge as free floating and unencumbered by its institutional connections. Questions such as 'From whom?', 'From where?' and 'From what institutional sources?' are integral to judgements about the confidence to be placed in this scientific knowledge, that is the 'public uptake (or not) of science is not based upon *intellectual capability* as much as socio-institutional factors having to do with social access, trust, and negotiation as opposed to imposed authority' (Wynne 1991: 116). In making these judgements, other, often more local and personal, knowledge is likely to be taken into account. Wynne gives the example of sheep farmers who, after the Chernobyl disaster, were advised by agricultural scientists that radiocaesium in their stocks would be flushed out more quickly if sheep were grazed on the lusher pastures of the valley rather than on the grasses of the high fells. Both the practicality and credibility of this advice were questioned because the farmers' local knowledge had shown that intensive grazing on valley grass could damage a fragile resource of critical importance for the future breeding cycles of their sheep (Wynne 1991). Likewise, Layton and his colleagues have shown how the domestic energy practices of elderly people are guided not only by the physics of heat conservation but also by aesthetic, personal convenience, financial and other considerations (D. Layton *et al.* 1993).

The 'public understanding of science', therefore, cannot be equated with understanding science on the scientists' own terms, not least because

processes of negotiation and evaluation are involved, although not necessarily explicitly. The consequence is that, far from scientific knowledge
occupying a central position in relation to everyday life practices, the
processes of integrating it with personal judgements and values and with
situation-specific knowledge frequently relocates science as a peripheral
player (as in the domestic energy practices of elderly people). Such
knowledge may even be removed from the scene altogether (as when the
relevant fundamental science is built into the routine practices which
others, such as car mechanics or television repair personnel, are required
to follow). This is not necessarily an indication of the relative un-
importance of scientific knowledge in the realm of practical action, but it
underlines the necessity of reworking or translating it, if it is to become
instrumental. This reworking or translation is no more a straightforward
application of the scientific knowledge acquired at school or in other
formal contexts than technology is merely applied science. Rather it is
about creating new knowledge or, where possible, restructuring, reworking and transforming existing scientific knowledge into forms which serve
the purpose in hand. Whatever that purpose (political, social, personal,
etc.), it is essentially concerned with action or capability, rather than with
the acquisition of knowledge for its own sake. It seems likely that this
'everyday thinking' and 'knowledge in action' are more complex activities
than scientific thinking and much less well understood.

SOME IMPLICATIONS FOR SCIENCE EDUCATION

The various studies of the ways in which adult members of the lay public
engage with science suggest strongly that their interaction with science is
rarely, if ever, narrowly cognitive. Importance is commonly given to the
source of the scientific knowledge, and particularly to the extent to which
it could be judged trustworthy and reflective of understanding of their
situation. Emotion, other knowledge, social relationships and social structures all play a significant part in determining the course of practical
action, if any, which adults deem most appropriate in their particular
circumstances. Expressed differently, their thinking is inextricably woven
into the context of their perceived problem so that the process of 'coming
to know' science is, inescapably, a social one. As for the adults, so for all
young people in schools up to at least the statutory school-leaving age,
that is those for whom a general, rather than a pre-professional, education
in science and mathematics is appropriate. For these young people, it is
suggested, scientific knowledge should be as much a resource for the
construction and maintenance of personal identity, a sense of 'who they
are and what they wish to achieve', as an external instrumentality for
understanding and manipulating the natural world.

This, of course, is not to deny science its place as one of the supremely

147

imaginative, creative and intellectual achievements, worthy of study in its own right. While, to borrow Redner's phrase, this may be seen as promoting the 'high church' position of classical science (Redner 1987), it is surely beyond contention that students should leave school knowing something of what science has to say about a number of matters of widespread interest and great importance, for example the nature and origin of life or the cosmos. It seems equally important that attention be given to the scientific dimensions of the modern world, such as the manufacture of chemicals or the distribution of electricity, with proper consideration of who gains and who loses in each instance. Ogborn (n.d.) has described this as vulgarizing science and has drawn attention to the importance of adopting effective and attractive teaching strategies. Those strategies, which will require the rearticulation of science education with values, are likely to be much more diverse and less anchored in laboratory work than is presently the case in science teaching.

Arguably, those studying science should also have some insight into the difficulty of generating reliable and consensible understanding about the natural world. Addressing this issue will call for more than a redirection of practical teaching in the school laboratory. A genuine evaluation of evidence, vicarious and/or first-hand as appropriate, and the deployment of pedagogies and new teaching technologies more familiar to many teachers of the humanities, would seem to be essential if students are to be helped to understand that there is nothing inevitable about a now standard scientific explanation and that such explanation requires agreement about what constitutes reliable knowledge. The nature of this agreement needs to be illustrated using a variety of examples drawn from different contexts, from phlogiston and the nature of light to cold nuclear fusion and polywater. Inevitably, this latter consideration raises the important issue of how science is to be distinguished from non-science and offers an opportunity for discussion of the organizational forms of ownership and control of scientific knowledge, identified by Wynne (1991) as the third of three elements which, along with content and research methodology, constitutes the public understanding of science. While all three elements are necessary if adults are to use and act maturely in relation to science, it is this third element which, in Wynne's judgement, has been largely ignored, despite the fact that its neglect undermines any attempt to improve the other two (Wynne 1991: 120).

Crucially, however, school science education needs to be restructured to provide opportunities for young people to understand what science can do to ameliorate and improve the quality of life for all those on the planet. Baez has elaborated this theme, referring to the 'quality of life in terms of environment, health, nourishment, shelter, resources, meaningful employment, rest and recreation, educational opportunities and cultural achievements ... the reduction of fear and anxiety, and learning to cope with risk and decision-making' (Baez 1980: 282).

A number of objections can, of course, be levelled at a restructuring of this kind. Some will object that it confuses science with technology or with environmental, social and political concerns that are necessarily contentious. Others may comment that it is not the responsibility of science educators to offer visions of the future or add that science teachers are ill-prepared to teach a curriculum of this kind. However (as noted above), science in the late twentieth century is not the heroic science of the school textbook but part of a new dynamic between research and society which amounts to a new system of knowledge production.

> science has changed its ends. It is no longer the old science of the last few centuries. That old science is coming to an end in the sense of approaching the limit of its potential scope. ... Contemporary science is worldly in every sense of the word and quite different in its essential character from the European science of the recent past. ... these differences are apparent in all dimensions of scientific research, intellectual, instrumental and organisational. They are also revealed in the changed relations of science, technology and production.
>
> (Redner 1987: 15)

It is significant, therefore, that Shamos (1995), having dismissed scientific literacy as a futile goal for science education, should offer as one of his 'three guiding principles for presenting science to the general (nonscience) student', the central theme of 'technology as a *practical* imperative for the individual's personal health and safety', coupled with an awareness of both the natural and the man-made environments (Shamos 1995: 217). Writing principally for a readership in the USA, Shamos's comment is indicative of a somewhat narrower perspective than that of Baez (1980), who rightly draws particular attention to the contribution that science in the context of action can make to raising the quality of life in the developing world. None the less, each has reached essentially the same conclusion, namely that if science education is to capture the interest of the majority of young people, it must engage with their aspirations, motives and concerns. For Baez, such a science education offers the possibility of encouraging the important attributes of curiosity, creativity, competence and compassion.

A more substantial objection to 'science education for action' is that such an education confronts many of the assumptions upon which schooling traditionally rests. In promising to weaken the traditional insulation of the school from the 'real' world beyond, it helps to fuel the broader debate about the nature and purpose of schooling at the end of the twentieth century in a world increasingly shaped by information technology and confronted by environmental and other problems of global significance. However, the severity of this challenge to the long-established tradition of schooling should not be underestimated. Science teachers, in particular, are unlikely to take readily to new strategies which involve addressing issues which, like most real issues, are controversial, messy and have to be brought into focus only to lack a unique or even (initially or eventually) an agreed solution. Issues of this kind, of course, characterize all reasoned practical activity, including the doing of scientific research, a fact that has led Brickhouse and her colleagues (1993: 373) to argue for practical reasoning, 'similar to everyday thinking, and required for the realisation of human interest', as a fundamental, if neglected component of school science education. There are, too, deep-seated problems of assessment, Posch (1993) quoting Austrian students who regarded the grading by their school of their science-based work in the local environment as a 'devaluation' of what they had done. Their own assessment criterion was the 'real life' evaluation they had encountered in dealing with people with whom they had come into contact during their project work within the community (Posch 1993). The response of these students has an important message for those who seek to assess knowledge in action by reference to an abstracted, even reified, procedural account of what is supposed to be involved in acting wisely in the realm of the practical. It also serves as a reminder of the more general importance of not underestimating student reaction to science curriculum change (Delamont 1990).

It is evident that schools or other formal educational agencies cannot bear the sole, perhaps not even the main, responsibility for promoting a functional public understanding of science. For many adults, science is but one resource, among others, to be drawn upon in pragmatic ways to serve the purpose in hand. In these circumstances, the coherence and progression of traditional science courses are neither appropriate nor welcomed. When adults need scientific expertise to help them address a problem, the evidence suggests that they are often remarkably successful in securing access to it. Such success seems to owe less to a basic understanding of science than to curiosity allied to purpose, to persistence and creativity in seeking access to data, and to a willingness and confidence to engage with scientific matters of interest to them. It is these qualities, coupled with a more generous perception of what is meant by the public understanding of science, that a general education in science should perhaps seek to foster.

11

SCHOOL SCIENCE AND THE FUTURE OF SCIENTIFIC CULTURE

Joan Solomon

WHAT SHALL WE CALL IT?

In Britain people are more accustomed to speaking about the 'Public Understanding of Science' than about 'Scientific Culture'. In the USA the term 'Scientific Literacy' is used. It is not hard to show that these three expressions describe the same general field, but they are subtly different in their attitude towards its nature and purpose. In this chapter I shall be suggesting that using the word 'culture', in many ways a term so all-embracing as to seem vague and almost useless is, on the contrary, the most helpful and illuminating of the three. In particular it can even be used to help guide the organization and delivery of school science so that it can spread to the population as a whole.

La culture scientifique is the term in use among the European nations which pride themselves on their long history of culture, such as that of the arts and humanities, without a knowledge of which a person might be considered unable to take an honourable place in educated converse. 'Culture' in this sense holds a far higher place, even an elitist one, in general estimation than does the more plebeian term 'literacy'. Scientific literacy is the name most commonly used in the USA. When the American Association for the Advancement of Science launched Project 2061 for the guidance of school science, they decided to work out 'benchmarks for scientific literacy'. This usage is beginning to penetrate Britain too. It is now commonplace to find it redescribed as 'scientific and technological literacy'. Jon Miller (1983), who has written extensively about scientific literacy and set up indicators to measure it in different fields of science, has defined the term in two ways:

• being knowledgeable about science
• being able to respond to messages about science.

The first of these meanings corresponds very closely to the British plain, no-nonsense, term 'public understanding'. It asks questions about the movements of the sun and the earth, or whether antibiotics act against viruses, and has the advantage that it is very easy to measure by means of questionnaires.

From the point of view of schools and science education, the idea of public knowledge and understanding is strangely unhelpful. Providing these commodities is clearly the business of school: it always has been, and it is not hard to show that more of it is being generated in the modern schools of Europe and the USA than was the case in the past. The statistics do not disagree about this (Durant *et al.* 1989). In both the UK and the USA questionnaires testing what knowledge 'lay' people have about science show that there is more of it among the young who have had modern schooling than among older people. It is also greater for those who continued their education in science to a higher level than for others who stopped learning it earlier. These are simple answers to a question about how much school knowledge persists into adulthood. It is, however, a question which is rather too simple to hit the mark. Having correct bits of knowledge about science, although useful enough in quiz games like 'Trivial Pursuit', seems a very long way away from what we could possibly call a 'scientific culture'.

Responding to messages about science is a much more difficult capability to measure. It requires interest enough to listen to the message, on the television, in books, or in newspapers. Data from the USA number the 'attentive minority', which follows science in this way, as little more than 18 per cent of the whole population. The attentive receiver needs to feel the wish to respond. Those not interested in science may neither hear its messages nor reflect upon them. Even if a spark of curiosity is awakened it may be that individuals will have difficulty in knowing how to formulate their own reactions so as to ask further questions in order to obtain the kind of answers which could be useful to them. This, I take it, is the second sense in which Miller uses the phrase 'being literate in science', which includes both attitudes to science and also an interest in it.

However, the phrase 'scientific literacy' also brings with it a lot of unfortunate baggage. It was only when I came across its translation into a newly devised word to be used in an education conference in Brazil that I realized one other dimension of its meaning which distinguishes it quite sharply from our 'Public Understanding of Science'. That word was 'Alfabetizaceao'. It has the same basic sense as in an adult reading campaign for those who do not even know their alphabet. The use of this term seems to be claiming that there are people who are literate and can 'read' messages in science, and other people who cannot. To be illiterate is to have missed out on very basic education, and may well be a matter of both national and private shame. In that sense it cannot be a helpful term.

Culture, even 'scientific culture', can suffer the same fate and get lost in elitism. There is little doubt that it did so in the hands of C. P. Snow (1965) who inaugurated the curious flare-up of interest in this subject in the mid-1960s with his book about *The Two Cultures*. To know about the Second Law of Thermodynamics, it was suggested, was like knowing about Shakespeare and Beethoven. It was an indicator of top people's culture. The singers and librettists Flanders and Swann responded with a splendid send-up with, as I remember, a strong chorus line of 'Work is heat, and Heat is work'. Having a somewhat broader view, in the 1990s, of what might constitute public culture, we can probably afford to ignore that unfortunate aspect of the word 'culture' and look at the subject in much broader terms.

SCIENTIFIC CULTURE

As an import from the study of anthropology 'culture' is used to describe inarticulate popular knowing, beliefs, proverbs, and ingrained habits of mind. In Bourdieu's words it is the 'habitus' is which we live. But we must remember that anthropology is no longer a study of the primitive society's belief in witchcraft and totem rites which assumes that these derive from some pre-logical stage of the people involved. That would be equivalent to the unfortunate overtones of Snow's version of scientific culture. Contemporary anthropology now rests on a much more empathic and respectful exploration of everyday beliefs and attitudes. The pioneer of this kind of anthropology, Sir Edward Evans-Pritchard (1902–73), insisted that it was possible to understand other belief systems only by becoming personally immersed in their way of living and absorbing their meanings. In our pursuit of scientific culture we shall need to see western science as our way of explaining happenings, and our way of finding answers. Witchcraft is the way in which, for example, the Azande of the Sudan, who were so extensively studied by Evans-Pritchard, did the same. All human beings need to explain and give meaning to the phenomena around them but the exact questions asked depend on the particular culture. People may ask 'Why are things going so badly for us?' rather than 'What atmospheric conditions cause rainfall, and by what mechanisms?' Nevertheless the questions that anthropologists hear are inquiries about phenomena; indeed they may not be very dissimilar to many that we ask ourselves, from the basis of our own non-scientific ways of thinking.

Since that time there have been rather similar ethnographic studies in both the science classroom and the science laboratory. These peer closely at how people behave and how they construct their understanding. The terse words of the American anthropologist Clifford Geertz (1993), in his study of *Local Knowledge*, nicely turn the tables on the earlier deprecating view of anthropology, 'We are all natives now.'

One thread in this exploration of scientific culture would be a description of the specific knowledge-related behaviour of professional scientists, who have become a group so tightly socialized as to have acquired their own meanings for words and practices. This exploration has been carried out (Latour and Woolgar 1979), but has little direct bearing on school science. For our discussion, teaching is the process of socialization by which pupils, like anthropologists watching alien people, or primatologists studying apes, are helped to see the world in some completely different way. Teachers are 'the natives' observed by their pupils and their types of explanations taken note of. Pupils try to understand why and what their science teachers consider sound evidence, and they generally find that good imitations of the teachers' culture are generously rewarded with praise and high marks. Science lessons show children a need for explanation where one did not exist before, and explanations of a type which can sometimes seem alien almost to the point of incomprehension. My feeling is that Evans-Pritchard, if asked whether children could be introduced to such a different culture by means of the twice-weekly science lesson, would have pronounced the whole notion quite hopeless. Two or three hours a week are very little from which to start understanding new habits of thought from scratch. No wonder then that school teaching has met with only moderate success in demonstrating and passing on the complete high culture of science.

Explaining failure is always much easier than trying to suggest methods which could lead to success. To do that we need a rather more precise definition of the word 'culture' which could be used to understand its functions. We know that it varies from one locality to another. We may also suspect that it is implanted in us through the complete range of mechanisms of growing up rather than through cognitive development or from the totality of school education. In *The Interpretation of Cultures*, an earlier seminal book by Clifford Geertz (1977), a description is given of the essence of 'culture' which is broad enough to encompass popular, national and scientific culture.

> Believing with Max Weber, that man is an animal suspended in webs of significance he himself has spun, I take culture to be those webs and the analysis of it, therefore, to be not an experimental science but an interpretative one – in search of meaning.
>
> (Geertz 1977: 5)

In the rest of this chapter we shall be able to use the two aspects of this wonderfully visual definition of culture to help us think about teaching science in school. One notion is 'significance' which must always refer to the subject and not necessarily to the reader or some authoritative figure. The other is the 'webbishness', or the interconnectedness of things. By 'things', that word we were always discouraged so strongly from using in school, is meant phenomena, activities, thinking, explaining and doing, but above all our own perceptions of these.

154

SCIENCE EDUCATION IN THE SCHOOLS OF THE EUROPEAN UNION

We are rapidly approaching the position in Europe and North America where all children from the age of 5 or 6 until 16 will be learning science. Will that change the nature and extent of popular scientific culture? The problems that face those of us who design syllabuses and curricula are first, what science should be taught, or could be taught, and second, in what ways. Our aim is that the science so taught may serve our children for a lifetime. In the newly emerging European Union there is also an operational aim: to encourage the growth of a scientific culture uniform enough for ideas to travel from country to country as freely as they did, by all accounts, in the days of the great Dutch travelling scholar Erasmus (after whom the EC project to encourage travel among contemporary European students is named).

The incentive for thinking again about scientific culture was taking part in a large collaborative project, set in motion by the European Commission, to examine 'School science and the future of scientific culture in Europe'. While the EC is interested in the scientific culture of the future citizens of Europe for both political and economic reasons, the Treaty of Rome, which began the slow process of building the new Europe, contains a strong recommendation to respect the 'linguistic and cultural diversity' of European countries. This produces a substantial dilemma for those who might like to see scientific culture as an unfractured whole across the continent. From the start of this project cultural diversity in the different member states was to be expected, but what kind of diversity and how important it might be, was part of the brief to be explored. The research programme, set up in 1993, commissioned national reports from a wide range of European countries, not all of whom were already in the EU, and then it used the data about science education being carried out in these different countries to argue about those aspects of practice which might be most powerful in their contribution to the future of scientific culture for the citizens of the new Europe.

If the foundations for scientific culture do stem from school science, and it was clear enough that other influences like the media, home attitudes and science museums must contribute too, then they must derive from a mixture of the intentions of governments, programmes within schools, how the teachers of different countries perceive science and science education, and how much of this they manage to convey to school students.

The intentions behind science education in each member state should have set the scene for the whole project. However, it seems to be almost impossible for any country to define its ideology so clearly and uniquely that all the processes of education follow from it. This is because science education serves several quite different purposes for each society. The project was to look at just one of these purposes, that of forming the popular scientific culture. Science education also has to train young people for work in which there is a scientific component, and to pass on to a gifted few the capability, as Isaac Newton is supposed to have said, to 'stand on the shoulders of giants'. In other words we need a continuing small group of innovative research scientists armed with as complete a knowledge of science and its theories as we can manage. As well as all that we want a trained workforce and a public steeped in scientific culture. If that programme is at all possible then it is certainly composed of three different tasks. It is the last of these that we shall concentrate upon in this chapter.

The contents of a National Curriculum might be expected to conform to both what national economic and technological purposes science education is thought to serve, as well as leading to some measure of understanding of the nature of scientific thought itself. However, national curricula rarely stipulate how science lessons are to be conducted in the schools, and it is this process of teaching and learning which colours young people's perceptions so vividly. It is crucial to the formation of their attitudes towards the nature of science. It is no good teachers telling their classes that science is an empirical activity (and even explaining the meaning of that word) if their pupils' experience of learning science is confined to dictation and rote learning. The conduct of lessons is affected by the teachers' perceptions of the nature of science as a system of thought – abstract and mathematical, or empirical and technical – and research shows that this is conveyed to children even when not explicitly taught (e.g. Brickhouse 1989). The students' perceptions of science will also depend on educational traditions, such as whether children should be positively encouraged to co-operate in their study (very strong in the Scandinavian countries but weak in eastern Europe), and what is a suitable activity for a teacher to perform within the school. In Switzerland, for example, teachers are simply lecturers who have no pastoral commitments at all; in the UK teachers are expected to exert discipline and serve as a moral example as well as teaching the contents of science; in Sweden moral purposes head the list of expected priorities.

The discipline of science itself might have been expected to possess far more commonality across the different member states, in terms of both content and philosophy than does, for example, literature and history, both of which are much more in the gift of a country's language and tradition. Curiously, this is not quite so at school level. Since the Scientific Renaissance of the sixteenth and seventeenth centuries it has been common to speak about the universal Invisible College to which all scientists belong by virtue of their common study. This is the aspect of science referred to by Robert Merton (1943), as the scientific norm of 'universality'. However, there have been notable and even scandalously chauvinistic controversies within Europe about scientific matters (e.g. the nature of light, or the invention of the calculus). At school, however, there are other deeper differences. Some of these are general factors which affect personal and institutional practices across all education. These include national and political attitudes towards

- personal autonomy and moral education (e.g. Scandinavia)
- standardization and uniformity (e.g. France)
- efficiency and market forces (e.g. UK).

There are also more subtle differences between the European countries, or groups of them, in the most admired ways of thought. This cannot but affect all education, and science in particular. These systems of philosophical arguments include humanism and rationalism (especially in the Netherlands and Germany), the inductive/heuristic/empirical approach (found only in Britain) and the deductive/abstract/mathematical approach (which is so highly prized in Cartesian France).

The study of these different preferences is far too vast a subject to be treated here (see Durkheim 1977; McClean 1995). Nevertheless a reading of the national reports for the European project showed the effect of these different modes of thought in ways which range from the definition of the boundaries of school 'science' to the possibility of local communities influencing the contents of the curriculum. There can be no doubt that there are basic regulative principles of thought which are integral and valued in each national culture and which colour their methods of education and the resulting scientific culture.

NEW TRENDS IN THE SCIENCE CURRICULUM

Science has become a compulsory subject in primary schools in most member states of the EU, or else is just about to be so. In most European countries (e.g. Sweden, Spain, Denmark, Portugal, Germany, Greece and Poland) an integrated or 'topic' approach is recommended for the teaching of science at primary level. Often the emphasis is now on 'the environment' (Scandinavia) or on 'nature study' (France). A range of arguments and concerns surround this integrated delivery of primary science. This whole movement began long ago with the regime of 'object-centred' lessons before the First World War. Its influence may now be seen in the interest shown in 'natural finds' and local environmental concerns. It is often argued that the integrated environmental approach is more appropriate for young children who learn holistically, and gain a better understanding of what they are being taught when the knowledge is embedded in everyday contexts (Donaldson 1978). It is also thought to be more appealing to the sensitivities of young children and to their concerns with animals and plants. As we shall see, however, it is not without its critics.

There is enormous diversity in the teaching of Technology – or Design and Technology – and indeed in its very meaning. Nevertheless it is at the centre of educational innovation in many countries. Sometimes it is based within the science curriculum (e.g. Sweden, Greece, France, Denmark and the Netherlands). In other countries (such as Poland, Spain, Portugal and the UK) it is a separate subject in the National Curriculum. In Sweden there has been a recent move away from technology as applied science so that it now has all three of the meanings below, as a separate curriculum subject. The three different educational approaches are:

1 A study of the main industrial means of production (e.g. Italy) with or without a discussion of social effects and civic implications.
2 Information Technology and the use of computers.
3 The acquisition of workshop skills for the designing and making of technological artefacts (e.g. the Netherlands, Denmark and the UK at junior secondary level).

The history of science is not very widely taught in the schools of Europe. The use of stories of discovery and controversies about explanations may be mentioned during teaching, and is occasionally recommended in some advisory documents, but not usually at the mandatory level. The main exceptions to this are Denmark (in physics at higher levels) and the UK at junior secondary level (although this is rarely observed in practice).

These three aspects of the science curriculum – primary science, technology, and historical references – have been singled out because they may each contribute in a special way to future scientific culture. To support this claim we need to use Geertz's picture of culture and show that each one is either connected to the common 'significances' of school pupils (environment, computers, or making artefacts), or that it interconnects different areas of learning or being (history, home activities, or technology). Technology, history and everyday primary science experiences all relate to people; this is where most children find learning and understanding at its easiest. Primary science connects to everyday life and people in another way. It is taught to children while they are still at an age when they discuss at home with their parents what they have learnt during the day at school, and can so produce a strong element of 'webbishness' in their knowledge. The features all help to embed science in the wider and more general culture of the population (Solomon 1994).

NEW TRENDS IN THE ORGANIZATION OF SCHOOL SCIENCE

From the time of Plato or before, education has been a well-recognized way of controlling the affiliations and national consciousness of the next generation. Minority groups within European nations often press hard for some measure of educational control. Countries such as Belgium, Germany and the UK contain stable and distinct communities, sometimes with national identity closely tied to their language, who have claimed the right to design their own syllabuses. In Spain and parts of the UK (e.g. Wales and Northern Ireland) the regions have only partial control over their own curricula. Indeed the whole subsidiarity (diversity) debate becomes especially heated when control of education seems to be passing out of the hands of any cultural community, large or small.

The location of power in education is never easy to pinpoint. Central government will generally pay teachers' salaries but the number of lessons in each subject may vary from region to region, from town to town and even from school to school. In Italy, for example, the curriculum is centrally determined and yet there are very large differences in the educational provision in the rich northern regions and the poorer southern ones. The UK system prior to 1989 had been predominantly run by local authorities which often had very different educational policies but now, going against the EU trend, much of their power has been taken from them by central government, even though there is devolvement of budgets to the schools themselves.

In Norway, Italy and the Netherlands there are movements under way to decentralize power either to the schools themselves or to a local board. In Greece, Ireland, Spain and Portugal, where the school-leaving age has been raised – with all the problems that raises – control is still exercised centrally, but reform in this area is being discussed. Poland, like most eastern European countries, is just emerging from a centralized political system and trying to organize a more local structure of control, and Ireland is moving in the same direction. Even French education, once a model of central control, is now allowing schools a little more autonomy in the delivery of their curriculum and its timetable. Sweden and the Netherlands have removed some of the detailed state regulation. It is important to note that decentralization may result in local groups exerting just as much control over the management of schools as central government did before the change. The emphasis here is only on the locality of the control.

Schools have increased in size wherever the populations of towns have grown at the expense of the villages. Large schools inevitably become more powerful units of management. Sometimes they see themselves as representatives of their community, and may designate themselves as centres for community education (e.g. the UK and Sweden). In such cases school laboratories and other scientific resources can act as a vehicle for spreading scientific culture. This will depend not only on popular demand but also on whether they are controlled by the governors of the school, by local interests, or by the central government.

Using Geertz's criteria for culture, it is possible to see this whole process of the democratization of schools as another step towards involving science in what is significant to students. Local influence, whether or not it is altruistic, provides pupils with a science more relevant to local interests and local industry. From the opposite direction, local control might allow the community to express their evaluation of science education in the most tangible way – through increased resources, parental involvement, and local industrial influence. The interaction between school and society then becomes more powerful. Thus this whole trend could both express and formulate an increasingly public scientific culture.

PROBLEMS AND HOSTILITIES

All in the garden is not rosy. There are, inevitably, some aspects of science education which might have made a significant contribution to popular scientific culture in Europe but are not often fully implemented in science teaching. First, practical work carried out by the students themselves, in ways that would promote better understanding of the nature of scientific knowledge and scientific evidence, is too rarely practised. This is unfortunate from an epistemological point of view, but there is also another advantage to be accrued from practical work. Since practical hands-on experience is usually considered much less demanding than more theoretical work, this diminishes the perceived inaccessibility of science. The widely held perception that science, especially physics, is very difficult to understand, apparently linked with a similar or even greater perceived difficulty associated with mathematics, is discouraging to very many pupils and adults. Any image of science which portrays it as arcane and comprehensible only to the very few, effectively removes it from the domain of popular culture because it links with nothing already known and is not thought to have significance for lay members of the public.

Second, linked to that very worrying problem is one already mentioned in the context of primary science. The environmental topics usually taught in primary schools seldom include physics and chemistry. Since these are commonly considered difficult subjects in secondary school, this omission at the elementary level, where the content is more accessible, is unfortunate. It rejects a simple way of attacking the problem of perceived difficulty by making physics and chemistry part of what young children talk about in their homes – the places where lifelong significances are constructed.

There are other enemies of scientific culture. In particular I would like to mention two which hail from the opposite ends of the spectrum of interest in science. No one would be surprised at the first of these: it is the extremist end of the Green movement. While many of those in Friends of the Earth have told me that they no longer feel that science is responsible for the pollution of the globe, there are some who still do. To them ecology is not science; on the contrary it is anti-science, and thus good and green all the way through. About *Science and Culture in Germany* Renate Bader (1993) wrote 'While science is seen as intellectual and academic, a strong environmental movement has caught the public fancy. It is driven by political and moral concerns. . . . Science for them equals risk; ecology is the saviour' (Bader 1993: 49).

This is in the tradition of Theodore Roszak's theme which goes back to the flower-power days of the 1960s and 1970s. In *Where the Wasteland Ends*, Roszak (1972) wrote of 'the rape of nature' and accused the practices and applications of modern science of this despoliation. But I have the impression that these attitudes are now changing. Popular culture contains so many contradictions that it is always hard to identify any predominant aspect. Science itself may be intolerant of contradictions, but popular thinking is not. There are proverbs and maxims in everyday life which contradict each other, and no one worries about it (Solomon 1992). In the same way science may both be the ravisher of the environment and also a tool with which to heal its pollution. The main thrust of science teaching must be to make science link in a positive way with what students feel is important and significant. One way to do this is to note the phrase 'political and moral concerns' in the extract above from Bader, and to ensure that the anti-scientists do not have a monopoly of this. The Science, Technology and Society movement which began in the classrooms of the Netherlands and the UK, and is now infiltrating most of the other European countries, has been foremost in this attempt (see Solomon 1988). Moral and political connections are clearly another strand in the web which is popular culture.

Finally and briefly I want to mention those who have seen fit to write about science as a difficult and totally unnatural way of thinking. The heights of scholarship in history, literature, theology and art, to name but four, would all seem equally odd to the uninitiated. High science certainly asks questions in particular ways and sometimes provides answers which seem like something out of *Alice's Adventures in Wonderland*. But then that is itself a popular book. Mysteries, like black holes, can be intriguing to young students precisely because they are beyond everyday experience and they stimulate the imagination quite wonderfully. To designate them as dry, difficult and unnatural is to extinguish interest in the mysterious and decrease the joy of science.

Nevertheless, almost all of those who have spent their life in science education believe that children from the complete range of ability can enjoy aspects of learning science. A few European countries, including England, are finding ways to teach science to children with special educational needs. Here it becomes a natural extension of their perceptual experience, however limited. The aim is not so much to increase the numbers who study for a degree in science as to increase popular scientific culture. Hands-on science centres which encourage play and family

161

participation are also growing up in most countries. As in the nineteenth century, when the British Association for the Advancement of Science first began holding its yearly meetings in different cities, our science is spreading its culture both geographically and also democratically to all students of the new Europe.

Science teachers themselves mostly started their careers by learning the high cultural knowledge of science, and only then chose to work in the world of children's ways of thinking and learning. Thus their empathic understanding spans several cultures. When they buttonhole you with anecdotes about children's insights, play and happy discoveries in science lessons or expeditions, it must have some credibility. These, after all, are the adults who can best make a guess at how the future of scientific culture may unfold.

12

INFORMED AMBIVALENCE
Changing attitudes to the public understanding of science
Jeff Thomas

The Royal Society report on the *Public Understanding of Science* (Bodmer 1985) was influential and timely – as other contributors to this volume will testify. It identified numerous advantages to be gained from greater levels of public understanding of science – ranging from more informed personal decision-making to greater national prosperity – and concluded that 'everyone needed some understanding of science'. The scientific community was urged to learn how to instruct and inform the public and to regard such communication as an unavoidable duty.

Given its evangelical tone and purpose, the Bodmer report can be excused for sidestepping a number of issues linked with its recommendations. It defined only very loosely the type and volume of science that the public needed to know. But it recognized that public knowledge needed to include not only the 'facts of science' but also its accomplishments, limitations and its methods. Understanding also included a basic knowledge of statistics and an ability to assimilate numerical data. This represented an ambitious programme of public education – indeed some have argued that educational goals on this scale are neither feasible nor appropriate (e.g. Shamos 1995).

The philosophy that underpinned the Bodmer report was later termed the cognitive deficit model (see Wynne 1991), which characterized the public as lacking in the fundamental knowledge of science. This model assumes a public eager to absorb more science; the traditional unwillingness of scientists to engage with a wider audience was seen as a major reason for limited public understanding. The deficit model of public understanding of science (PUS) is commonly interpreted as a shortfall of knowledge of facts – what Gilbert Ryle (1949) termed 'knowledge that'. As Nott and Wellington (1996) also point out, PUS is sometimes extended to include 'knowledge how' and 'knowledge why' and much more rarely the domain of views, values and feelings about science. The Bodmer report has therefore become synonymous with the deficit model – perhaps unfairly, given its references to the 'social implications of science' and science's 'limitations and methods'.

Bodmer does, however, express the hope that higher levels of public understanding would lead to greater appreciation of science and identifies 'public ignorance' as the sole target of concern.

This chapter argues that the relationship between public knowledge and public attitude towards science is more complex and problematic than Bodmer implied. The early part of the chapter rejects the deficit model of PUS, first in the context of current controversies that are scientifically based and then looks at examples of public 'reconstruction' of science. The second part of the chapter looks critically at the view that understanding of science is positively correlated with attitude. While there are convincing arguments in support of greater PUS, a scientifically literate society is unlikely to be uncritically supportive of science. Indeed, if public views are built on the basis of greater scientific awareness, public attitudes are likely to be increasingly divided and ambivalent. What are the grounds for claiming this?

THE INFLUENCE OF CURRENT CONTROVERSIES

The public's view of science is shaped substantially by controversial current events. As Millar explains in Chapter 7 in this volume, 'socio-scientific' issues such as nuclear testing present particular challenges to teachers of school science because such issues are inherently uncertain and complex. Topics such as global warming and public health scares show science is often incapable of providing clear answers to the 'cut and dried' questions asked by public and politicians alike, for example, the magnitude of any risk to health. Statements about the likelihood of global warming are necessarily couched in terms of probabilities and projections. The science that underpins the construction of computer models of the climate system is as complex and fraught as the assessments of social scientists that form the basis of projections about future energy needs. A fully 'informed' assessment of the risks associated with nuclear power generation would require a grasp of the physical nature of different forms of radiation, their effects on different human tissues, the relationship between radiation dose and evoked response, the legitimacy of extrapolation from high dose to low dose effects. Whether an agreed level of risk is socially acceptable requires deep thinking in areas beyond the realm of science. When complex science of this type enters the public domain, uncertainty in the public's mind about the processes of science can compound the confusion (see Millar and Wynne 1988).

For each of these issues, and others like them, a range of defensible and informed 'expert' positions can be adopted. Urging the public to feel at ease with such a bewildering array of facts and opinions, to the point where enlightened understanding leads naturally to informed personal decision-making, smacks of naive optimism. An Open University student's comment comes to mind, leaving a successful seminar on the prospects of global warming – 'still confused after all that, but at a higher level'. Little wonder therefore that Shamos (1995) more cautiously restates the aims of science education for democratic involvement as the ability to make an informed choice about which expert to believe. The key point in the present context is that greater public knowledge of the science that underpins socio-scientific problems is unlikely to lead to more harmonized public debate – if ignorance among the public provides the basis for uncertainty, lack of trust and ambivalence, then such feelings can be evoked just as readily by knowledge.

The current controversy in the UK, where science is caught uncomfortably in cultural cross-fire, relates to the likely link between BSE and Creutzfeldt-Jakob Disease (CJD). It was ironic that the controversy arose in the midst of set96 – what was intended to be an unproblematic nation-wide celebration of science, engineering and technology (set). The set96 events aim to 'raise the profile' of science – the resurgence of the BSE saga did this more effectively, though not in ways that 'deficit-modellers' would approve of. As the debate developed over the early months of 1996, there was every indication that the controversy was shaping the public's and the media's opinion of the credibility of science (see e.g. Durant 1996). For at least three reasons, the status of science is unlikely to be improved by the saga. First, despite the fact that the intensification of agriculture is more a technological phenomenon than a scientific one, the two sides of the coin are not normally separated in the public's mind (see Casti 1992). Second, where political and public pressure demands of science a clear, unqualified answer – in this instance, whether beef is safe to eat – responses are necessarily cautious and qualified. Where reason and science cannot be enlisted in the support of policy, political imperatives suggest that ways must be found of regaining the public's confidence in steps that go 'beyond the science'. Thus the policy of a culling of a fraction of the UK dairy herd that began in April 1996 was based in the need to reassure the public, not on the scientific pronouncements of the public health specialists that comprise the Spongiform Encephalopathy Advisory Committee. Third, science understanding is revealed to be transitory and incomplete. Policy-makers adopted a 'safe until proved guilty' approach, pointing out that, until March 1996, there was no convincing scientific evidence of the transferability of the BSE infective agent to humans. When the scientific case switches overnight from 'no evidence of transfer to humans' to 'cause for concern', the reliability of science for policy-making and public guidance is inevitably questioned.

Public perception of science is subject to the well-recognized phenomenon of 'asymmetry of trust'; episodes which threaten trust in science are more significant (and memorable) than those that generate support. In the BSE saga, some scientists and many politicians may bemoan the public's ignorance of science, categorizing the public's views as largely emotive and irrational. Such deficit-thinking neatly places responsibility for confusion with the public, and implies that the science is unequivocal and compelling. More than likely future public choices and dilemmas that are rooted in science will be equally messy. Episodes such as BSE may inform the public about the limits and uncertainties of science, but it is questionable whether such shifts in public perception will result in a greater regard for science, of the type anticipated in the Bodmer report. Judging by the tone of editorial comment in the wake of the BSE crisis, there are more voices now improperly accusing science as 'failing society' (see *The Independent* 30 March 1996). At the very least, the public is reminded that science and politics are uncomfortable bedfellows.

IN WHAT WAYS DOES THE PUBLIC USE RECEIVED INFORMATION?

Inherent in the most extreme form of the deficit model of PUS is the belief that science is delivered to a receptive public in a detached and value-free form – arriving in Irwin and Wynne's (1996) memorable phrase 'as if by parachute', to be assimilated and faithfully reproduced, independent of context. The implication is that new science understanding retains a revered status, stops deficit-thinking and shifts attitudes – and enhances the public's appreciation of science in the process. For example, knowledge about the benefits of biotechnology and the techniques that underlie genetic manipulation is sometimes thought to defuse anxiety about potential misuse – a point that Levidow touches on in Chapter 8 in this volume.

In reality, a variety of local contexts and personal value systems unrelated to science influence how science is interpreted. Although the research findings are well established, they appear to have made little impression on the scientific community, partly because some of the language is sociological in style and the conclusions uncomfortable for those who subscribe to the 'deficit model'. The outstanding work of David Layton, Edgar Jenkins and their co-workers (Layton *et al*. 1993) has a substantial but largely unrecognized significance for the PUS movement. (Jenkins explores the broader significance of these findings in Chapter 10 in this volume.) Alan Irwin and Brian Wynne (1996) provide a further set of examples of 'science-in-action' that need to be taken to heart by science educators and PUS practitioners alike.

Case studies of this type investigate how science information is received, evaluated and reinterpreted by sectors of the population that share a common concern. A central issue is how specific science knowledge engages with routine concerns. Irwin, Dale and Smith (1996) for example used questionnaires to establish the kinds of technical information that would be sought by residents in two specific locations within Greater Manchester, where housing complexes are close to potentially hazardous chemical industry. Irwin and his co-workers were concerned with the interaction of technical expertise with other forms of local knowledge and with the motivations of residents for seeking out new information. Discussions within the community related to pollution made little use of the facts or language of science, nor did scientific experts feature prominently in discussion within the community. Science largely 'disappeared from view' when local discourses began. The conclusion was that formal science knowledge enjoyed no special authority. When expert knowledge was sought, the delivered science often had negative connotation for many citizens; it was unable to answer key questions and tended to promote dissatisfaction, enhancing the individual's feelings of powerlessness.

This view of 'science-in-action' is far removed from the deficit model reflected in Bodmer (1985). It also sits uncomfortably alongside the claims of scientism – that science is the best (if not the only) form of knowledge about the natural world. It may be so in the eye of the practitioner (see Wolpert, Chapter 1 in this volume) but the public sees it differently. Science put to use always has connections – alone it is of limited influence in shaping thinking. Examples of this type prompt David Layton *et al.* (1993) to reject the cognitive deficit model and replace it with an *interactive* model of the relationship between the science and the public. Rather than conveying science as unproblematic, objective and coherent, Layton seeks to emphasize science's problematic boundaries and its inability to answer key questions with certitude. An interactive model of PUS shifts the problems that science educators and PUS enthusiasts face on to a much broader footing; science and its understanding become the problem, rather than the public. The debate is moved into areas that most professional scientists regard with suspicion – what is science information for, who owns and controls the products of science and in what way is science socially constructed – questions that we return to at the end of this chapter.

THE RELATIONSHIP BETWEEN KNOWLEDGE AND ATTITUDE

There now exists a wealth of large-scale survey data that assess levels of science understanding in the public. Many are sufficiently similar in format and intent to allow country-by-country comparisons of science literacy (e.g. INRA (Europe) 1993). Most assess knowledge of fundamental science facts, while some have sought to assess public understanding of the scientific method (for a review and critique of such surveys, see Wynne 1994). An increasing number of comprehensive surveys are concerned with both knowledge of and attitude to science, and have therefore

JEFF THOMAS

provided information on the links between understanding of science and levels of support.

Miller's US data imply modest support for the notion that greater understanding prompts greater approval. He found that individuals with a greater understanding of science are more likely to approve of research involving animal experimentation, the genetic modification of organisms and to endorse government support for basic research (see e.g. J. Miller 1982; Turney 1996). But age, gender and the general level of education are also important determinants of attitude so the links between understanding and approval are not strong. The UK data of Evans and Durant (1995) also imply that the link is unconvincing. Their data relate both to the knowledge dimension – respondents were asked about the theoretical and factual aspects of science – and their understanding of science processes, in particular an awareness of the methods of science. Questions related to attitude revealed the degree of support that was evident for science, scientists and their associated activities. Their analysis of the data sought to distinguish between attitudes to science in general and attitudes to specific areas of scientific research, such as cancer research, genetic engineering and space exploration.

Evans and Durant (1995) report that understanding of science is only weakly related to positive attitudes in general and to areas of research classified as basic and useful, such as searching for a cure for cancer or doing basic research in physics. However, a different pattern emerged with research that was morally contentious, such as creating new forms of life or producing human embryos for medical purposes, or non-useful, such as searching for new stars and galaxies. In these instances, the most knowledgeable members of the public were in general more strongly opposed to such research than were the less knowledgeable. In general, the more knowledgeable members of the public are likely to be the most discriminating in their support. This implies that attitudes to controversial issues involve value-judgements far removed from science understanding alone and that the acceptance of controversial lines of research will not naturally spring from scientific understanding. Evans and Durant recognize the dangers of inferring too much from attitude tests of this type, but they speculate that a better informed society is likely to be distinguished by increased resistance to certain forms of research. They conclude that 'in so far as scientists and educationalists are motivated by the desire to mobilise public support for science, the results presented in this paper suggest that such attempts cannot always be relied upon to be straight-forwardly beneficial' (Evans and Durant 1995).

This interpretation is supported by Martin Bauer (1995) in his preliminary analysis of the European Union-wide Eurobarometer data of 1989 and 1992. This data-set records the response of about 1,000 respondents in each EU country, assessed on attitudes, interest and knowledge of science. His analysis of the data differentiated countries in terms of their level of industrialization – those with the highest levels of industrial output are post-industrialized. When the national average levels of science know-ledge and the degrees of industrialization of different countries are compared, post-industrialized countries are characterized by an increased level of science knowledge. But when average interest in science and technology is measured against degree of progress towards the post-industrial society, the populations of the most industrialized societies record *less* interest in science than do those of countries that have lower levels of industrialization. A likely implication is that in these highly industrialised societies, lack of interest in science is more apparent, together with more active hostility to science, that is anti-science sentiment.

The suggestion that knowledge and approval of science are not simplistically linked is supported by a range of findings. The work of Hans Peters relates to technological developments in Germany in the late 1980s (personal communication, 1995). His work suggests that there is no significant correlation between knowledge level and support for nuclear power. He tested by questionnaire the knowledge level of those opposed to and those who supported nuclear development and those in favour of or opposing the construction of a local waste incinerator in 1989 and 1990. In general, those with very firm views about the desirability or otherwise of the technology had the greatest knowledge; those who were very opposed often made a deliberate effort to seek out more information and therefore had levels of knowledge that approached, or exceeded, that of the proponents. This suggests that opposition to technology is not based on ignorance. Peters concluded that the operation of wisdom and common sense played a far greater role in determining attitude than scientific reason. In particular, individuals use experiences from everyday life in making scientific judgements. A similar conclusion is evident from data on attitudes to biotechnology in the UK: levels of knowledge were roughly equivalent in those two groups of strongly contrasted attitude – those strongly in favour of the new technologies and those against. Martin and Tait (1992) found complex relationships between attitude and under-standing. Attitudes did not reflect a simplistic view of biotechnology as a whole – respondents differentiated between distinct aspects of bio-technology, treating the different risks, benefits and implications separ-ately. They remark on the relative stability of views on biotechnology once they were formed by members of groups with an integrated and coherent set of attitudes. In their view, such groups place new informa-tion within ready-made conceptual frameworks, where compatible atti-tudes are neatly housed, and once formed such attitudes become hard to shift.

HOW MIGHT INTERVENTION SHIFT ATTITUDES TO SCIENCE?

Intervention in this sense implies informal or formal instruction in science, of varying intensity and duration. There is only a modest amount of published work on how such programmes influence attitude to science, though the data we do have range across a wide variety of contexts and educational levels.

Only limited data exist at school level, some relating to the socio-scientific examples touched on earlier. Even the limited findings on the pre-existing attitudes of school pupils reveal a complex interrelationship (see Dulskie *et al.* 1995). Lock (1996) found that teaching of genetic engineering reduced the proportion of school pupils who responded 'Don't know' when asked for examples of the technique. Pupils were also inclined to more definite opinions about the acceptability of certain genetic engineering procedures. The reduction in the number of uncertain responses suggests that teaching can help pupils clarify their position. In general, the shift was away from 'I'm not sure' towards support for genetic engineering. This work implies that the construction of attitudes towards science-based issues is an inevitable part of early science learning; it is all the more worrying, as Lock (1996) points out, that the UK National Curriculum currently excludes issues that have a social, moral or ethical basis. Such 'higher level' issues are likely to be the province of only a small fraction of the most able pupils. An added complication, derived from USA data, is that science learning at school level is seldom directly transferable to the adult context (Shamos 1995).

There is even less known about adult learning of science, for example how attitude and formal learning are related. The very limited data that are emerging suggest that the simple cognitive deficit model of learning – more information leading to a more enlightened view – is once again not supported. In the Open University, the course *Science Matters* covers a range of controversial issues that represent the banner headlines of the day – notably nuclear power, genetic engineering and climate change. Its audience consists of mature adults with a high motivation for learning and a particular interest in science; the great majority recall their experiences of science at school level to have been positive. Nearly all students will have some prior knowledge and experience of basic science, which provides the foundation upon which the course builds. The course uses television, texts and radio and represents about 200 hours' work through the Open University academic year. It aims to provide a balanced presentation of the key scientific facts behind these controversial areas; the overall aim (expressed in the optimistic words of our original formulation) is to provide 'a base of science understanding that allow students to construct coherent and defensible points of view about these contentious issues'.

Preliminary work involved thirty-item questionnaires sent to a representative sample of the students. Students were asked if their formal learning of the course material had no effect, confirmed their views, made them more ambivalent or changed their minds. The predominant response was that formal learning had confirmed their pre-existing opinions. For example, 43 per cent of those who responded said that their opinions about nuclear power had been confirmed (as opposed to 12 per cent who stated that their views had substantially changed), while 38 per cent reported that the course text had confirmed existing attitudes on the likelihood of global warming, as opposed to 22 per cent for whom the study had shifted their view. Attitude change was declared most frequently as a result of studying the text of genetic engineering. As with the data of Martin and Tait (1992), this preliminary survey suggests that, more often than not, new information is assimilated in ways that support pre-existing views. It also implies that the response to learning depends upon the particular case at issue. Further work is currently under way to establish with more certainty what factors within formal learning cause attitude shift. If the more substantial study supports this interpretation, it would be consistent with much of the published work on the effects of formal teaching of environmental issues. For example, Kinsey and Wheatley (1984) and Yount and Horton (1992) found that the most likely response to formal teaching was confirmation of pre-existing views. It is notable that Joss (1995) reports that although members of the lay panel within the Consensus Conference on Plant Biotechnology increased their *knowledge* of the subject, the preliminary analysis of patterns of agreement with assertions before and after the conference suggests that the panel did not undergo any significant change in their *perceptions* on plant biotechnology.

There is little other information on the effect of more modest learning programmes on attitude, other than the thorough work of John Doble and colleagues. They established a number of Citizen Review Panels which meet in a variety of locations in the USA for intensive three-hour sessions (Doble and Johnson 1990). Questionnaires are completed by panel members before and after their watching two fifteen-minute videos describing two contentious contemporary issues – the disposal of solid waste and the prospect of global warming. Doble compared the responses to these issues among the lay public with those of US scientists. He reports that 'the public's judgement about both issues ... is strikingly similar to the scientists" (Doble and Johnson 1990). The implication is that the lack of technical knowledge does not inhibit evaluation of complex issues. The manner in which these informed opinions were established was of interest. Areas of divergence between lay persons and scientists were more closely linked to differences in value systems than in expertise. Uncertainty was dealt with by relating circumstances to their own personal experience. It is striking that opposition to a particular option – notably nuclear power –

did not change no matter how much technical information was provided. Opposition to nuclear power plants rested not on technical information, but on a combination of intellectual and emotional assessments involving a complex variety of concerns. The conclusion was that opposition to particular policies rested on factors that were essentially non-scientific, for example, concern about taxes, or trust for organizations on the basis of past experience.

A PLEA FOR DISCOURSE

Jon Ogborn refers perceptively to what he sees as a 'loss of nerve in science education' (Ogborn 1995). This comment relates to what he sees as the impossible dream of uncritical acceptance of the rationality of scientific method and the certainty of scientific results. Ogborn urges a return to pragmatic realism – that the pretence of science 'knowing for certain and for ever' be rejected. But he also urges scientists to recognize that science is a human product, built up through social processes. Certainly some sociologists are guilty of a misreading of science. To classify all science knowledge as a social invention, just one more invented story, is deeply unpalatable and likely to inflame the average bench scientist – nuclear physicist and structural chemist alike, and for good reason. But it is also unhelpful when scientists use the term 'social science' as a form of abuse. An effective intellectual discourse between these two camps has to be created, for the good of each. As Ogborn and others (see Rose in Chapter 4 in this volume) have demonstrated, a meeting of minds is possible, assuming that both sides can abandon their most extreme entrenched positions.

The PUS programme has much to gain from a greater appreciation of the 'social' factors that influence learning and attitude formation. This would encourage enthusiasts to depart from the 'conventional wisdom' of PUS – that remedial instruction reverses the deficiency of knowledge and ensures greater commitment to science. What this chapter has shown is that individuals are not passive recipients of raw science – neither is science seen as a superior form of natural understanding. Knowledge of science becomes situated within a broad web of complex social and emotional factors. None of these concerns necessarily detracts from the case for greater PUS, but they suggest that in the post-Bodmer era, new aims and practices should be established that are more in keeping with social reality. A scientifically literate public is perhaps one where science attracts an emotional mix of dispute, ambivalence, anxiety and appreciation in ways no different from other human pursuits.

Part IV

SCIENTISTS AND THE PUBLIC

INTRODUCTION

Previous chapters have implied that critical assaults on the institution of science have left it a little bruised, with its traditional self-confidence dented. Concerns about the popularity of science abound – particularly in relation to the levels of uptake of science post-16. But exposure to science has probably never been greater – for children and adults, science is accessible via a number of informal channels. Graham Farmelo in Chapter 13 reflects on the effectiveness of science communication, which includes television, radio, publications and museums. He argues that in some respects, science is well served by 'the media', but that the situation would be even better if scientists took more advantage of the available opportunities. In this sense, the traditional skills of communication developed in conventional scientists – the etiquette of conferences, lecture techniques and peer review – seem at odds with the new demands of instant and global communication.

The title of Richard Gregory's Chapter 14 reflects his view of the importance of science learning being enjoyable. Play in science involves directed observation and the following through of intelligent hunches. A hands-on experience is an immediate common-sensical beginning point for more sophisticated learning. This highly creative philosophy has been the driving force behind the development of the Exploratory in Bristol – where future expansion is now set to build on great successes of this past.

Increasingly, scientists are being urged to communicate directly with the public, both adults and children – for example at exhibitions and festivals – and to take their expertise into the classroom. What type of communication works effectively and what does one communicate about? There is an increasing expectation that scientists will see interaction with the public as a duty – in which case, is there any evidence that scientists share this sense of urgency and commitment? The evidence that has come to light so far is discussed by Sue Pringle in Chapter 15. The picture is encouraging, but progress will not be maintained unless PUS activities

173

develop from their current uncoordinated and under-resourced state into something of widely recognized value. PUS activities become all the more worth while when empirical research of the type that Pringle reports shows that communicating science can bring measurable benefits to scientists and public alike.

13

FROM BIG BANG TO DAMP SQUIB?

Graham Farmelo

It's all very well giving us pictures from the beginning of time, but if science cannot help us to explain why and when a hamburger is unsafe, then we are bound to ask what use it is.

(Leader in *The Independent* 30 March 1996)

'The big bang happened in 1988,' the journalist Anthony Gottlieb has observed, 'as everyone in publishing knows.' He was referring to Stephen Hawking's *A Brief History of Time*, whose world-wide sales of more than 5 million have bemused most science popularizers. They generally hold the book in low regard and have probably spent more time trying to understand its success than the public have spent trying to read it.

One day, no doubt, a media studies student will rigorously study the Hawking Phenomenon (see e.g. Rodgers 1992) and explain it comprehensively in a widely unread PhD thesis. Until then, everyone involved in the public understanding of science will be free to press the phenomenon into support for their own pet theories about the public's perception of science. The book's success can be used to argue that the non-specialist public are happy to wrestle with abstract ideas that have little relevance to everyday life. It may also be demonstrating such a strong public belief in the worthiness of basic science that people will buy a token of their commitment for display on their bookshelf, in the same way as the possession of the complete works of Shakespeare can imply an endorsement of high British culture. Or, perhaps, the public do not give a damn about science but are fascinated by the power of the intellect to transcend physical infirmity.

Whatever the truth, there is no doubt that the singular success of *A Brief History of Time* made science a prospectively lucrative branch of publishing and also made it respectable for scientists to try their hands at reaching a non-specialist audience. (In 1989, you could almost hear Hawking's colleagues in the scientific community muttering *sotto voce*: 'If he can do it, why shouldn't I?') Before the big bang, talking to the masses was generally regarded as *infra dig*, something you normally did in your dotage

175

or when you had run out of ideas for your most important activity – research.

Also, the phenomenon made the very topic of science popularization popular with the chattering classes – how many of us have not been involved in at least one conversation about explaining the Hawking Phenomenon? Scientists had, however, been concerned for decades about the public's appreciation, understanding and support of science, engineering and technology (the disciplines are often collectively labelled 'science', a convenient if rather broad-brush shorthand that I shall normally use here). In the early 1980s, the Council of the Royal Society took the first step towards addressing what was perceived by some as a problem and by others as a crisis by appointing an *ad hoc* commission, chaired by the leading geneticist Sir Walter Bodmer. The aim of the commission was to review science's relations with the public and to make recommendations that would lead to improvements.

The report, published in 1985, was impressively thorough (Bodmer 1985). Amid its forty-one pages of dense reportese were dozens of suggestions for taking science and technology to the public, together with many an implicit rebuke for the majority of scientists who had not seen public communication as part of their job. The authors left to the very end of the report their 'most direct and urgent message' which was neither for the public, nor for the government, but for the scientists themselves: 'learn to communicate with the public, be willing to do so and consider it your duty to do so'.

This adjuration, supported by the numerous specific recommendations in the summary of the report, launched a host of initiatives under the banner of 'the public understanding of science' (PUS). This quickly became a new cottage industry, with its special events, its own professors and university courses, its own journal and conferences which almost always feature an unproductive discussion of what is meant by the terms 'public', 'understanding' and 'science'. Many of these activities were co-ordinated or sponsored by the publicly funded Committee on the Public Understanding of Science (COPUS), a tripartite committee of the Royal Society, the Royal Institution and the British Association for the Advancement of Science. It was set up in 1985, in the wake of the Bodmer report, to facilitate initiatives that promote the public understanding of science. In some ways, the setting up of COPUS was analogous to the founding of the Arts Council in 1948. For the architect-in-chief of the Council, John Maynard Keynes, its purpose was to nourish the artistic taste of the public and to make the arts more widely accessible – roughly the artistic counterpart of the cultural *raison d'être* for COPUS.

Only a churl would deny that since those post-Bodmer report days, communicating with the public has come to be seen as a worthwhile part of the scientist's duties and that there has been an extraordinary growth in the range and depth of activities that link the scientific community with the public. There are the television and radio programmes, well-informed science columns in the press, science festivals and a national science week, a prize for the best popular science book, scientific consensus conferences and a slew of other initiatives. Yet doubts remain. After a reception marking the umpteenth PUS conference, one luminary, having downed perhaps a little too much of the house Sauvignon, wearily muttered to me: 'You know, I sometimes wonder if everything we do makes a blind bit of difference'.

In this chapter, I shall take an opinionated look at some of the ways in which science reaches the UK public informally, that is, outside the formal education system. How effective are the links between scientists and the public? Do scientists protest too much about the alleged lack of scientific coverage in the media, and how effective are scientists when they *are* given the chance to present their work? And what of the future – will science be increasingly perceived as an important part of our culture or is it destined to be viewed merely as a boffin's corner in the moronic inferno? A decade after the UK scientific community clambered off its laurels, is the problem that Bodmer's committee tackled still with us, has it been solved or do we have a crisis on our hands?

Until quite recently, we had little or no idea about how much the British public know about science. All this changed in the late 1980s with the publication of several widely publicized surveys that sought to find out what facts the public know about science and what they think about the way it is practised. Broadly speaking, the results indicate that while most members of the public do not know much about science and would not be able to pass a science GCSE (see Durant *et al.* 1989) they do have some fairly extensive, informal knowledge about very specific areas that are an obviously important part of everyday life, for example, medical science and environmental matters (see e.g. D. Layton *et al.* 1993).

John Durant, the Professor of PUS at Imperial College and an expert in the field of public science surveys, believes that

> we are only just beginning to understand and come to terms with what the public actually know about science. This knowledge is a complex mixture of ideas, beliefs and associations – an informal 'common-sense' knowledge base which scientists need to take more seriously if they are to engage more effectively with the public.
>
> (Personal communication 5 October 1995)

There is no doubt that, among the UK institutions that enable and promote informal communication between scientists and the public, the BBC has by far the greatest influence. Since John Birt became its director-general in 1992, the Corporation has successfully undergone an image make-over, and it is now seen not so much as the nation's auntie as its street-wise elder sister. During these years of change – probably no more radical than those of other public institutions – the BBC has taken a good deal of stick for its management policies and style. Whatever the rights and wrongs of the arguments, there is no doubt that science has done well in the new climate. Given its obligation to provide a high-quality public service and, at the same time, to maintain its audience share in competition with radio and television channels that can go as down-market as they like, the BBC must be judged to be doing a first-rate job.

As it expands its role as a global broadcasting institution, it will be hard-pressed to maintain the benchmark quality of its specialist programming. There is little hope that the standards set by the BBC will be as influential as they were in the days before satellite television. As Anthony Smith (1996: ch. 3) has remarked in his perceptive summary of the place of the BBC in contemporary culture: 'In the new context, public service broad-casting can only set examples; it cannot make them prevail.' As com-mercial forces are let loose in the increasingly global market-place of the broadcasting media, all we can do is hope that the BBC's science coverage is maintained and not squeezed out by attempts to make the organization more competitive in terms of audiences. Anyone who thinks this is going to be easy should go to the USA and spend a day watching television.

On radio, science is flourishing, and Liz Forgan has proudly pointed out that between 1993 and 1996 the BBC's science unit doubled its output. (This remark was made by the Outgoing Managing Director of BBC Network Radio at the Science Museum on 18 March 1996 at the BBC's reception for set96 (Science, Engineering and Technology) week.) Now, almost every day, there are examples of first-rate science journalism on the BBC's national radio channels, especially in news items and in Radio 4's *Science Now, Medicine Now* and the *Natural History Programme*. Each of these flagship programmes has about half a million listeners, many of whom tune in on the off chance of hearing something they might enjoy. In common with the regular science features on Radios 3 and 5 Live, these programmes use the unique attributes of radio: they are a splendid forum for both intimate personal presentations and for lively group discussions, and are a wonderfully effective medium for telling good stories. A 'talking head' can be as entertaining on the radio as it is dull on the television.

The key challenge to the radio producer is not so much lack of opportunity to secure air-time as to find scientists who will speak openly and engagingly about their work. Deborah Cohen, editor of the BBC Radio science unit, says that

We have to avoid being bland and dull as otherwise our listeners will simply switch off. One problem that we have is that very few scientists are prepared to stick their necks out and criticize each

other's work in public . . . chemists and engineers are particularly
short of good stories.

(Personal communication 11 October 1995)

It is quite possible that the pattern of listening to science news and
features on the radio will be revolutionized by the introduction of digital
technology. Digital Audio Broadcasting (DAB) will take radio 'into a new
age just as CD has transformed the music industry', enthuses the BBC
(1995), whose DAB broadcasts to south-east England began in September
1995. If broadcasting organizations and manufacturers of radio sets take
full advantage of the technology, DAB will enable listeners to have access
to text and data for every radio programme and they will be able to turn
off a radio programme half-way through and listen to the remainder when
it is more convenient (see e.g. Price 1992).

Listeners will also be able to tell their radio that they have a preference
for particular types of material, instructing the radio to fade into the
programme to which they are listening any science stories that are being
broadcast at the same time on other channels. Who knows whether listeners
will take to this less passive mode of radio listening? We shall know the
answer within the next few years, if manufacturers can produce digital
radios of this type at prices that can tempt sufficient people who are used
to spending £20 on an ordinary analogue radio, and if broadcasters can
provide services that listeners actually want. The BBC is plainly confident
of DAB's potential: it is committed to building transmitters by mid-1998
that will make digital radio accessible to 60 per cent of people in the UK.

The digital revolution is also just round the corner in television, where
there are much higher audiences and advertising revenues to be won and
where, in consequence, science occupies a much smaller proportion of the
total broadcasting time. Even a modestly popular science programme on
one of the terrestrial channels is watched by only a few hundred thousand,
while a popular programme broadcast in prime time usually reaches
millions. In its last series, the highest viewing figures for *Horizon* were 2.2
million, for *QED* they were 6.6 million, *Tomorrow's World* 4.2 million and
the *Royal Institution Lectures* 1.3 million. The viewing figures for *Animal
Hospital*, 11.4 million, made it the most successful factual series ever shown
on UK television. One of the flagship radio programmes on Radio 4, such
as *Science Now*, typically has half a million listeners.

Apart from Channel 4's *Equinox*, there are very few science series on the
independent television channels. Nor can we expect many to be made,
except possibly in the run-up to a franchise renewal. A well-known
scientist told me recently that he was summoned to the offices of a leading
independent television production company to discuss the possibilities of
making some new science programmes only to be told that they had in
mind two topics, astrology and the paranormal.

179

Not counting the science items on the news, in 1996 BBC television presented 100 hours of science programming, a 50 per cent increase on the time allocated in 1993. Often forgotten is that the BBC also broadcasts about the same amount of Open University science material, as part of its science, technology and mathematics degree courses (let us hope that these programmes will not be squeezed out of the schedules). About 50 hours of the mainstream broadcast time is devoted to the flagship programmes, *Horizon, Tomorrow's World* and *QED,* which all concentrate on contemporary topics with wide public appeal. Many scientists look down their noses at these and other productions which try to make science snappy and entertaining: just look at the critical shellacking given to *How Do They Do That?*, the most overtly populist of the new science-based series, which has more than 7 million viewers. The approach of this programme is to use simple scientific ideas to answer questions that viewers may well have asked themselves such as 'How does a CD player work?' and 'How can you take a DNA fingerprint?'

According to the BBC TV producer Caroline van den Brul, 'it may well be possible to introduce more science on television if the relevance of its ideas is regularly picked up in every programme area. There is a good deal of scientific content in cookery and gardening programmes – other topics, such as sport and wine-tasting, could make equally fruitful links with science.' For this to happen, the commissioning editors and the producers have to be persuaded that science need not be a 'turn-off'. This is not the issue it was a few years ago: van den Brul says that it is no longer correct to say that the BBC is run by an 'arts Mafia', *bons mots* she coined in 1992 (van den Brul 1992), to the outrage of some of her colleagues.

The importance of the BBC's backing of science news and features in its programming is nowhere better displayed than in its role as a key supporter of the UK's Science Weeks. Conceived in 1994 by the British Association for the Advancement of Science (BA, formerly BAAS) and supported by the government, Science Weeks provide a framework for a national celebration of not only science, but also engineering and technology. For reasons that have never been entirely clear, they always take place in late March, shortly before Easter. This is rather unfortunate timing as most schools are winding down at the end of term, and many families can participate in the Week's activities only during the weekends.

For most people, Science, Engineering and Technology Week has proved to be too much of a mouthful and a remarkable total of 27 names for the Week have appeared in the media. Among these, the truncation 'Science Week' has caught on, and this is perhaps one reason for the lack of engineering and technology activities during the first two Weeks. Another might be the feeble financial support for the weeks proffered by the engineering and industrial community. The BA's Brian Gamble, *Obergruppenführer* of each of the Science Weeks, acknowledges that 'industry has been slow to grasp the opportunities presented by the Weeks, perhaps because they do not fit comfortably with the public relations campaigns mounted by industry.' He adds, however, that 'support has gradually risen: only twenty or so companies supported the 1994 Week, whereas the 1996 Week saw the involvement of 70 or so business-oriented events'.

The first three Science Weeks, which featured thousands of special events up and down the UK, had considerably more impact than most other 'national weeks' (see e.g. Evaluation Associates 1995). This is despite the fact that the 1996 Week unfortunately coincided with an explosion of public concern over the edibility, or otherwise, of British beef – for most of the UK public, the third week in March was devoted not so much to set96 as BSE 96.

The overall success of these Science Weeks in bringing a high concentration of science stories to the public has in large measure been due to the strong backing given to the idea by the BBC. Without this support, Science Weeks would scarcely be viable.

As with television, commercial pressures are currently squeezing the science news coverage in the press. Many science journalists complain off the record that it is now a good deal harder to get their stories past their subeditors than it was in the mid-1980s, now fondly remembered as the heyday of science coverage. It may not be a coincidence that this occurred around the time of the launch of *The Independent* (1986), which set a fine example, with superb science news coverage and equally solid feature articles. Around that time, there were also some strong science-related news stories, such as the Chernobyl and Zeebrugge disasters, and these were duly covered thoroughly, although with some revealing differences of emphasis (see e.g. Clayton *et al.* 1993). Although all the 'heavy' newspapers still have at least one science correspondent, science news pieces are now regularly failing to pass the desks of the sub-editors, who nevertheless still have a strong appetite for health stories. On the literary pages, there has also been a precipitate drop in the number of reviews of science books.

Roger Highfield, science editor of the *Daily Telegraph*, explains this trend in terms of two principal editorial forces that influence the content of the features pages in a quality newspaper – the need both to have authoritative material and to attract advertisers. The ABC1 readers expect science to be covered in their papers, just as they expect enlightened political comment, whether they read it or not. However, in the fiercely competitive newspaper market of the 1990s, commercial pressures hold sway, so features that attract advertising revenue are becoming increasingly popular. The increase in coverage of IT-related topics relative to science coverage is exemplified in the *Guardian*'s OnLine supplement. This lively mixture of accessible science features has a distinctly technological flavour and gives much of its space to IT coverage that is cleverly written to appeal as much to the cybersurfer as the cybertyro.

The *Guardian's* science editor Tim Radford argues the importance of making all science stories appealing to all readers, not only those who are disposed to read about science. He stresses that 'there is no such a thing as science journalism, there is only journalism. When you write a science piece, the priorities are the same as they are for any other story – it must be fair and accurate but, above all, it must be read' (personal communication 10 October 1995). Radford plainly agrees with the conclusion of Anders Hansen's (1994) absorbing study of science reporting in the British press: 'although the specialist reporters who report on science and related subjects do differ from other types of specialist reporters in some respects, it is their overriding and fundamental commitment to the practices of journalism which stand out'.

All this would make most scientists blanch because, for them, the readability and accessibility of their writings are optional extras, not necessities. As Roger Highfield observes, this failure to appreciate the need for dramatic impact is manifest as 'an alarming lack of wherewithal on the part of many scientists to come up with a snappy quote to grab the interest of Jo Public' (personal communication 19 October 1995). Caroline van den Brul (1995) agrees; she believes that 'most scientists don't know what makes a good story because they don't read newspapers and don't watch TV with an eye to what makes them newsworthy. Many scientists mistakenly believe that new information is self-evidently interesting, but the public want to know *why* it should be of interest to them.'

The sheer lack of *nous* demonstrated by scientists in their relations with the press is perpetually astonishing. Tom Wilkie, former science editor of *The Independent*, recalls a memorable example from 1988, when the British computer firm Inmos was sold off to a Franco-Italian company. 'The sale raised a host of issues concerning short-termism and the national commitment – or otherwise – to research and development. I wrote an op-ed piece about these issues and the response consisted of a single letter, where an academic pointed out that I had given the wrong number of megaflops for one of Inmos's transputers'. Wilkie believes that this illustrates 'the startling lack of perception on the part of scientists on how to participate in a public debate', and that 'most leading scientists have little or no idea of how to use their status to promote discussion about crucial issues such as the relationship between science and wealth creation' (personal communication 20 October 1995).

Even if scientists do manage to hone their debating skills, there will always be a clash between their interests and those of the media. For journalists, a science story is 'hot' only if it is likely to interest their news editor and their audience, regardless of whether it has the imprimatur of the scientific community. However, most scientists are much more cautious and will release a story to the press only after it has been written up and been peer reviewed, in a process that usually takes aeons by journalistic standards. It follows that if scientists want to reach the public effectively through the news media, they will have to compromise on their tradition, some three centuries old, of making a story publicly available only after its content has been sanctified by fellow researchers.

Ideally such a compromise should have been carefully thought through and agreed by representative bodies in science and the media, so that it commands wide respect (this may seem to be making too much of the issue, but it is too important to be left to evolve in its present haphazard way). It is certainly in the interest of the scientific community to avoid repetitions of, for example, the 1989 cold fusion fiasco in which the protagonists went public before their apparently sensational results had been properly checked. This premature action later sullied not only their own reputations but also, arguably, those of their fellow scientists (see Close 1990).

In most media, the traffic of science communication is one-way – almost invariably from scientists to the public – a state of affairs that continually reinforces the view of scientists as an authoritarian and paternalistic lobby. Perhaps it would be a good idea if the traffic were once in a while allowed to flow in both directions? This was part of the motivation behind the idea of setting up consensus conferences, which are public inquiries in which ten to sixteen people are charged with the assessment of a socially controversial topic in science and technology. These members of the lay public are free to call experts, normally from a wide range of fields and with an equally wide variety of opinions. Having assessed the responses of the experts, the panellists negotiate among themselves with the aim of producing a statement of consensus. Shortly afterwards, in what is the culmination of the work of the conference, a written statement of the panel's consensus is made public in a press conference.

The idea originated in the USA in the mid-1970s as a method of assessing the benefits of new (and often expensive) developments in medical technology (see Institute of Medicine 1990). In Europe, the first such consensus conferences were organized in Denmark under the auspices of the then newly established Danish parliamentary office of technology assessment, whose first conference on the applications of genetic technology took place in 1987. There have since been thirteen of these conferences in Denmark and two in the Netherlands, on a wide variety of topics including air pollution, infertility treatments, sustainable agriculture, electronic identity cards and transport policy (see Joss 1995).

The first UK consensus conference, held in 1994, was sponsored by the Biotechnology and Biological Sciences Research Council. The somewhat surprising subject of the conference was plant biotechnology, which many researchers had long thought might be controversial but which was not particularly high on the public agenda at the time (the first genetically engineered plant products, notably those based on the Flavr Savr tomato, did not go on sale in the UK until over a year later). The panel, recruited after an advertising campaign in the national and local press, comprised eight men and eight women – including a factory worker, a marketing consultant and a roadsweeper – with ages ranging from 18 to 64. In preparation for the final conference, they were asked to read carefully selected material and they met in Oxford for two gruelling study-weekends, where they were briefed on the background to the technical and social issues that they were going to have to address.

The conference was held in public at London's Regent's College, 2–4 November 1994. An audience of some 300 people watched the panel cross-examine 21 experts, from industry, universities and other research organizations, environmental pressure groups, and so on. Chaired by the science reporter Peter Evans, the proceedings were by and large a model of measured and informed discussion, similar in many ways to the more cerebral debates in the House of Lords. What an ironic pity, then, that it was one of the noble lords who was one of the few who publicly cast aspersions on the conference (Lord Howie of Troon, letter, *The Independent* 10 November 1992).

Their final, twenty-page report was – as might be expected in a document that deliberately sought consensus – cautious in the extreme. No research programme was recommended to be foreclosed, no environmental lobby was attacked, no industrial company savaged; ergo, no headlines were made. Yet the conference did achieve wide coverage in the media, notably on the radio and in the press (a television programme based on the event was mooted but the plans had to be dropped when it became clear that the recording might have compromised the integrity of the discussion). For their part, the panel said that they 'consider that the provision of evidence by a consensus conference could add a whole new dimension to the democratic process of decision-making within our parliamentary system.' This is a telling point – our demoralized democracy would benefit handsomely if there were more forums like these, enabling informed non-specialists to talk directly *with* experts, rather than the opportunity to be talked *at* through the media.

One of the most striking aspects of the publicity for this first UK consensus conference was that no one commented on the fact that it was organized by the Science Museum. In the mid-1980s such a role for the museum would have been unthinkable: museums were much less conscious of their obligations to non-specialists apart from their public duty to conserve, study and present their artefacts. This attitude is rapidly obsolescing (see Miles *et al.* 1988), and it is now *de rigueur* for museums to acknowledge their public role and to act on it. In London, for example, the

Science Museum has its public responsibilities enshrined in its mission statement, which expresses its intention to 'promote the public understanding of science'. It is hardly surprising, then, that the museum has become a centre of PUS activities, many of them generated by John Durant, who in 1989 took up a joint appointment as one of the museum's assistant directors and the UK's first Professor of the Public Understanding of Science, at Imperial College, London.

The trend in UK science museums towards greater concern for the public's needs had, at root, several causes. Not least was the revolution in the attitudes of teachers – in every type of institution, from kindergarten to university – that science education had to broaden its appeal. In the conservative political climate from the late 1970s, this had a strong appeal for the government which, despite admission fees and a substantial increase in sponsorship income, remains the principal source of income for the national museums. The folklore has it that Mrs Thatcher, although not enamoured of museums, which she dubbed 'dingy, musty places', was surprised and impressed by the sheer number of people that visit them. The 350 or so national, regional and local museums in the UK that deal with science in some way have a total annual attendance of about 5 million.

Another factor that drove museums towards the non-specialist public was the extraordinary growth of science centres (see e.g. Gregory 1989 and Chapter 14 in this volume). These centres do not have collections of objects, rather, they present science mainly through hands-on exhibits ('interactives') which visitors are invited to explore as they please, sometimes with the assistance of trained 'explainers'. The principal challenge in designing interactives for these centres is to make them durable, educationally rewarding and to address topics beyond the familiar areas of high-school physics and psychology, which have lent themselves most easily to hands-on treatments.

The Exploratory, the first science centre in the UK, was set up in Bristol in 1987 by the neuropsychologist Richard Gregory. Soon afterwards, the Science Museum opened Launch Pad, which immediately became its most popular gallery and has remained so ever since. It soon became clear that if science museums were to hold their own in the new market-place of 'edutainment', they would have to find ways of integrating hands-on activities into their more traditional displays. Quite apart from the difficulty of allowing free access to objects (usually forbidden on conservation grounds), the full-blooded introduction of hands-on elements is offensive to a small but vociferous cohort who cherish the quiet, unchanging atmosphere of the traditional gallery.

A decade after the science-centre revolution in the UK, museums and science centres happily cohabit and there are enough of them all over the UK for most people to have a science-based day out if they are so inclined. The variety, depth and reliability of the hands-on experience that they offer the public has improved considerably and the best of the science centres are well established. Although the rate of growth in the number of science centres has abated, new ones are still being built – in 1996 the £7 million, state-of-the-art facilities opened at the Techniquest centre in Cardiff. Science museums are flourishing and their new galleries are more varied than ever: there are new object-rich displays (such as the Scientific Instrument gallery in Edinburgh), almost object-free, hands-on areas (such as the Ecology gallery at the Natural History Museum) and a host of galleries that feature a mixture of the two (Measuring Up at the Manchester Museum of Science and Industry is a good example).

Approximately 1 million people visit UK science centres every year and the number of people visiting science museums is steadily increasing (Department of National Heritage 1993). Yet, in the perennially harsh financial climate, science centres and museums face many challenges: both are labour-intensive and therefore expensive to maintain, both have to catch up with the possibilities of the revolution in information technology and both must somehow thrive in the leisure market-place in such a way that they retain their distinct identities and their academic credibility, while remaining popular with the public. Although there is plenty of anecdotal evidence for the long-term educational benefits of museum and science-centre visits, especially for children, there is worryingly little research evidence to back up these claims; a welcome exception is Stevenson (1991). This topic should prove to be extremely rewarding for educational researchers.

So how will science museums and science centres change over the next few decades? There is a good deal of talk of how the increasing availability of virtual reality technology and on-line access will change the expectations and behaviour of visitors, but much of this is probably fanciful, unless the financial climate becomes more clement. In the foreseeable future, it is likely that there will still be a thriving market for communal experiences of authentic science and technology, whether it is through objects or hands-on interactives. Science centres will have to find new ways of engaging their audiences if they are not to be displaced by the discovery areas that have proved so popular in the USA by exploiting the children's enjoyment of interactivity, while downplaying the scientific content or even removing it all together.

For museums, one of the key challenges is the presentation of contemporary science and technology. When visitors are asked, most of them say that they would like modern material to be covered, but such coverage has proved to be beyond almost every one of the world's science museums (science centres scarcely fare much better). Important modern developments often go completely unremarked in exhibitions, and references to science and technology news are often limited to mentions in public talks or to dog-eared xeroxes of newspaper cuttings pinned to a noticeboard.

There are now increasing signs that museums are taking more seriously their responsibilities of keeping up to date. The Science Museum, for example, is now planning a £45.5 million extension to be devoted exclusively to contemporary biomedical science and information technology, with 3,500 square metres of exhibition space. The key challenge to this Wellcome Wing project will not so much be to open the centre, but to ensure that it *stays* fresh – continual renewal on this scale has never before been achieved in the 150-year history of science museums.

Another of the PUS areas in which the Science Museum has become involved is the promotion of popular science books. In 1987, the museum became the first sponsor of the Science Book Prize which has since been awarded annually to the adult book that has done 'most for the public understanding of science' and to the best children's science book. From 1990, the French chemical company Rhône-Poulenc has sponsored the prizes and increased the prize money to £10,000 for both categories.

There is certainly a need to bring to the attention of the public the best popular science books, for, as any bookseller will tell you, popular science books are generally very unpopular. According to a survey carried out for W.H. Smith in the early 1990s, only 2 per cent of the UK population admitted to buying a non-fiction science book in the preceding year. Of the 10 million or so books sold by Dillons each year, only about 2 per cent were about science, slightly less than the 2.5 per cent about science fiction.

The prizes have undoubtedly been awarded to some outstanding books, but they do not include Hawking's, which was beaten for the 1989 Science Book Prize by Roger Lewin's long-forgotten but better written *Bones of Contention*. Subsequent winners have included Roger Penrose's *The Emperor's New Mind* (1990), Stephen Jay Gould's *Wonderful Life* (1991) and Jared Diamond's *The Rise and Fall of the Third Chimpanzee* (1992). Every one a marvellous book, to be sure, but for whom where they written? The authors all intended to write for a general audience and it is true that the books feature reams of elegant writing and generally avoid the forbidding jargon of the academic paper. Yet, although they are all excellent introductions for scientists working in other areas, they are not the sort of thing that most people would choose as their bedtime reading. Small wonder, then, that even with the publicity generated by the prize, a typical winner sells only about 10,000 copies in the UK, a figure dwarfed by a modestly popular cookery book.

The problem is, once again, that scientists are much better at talking to each other than they are at talking to the public. The Rhône-Poulenc prize committee have recognized this and have been emphasizing to the jurors that the prize is for general readers, not for aficionados (most of the jurors begin the judging process as self-proclaimed generalists, only to emerge, having read the books, as enthusiasts for 'popular' science writing). There has consequently been a trend towards books that could safely be recommended to the scientific greenhorn: in 1994 the judges chose Steve Jones's *The Language of the Genes*, the most accessible winner to date although, in the following year, John Emsley's less digestible *Consumer's Good Chemical Guide* controversially beat into second place the brilliant but demanding *The Language Instinct*, by the MIT neurolinguist Steven Pinker.

The fact that Emsley's prize-winner has been vastly outsold by Pinker's 500-page *tour de force* underlines the difficulty of making a safe recommendation for the public. Even more worrying is the paucity of books that can reasonably be said to be suitable for people who neither know nor care much about science. Is the popular science book an impossible dream? Has Hawking not pioneered the publishing equivalent of virtual reality?

So did my fellow tippler at that PUS conference have a point – is it possible that the work of the entire PUS community makes next to no difference to the public's perception of science? Alas, there are not enough survey data to draw any firm conclusions. What can be said confidently is that science communicators are now working in all the media – a crucial issue is not whether science is or is not available to the public, but whether scientists are capable of responding to the opportunities that the media offer them.

Talk about scientists to anyone in the media – newspapers, television, radio, publishing and so on – and sooner or later you will hear of the difficulty of getting a good story from most of them. There are many reasons for this, but perhaps the most important are the scientists' lack of media savvy and the cultural clash between science, in which accuracy and peer review are treasured traditions, and the media, in which entertainment and contemporaneity are key virtues (see S. White *et al.* 1993). To do anything significant about these problems, bold and urgent action is required.

If scientists are to stand a chance of holding their own in the media circus, it is crucial that their communication skills are developed as part of their education, from kindergarten to the common room. At every stage in a scientist's training, some time (a few days a year?) should be reserved for learning and practising methods of talking effectively to non-specialists and for training in the art of presenting technical material in the media. It is unfortunate that so many academics regard 'training' as a dirty word, especially as so many of them would patently benefit from it, not least in their dealings with the public and the media.

There has undoubtedly been progress in this area since the mid-1980s, but there is still a long way to go. A jump start would follow the long-overdue scrapping of conventional A Levels in favour of broader-based courses that enable teenagers to develop their communication skills – in this regard the Dearing (1996) report makes welcome suggestions – and by effecting a swingeing increase in the time allocated in first degrees to communication skills. It is important that students learn to talk to a lay audience, so it is important that the exercises are carried out not only with their teachers and fellow students, but also with people who neither know nor care much about science.

It is also important that communication with the public is valued much more highly in the academic community, as the Wolfendale Committee has argued (Wolfendale 1995). At the moment, public activities are being given more support, for example by the all-powerful research councils, but it remains for the promotion boards of most universities to do more than pay lip-service to the value of the work academics do with the public. Until such initiatives are taken seriously as part of a young researcher's career, most PUS work – policy and practice – will be done by academics who are nearer their retirement parties than the peaks of their careers.

But even if scientists could be persuaded overnight to double the time they spend presenting their work to the lay public, we would still be left with the problem of making the messages attractive and engaging. Science communication is a skill – you can take a master's degree in the subject – and few of us are really good at it, even after years of practice. Since the careers of editors and producers depend on the quality of the articles they commission and the programmes they make, they are understandably selective in choosing the scientists they are prepared to work with. In practice this means that, of the scientists who are keen to contribute to the media, few are regularly given the chance. Most stand in the wings watching the regular star performances of colleagues such as the media's current favourite scientist, Steve Jones, Professor of Genetics at University College, London. Not only is he exceptionally eloquent, with a sharp eye for a good story, but also, unlike so many of his fellow scientists, he dares to be bold, as in his *In the Blood* (1996).

Boldness is not the strong suit of most scientists in the media. Conscious of all the caveats and provisos needed to make most colloquial statements about their work rigorously acceptable to their most pedantic peers, many scientists find it well-nigh impossible to give an engaging account of their research. Nor is academic rigour the only problem: there is also the fear of offending colleagues and funding agencies, and of being politically incorrect. How many of the scientists who believe that PUS work is a waste of their time would be comfortable saying so in public? How many would dare to say a word that might offend their research collaborators, or even their competitors? Most scientists come across as noncommittal, bland and dull, so it is hardly surprising that they fail to cut much of a dash in the media.

If scientists are radically to improve their 'media image', they will have to be more ready to drop the formal presentational styles generally expected in academia and adopt more relaxed approaches. In practice, this will mean that they will have to be prepared to compromise more readily with the highest standards of scientific rigour. It is the question of how (or whether) to relax standards of rigour that is most difficult. Throughout their education, scientists are taught the need for precision – to reason logically while thinking imaginatively, to use theories only in their correct domains, to interpret data conservatively – so it is not easy for them to adopt the fast-and-loose style that usually goes down well in the media.

The need for caution is underlined whenever socially sensitive scientific information is confusingly presented to the public, who apparently find the uncertainties of scientific analysis deeply unsettling. Witness, for example, the uproar over the alleged dangers of using some types of oral contraception and of eating beef from cattle that may have been infected with BSE.

Somehow, scientists will have to find ways of presenting science that retain the essential features of good scientific analysis yet that are lively and engaging for the public. Among the obstacles to this are the profound public misunderstanding of the nature of science, notably the tentativeness of many of its theories, and the very concept of probability (the success of the National Lottery is a depressingly imposing monument to British ignorance of mathematics). Fundamental problems of understanding like these will be addressed properly only by better formal education in schools, with much less emphasis on preparing students for university work and more emphasis on teaching material that is relevant to the majority, who will not become professional scientists. Such changes will entail another unwelcome but necessary upheaval in school curriculum.

If scientists do manage to communicate more effectively with the public, they will still have to cope with consequences that will not all be to their liking. There is a fond and widespread belief that the more lay people know about science, the more they will approve of it, yet in practice this does not seem to be the case. The Eurobarometer surveys in 1989 and 1992 (see INRA (Europe) 1993) demonstrate that, other things being equal, the more contact and familiarity the public have with science, the more supportive they are of scientific work, although people who know more about science have markedly stronger opinions about specific issues. The opinions themselves are much less predictable.

It is not only scientists who are keen on promoting the scientific literacy of the lay public (see J. Miller 1983). Among the supporters of PUS activities in the west are politicians, whose motivation stems not so much from concern with issues of culture and democratic accountability, but from a near panic about the drift of the centre of gravity of the world's economy towards the East Pacific Rim (see e.g. Cresson 1996). The UK is very much party to this consensus and, as we have seen, there is no shortage in the media of initiatives in the field of science popularization. Yet these new ventures are manifestly struggling to hold their own in the media, as they have to compete with the more instantly appealing fare of entertainment that is always on offer.

If scientists really do want to share their work with the public, they will have to become much better at talking with – not at – lay audiences, much more skilled at popularizing their research and much more adept at participating in public debates. As far-fetched as it may seem, it is possible to imagine a much more prominent place for science in our cultural life, with the scientific community more demonstrably committed to its obligations to the public. This would entail scientists being more willing and able to make the most of their chances to appear on the television and radio, their writing books that the public actually want to read without being vilified by their colleagues for doing so, their collaborating more effectively with museums and science centres, their organizing more events that involve the public in the ethical aspects of scientific work, and so on.

All this would involve a good deal of risk-taking: the public may not always like what it hears and so may well want to have more of a say in the direction and applications of scientific research. Yet the risks are well worth taking – the alternative of continuing to accept a marginal role in society for science would be a tragic betrayal of every scientist's responsibilities to the public. Let us hope that the scientific community rises to the challenge soon, before the media and the public run out of patience.

14

SCIENCE THROUGH PLAY

Richard Gregory

If necessity is the mother of invention, play is the father of discovery. Science, indeed, starts with the play of children. The significance of play for cognitive development has a substantial literature (Hodgkin 1985; Görlitz and Wohlwill 1987). No doubt it is true that chance favours the prepared mind, but games prepare the mind. Games are safe try-outs for developing skills of response and prediction, and for making discoveries and inventing new solutions. Rather than play being trivial, it seems to be essential for cognitive development – for individuals and for science.

Children's toys are their laboratory. The American psychologist Jerome Bruner suggests some of play's uses – including for learning about oneself, and how one can relate to the object world and to other people:

> First, it is a means of minimizing the consequences of one's actions and of learning, therefore, in a less risky situation. This is particularly true of social play, where, by adopting a play face or a 'galumphing gait' . . . the young animal signals its intent to play. . . .
>
> Second, play provides an excellent opportunity to try combinations of behaviour that would, under functional pressure, never be tried.
>
> (Bruner *et al.* 1976: 38)

Thus chimpanzees play with sticks, leading to poking holes into trees for extracting termites. Yes – chimpanzees do use tools! It turns out that skills are learned both from watching adult behaviour and from individual play-practice. The use of sticks as tools by chimpanzees, especially for getting termites out of holes, has been studied extensively. Van Lawick and Goodall (1974) found that part-skills, or sub-routines, are developed by repetition, then put together to be effective. Bruner says that:

> One very crucial feature of tool skills in chimpanzees as in humans is the trying out of variants of the new skill in different contexts. Once Köhler's (1925) ape Sultan had 'learned' to use a stick to draw in food, he tried using it very soon for poking other animals, for digging, and

for dipping it through an opening in a cesspool. Once Rana had learned to climb up stacked boxes to get a suspended piece of fruit, she rapidly tried her new climbing routine on a ladder, a board, a keeper, and Köhler himself – most often forgetting the fruit in preference for the combinatory activity *per se*. . . . It is probably this 'push to variation' (rather than fixation by positive reinforcement) that gives chimpanzee manipulation such widespread efficiency – such opportunism for dipping sticks into beehives for honey, using sticks for clubbing lizards and rodents, and using branches for striking at or throwing at big felines.

(Bruner *et al.* 1976: 41)

It is not only particular skills that are learned: abstract concepts are created through play, as play is unfettered from immediate need and so is free to try out new possibilities. No doubt it is surprising outcomes that suggest – for children as for science – quite new ideas and need for new kinds of explanations. Thus Newton thought of what holds up the moon from imagining (or actually) throwing a stone further and further – and realizing that finally it would never land, but would circle the earth for ever. This was a key to his entire theory of dynamic astronomy.

Possibilities arise from questioning – in science from experiences including experiments, and of puzzles from philosophy. We may think of philosophy as sophisticated 'hand-waving'. No doubt it starts from puzzles in childhood. Do children raise what we see as philosophical questions? This has been asked and in some degree answered by an American teacher of philosophy, Gareth Matthews, in *Philosophy and the Young Child* (1990). He starts with Tim, aged about 6 years, who while licking a jar asked: 'Papa, how can we be sure that everything is not a dream?' His father said he did not know. Tim answered: 'Well, I don't think everything is a dream, 'cause in a dream people wouldn't go around asking if it was a dream.' More empirical is the example of a young boy, John Edgar, who had often seen aircraft take off and disappear in the distance as he lived near an airport. Flying for the first time at the age of 4 years, he turned to his father after take-off, and said in a puzzled voice: 'Things don't really get smaller up here.' This suggests some interesting experiments.

Ursula (aged 3 years 4 months) said: 'I have a pain in my tummy.' Mother: 'You lie down and your pain will go away.' Ursula: 'Where will it go?' All children ask questions like these. They arise by analogy with, for example, food, and so on, going somewhere else. Indeed, children do philosophize, though perhaps most people give up philosophy by the age of 10 or so. Plato approves of this:

It is a fine thing to partake of philosophy just for the sake of education, and it is no disgrace for a lad to follow it: but when a man already advanced in years continues its pursuit, the affair, Socrates, becomes ridiculous; and for my part I have much the same feeling towards students of philosophy as towards those who lisp or play tricks.

(Plato, The Dialogue, the *Gorgias*)

Do we discourage questioning and experimenting? Are most adults (as might appear from so many 'negative' articles in popular newspapers) intimidated by questions and discoveries of science? Is this why most of us have not grown out of the ancient 'common sense' of pre-modern science? That we are stuck conceptually in antiquity is well expressed by Bernard Cohen (1980). The physics of Galileo, Kepler and Newton has revolutionized scientific perception, yet has hardly affected how most of us see the world now. Considering early ideas of motion, Cohen says: 'Odd as it may seem, most people's views about motion are part of a system of physics that was proposed more than 2000 years ago and was experimentally shown to be inadequate at least 1400 years ago'. He continues:

In the inability to deal with questions of motion in relation to a moving Earth, the average person is in the same position as some of the greatest scientists of the past, which may be a source of considerable comfort. The major difference is, however, that for the scientist of the past the inability to resolve these questions was a sign of the times, whereas for us moderns such inability is, alas, a sign of ignorance.

(Cohen 1980)

Why are most of us stuck as adults – though as children, at least implicitly, we apply simple scientific method for our learning and discovery? This is the view of Jean Piaget (1896–1980). Piaget points out that children start with Aristotelian notions of physics, of motion and forces and so on, and with 'primitive' magical notions of cause – not distinguishing between their own responses and the behaviour of inanimate objects. In *The Child's Conception of the World* (1929) he describes children as having animistic views, believing that all objects capable of movement, such as bicycles and the sun and the moon, are alive. Piaget reported many experiments bearing on these questions, such as the famous studies on perceived conservation (or rather lack of conservation) of matter. Piaget finds that most children before the age of 9, given various shapes of a lump of clay, do not appreciate conservation of substance. But how good are adults? A well-known marketing trick is to use odd-shaped bottles to make the contents look larger. Piaget has a lot to say on child development: perhaps less on why most of us, as adults, are stuck in pre-modern science notions.

These pre-modern science notions are considered in Driver et al.'s (1985)

Children's Ideas in Science. It seems that children do not approach asking questions about phenomena from a vacuum. They generally have pre-formed ideas, which though not appropriate or coherent, may be held to survive robustly through life – in spite of school and their individual experience. Edith Guesne describes experiments with children on light and vision (Driver *et al.* 1985). She finds that many children of around 15 years do not conceive of light as moving. In terms of our science they have bizarre notions of light and shadows, yet these are where we all start from. Some children of 13–14 years conceive of light as sent out from lamp bulbs – but not from other objects, such as tables or books. Just as Plato and Euclid described light, a French boy thought of light as going out of his eyes like a glowing stick. Seeing a cardboard box:

> Here my eyes can go right up to the box ... it's my sight....
> If it [the box] was fifteen kilometres away, I couldn't see it, because
> ... my sight isn't strong enough.... Because a box doesn't move,
> it hasn't any energy. A lamp for example moves, the light gets
> there.... The box, it's stuff that isn't alive.

> (Driver *et al.* 1985)

Children often think of objects as in a 'bath of light' with no link between objects and the eyes. (This is essentially the medieval view. Thus for Thomas Aquinas (1225–74) seeing was '*grasping*' the forms of things, clearly an analogy to touching, implying that vision works directly, without links.) It is important to note that although children are very familiar with falling objects, with light from the sun and artificial lamps, they fail to understand basic concepts of physics from their individual experience. To a great extent, they fail also following years of schooling! Surely what is needed is directed play with immediately available explanations, and encouragement to question further and test hypotheses. This is hard for schools to do because it needs a wide range of apparatus to be available at any time, and instant answers to questions. At least, this would be the ideal. Something approaching this ideal may be given by resources for schools, such as hands-on science centres for children, and indeed for the public.

To return to the question: why are so many adults stuck with pre-scientific ideas – although as children we are behaving as scientists – is very important for education and in particular hands-on science centres. If we find it hard to escape from pre-Aristotelian ideas through play as children – why should hands-on science centres achieve more? The lesson is, surely, that hands-on experience, both for children and for learning science as adults, is extremely important – but it needs to be *interpreted* – by ideas and concepts which are not at all easy to discover, or, even from the best teachers, to understand. In other words: it is the hands-on experience of children that gives the 'common-sense' accounts of reality;

but it requires sophisticated ideas, that have taken thousands of years of philosophy and planned technology, as well as mathematics and organized science, to develop and appreciate. No doubt these come from shared and explicitly discussed experience, including specially directed observations and experiments directed to test hypotheses. This is beyond children's play, but is essentially the sophistication of the 'play' of science. So science centres must introduce concepts (which may be extremely counterintuitive) in order to interpret the discoveries of hands-on experience – to help child's play become science's play with adult understanding.

Introducing science and technology through first-hand experience is not a new idea. Francis Bacon (1561–1626), in his unfinished book *New Atlantis* (1627), describes his imaginary *House of Salomon* – open for all to share knowledge and harvest its benefits, through playing with the available science and technology and imagining future possibilities.

Bacon saw that science could and should be a social activity, with many kinds of contributions, according to individual abilities and interests (Ziman 1978). His *Novum Organum* (1620) set out rules for scientific method, with suggestions for applying it by co-operative experimenting: hence research laboratories. This inspired the foundation of the Royal Society, by Charles II in 1660. Nothing much came of his *New Atlantis* dream for science centres until over three hundred years later, yet his *New Atlantis* plan made a lot of sense then and today, having

> Perspective Houses, where we make demonstrations of all lights and radiations; and of all colours; and of things uncoloured and transparent, we can represent unto you all several colours; not in rain-bows, as it were in gems and prisms, but of themselves single. We represent all multiplications of light, which we carry to great distance, and make so sharp as to discern small points and lines; also all colourations of light. . . . We procure means for seeing objects afar off, and things afar off as near; making feigned distances. . . .

> We have also engine houses. . . . We imitate also flights of birds; we have some degree of flying in the air; we have ships and boats for going under water, and brooking of seas; also swimming girdles and supporters. We have diverse curious clocks, and other like motions of return, and some perpetual motions. We imitate also motions of living creatures, by images of men, beast, birds, fishes and serpents. . . .

> We have also a mathematical house, where are represented all instruments, as well as geometry and astronomy, exquisitely made.

Bacon was wary of errors of the senses. He distrusted the new-fangled telescope, which was hardly surprising at the time, as curved glass was associated with distortions. Some instruments had been used for avoiding limitations of the senses from antiquity, especially scales for measurement, which originated in the earliest days of the Egyptian civilization, 3000 BC; also rulers, set squares, and using water to establish levels for foundations of buildings go back to the earliest times. Spectacles, however, for hundreds of years associated weak sight with weak minds (and as for telescopes, they were invented by uneducated craftsmen and so had low social prestige). So this is a complicated business, where instruments both extend our abilities and understanding, yet also show up our weaknesses and infallibility. This makes the scientific study of illusion peculiarly significant. Bacon's House of Salomon was to include warnings of perceptual errors, with demonstrations of

Deceits of the Senses; where we represent all manner of juggling, false apparitions, impostures, and illusions; and their fallacies. And surely you will easily believe that we have so many things truly natural which induce imagination, could in a world of particulars deceive the senses, if we could disguise those things and labour to make them seem more miraculous.

It is sad that it has taken so long to begin to make Bacon's dream for sharing science come true. The modern pioneer of hands-on science centres is Frank Oppenheimer (1912–85), who founded the Exploratorium in San Francisco in 1969 (Hein 1987). He was inspired by visiting the mainly push-button though partly hands-on Children's Gallery of the London Science Museum, dating from the 1930s.

Frank Oppenheimer saw phenomena of perception (especially visual illusions) as significant and useful for introducing people to the universe through appreciating their own perceptual processes. This is now an important theme in most science centres – paradoxically linking us to the physical universe through perceptual departures from physics. I had the privilege of helping Frank Oppenheimer with some of the first demonstrations and developing the philosophy of the San Francisco Exploratorium. Oppenheimer wrote: 'I suspect that everybody – not just you and I – genuinely wants to share and feel at home with the cumulative and increasingly coherent awareness of nature that is the traditional harvest of scientists and artists.' He said of his exhibits: 'We do not want people to leave with the implied feeling: "Isn't somebody else clever?" Our exhibits are honest and simple so that no one feels he or she must be on guard against being fooled or misled' (Murphy 1985). This is easier said than done. It has taken thousands of years of science to avoid being misled by certain phenomena, from loadstones to the apparent motion of the stars, and science is still struggling to reconcile phenomena with hidden realities. Science centres are intended to be fun and to present phenomena and ideas so that they will be understood. They have, however, been criticized for appearing trivial. Michael Shortland (1987) criticized science centres for being too like fun-fairs. But one can learn a lot from fun-fairs! For here are to be found all manner of phenomena of physics, of probability, and indeed much of human behaviour, including skills and reactions to surprise, and even fear. Put a frame around a picture and it is transformed by being the centre of critical and admiring attention: perhaps a science centre puts such a frame around phenomena, even in a fun-fair.

Ten years after the start of the Exploratorium in San Francisco, we founded the first hands-on science centre in Britain, the Exploratory, in Bristol. This is now a rapidly growing international movement, which is surely important for making science part of everyday life by taking children and adults through 'common-sense' appearances to more sophisticated understanding. Should new techniques such as virtual reality be used? Will the patience, and almost infinite memory capacity of computers, serve to 'programme' human minds to be more knowledgeable, and able to use knowledge more creatively? As it is, understanding does not always increase skill, for it can distract rather than be incorporated. Conceivably a more hands-on approach to education will help to integrate understanding with perception and skill. Whether virtual reality (VR) will help is a moot question, presumably to remain mute until we have better VR systems, and experience of their effects (see Gregory 1983, 1988, 1989).

KEYS TO DISCOVERY

We have seen that there is evidence that young children are not blank slates, but have what are often bizarre notions of for example, physics, which can be hard to shift. The 'naive notions' of children are remarkably Aristotelian (Di Sessa 1982; Driver *et al.* 1985; G. B. Matthews 1990). Perhaps it is not clear whether children have their own thought-out theories, or whether when asked a question, such as 'What holds the moon up?' they say the first thing that comes into their heads. But whether their 'naive notions' are pre-formulated or invented spontaneously as occasion suggests, the conclusion is clear, that though hands-on experience is essential, it is not adequate for understanding. A great deal of explanation and help of many kinds is needed. For it is absurd to expect individual children to recapitulate much of the history of science by their own efforts.

It might be helpful to distinguish here for education and for science what seem to be three essentials: initial hands-on discovery; informal explanations; formal and especially mathematical accounts. The latter two may be very far from initial hands-on experience. The keys to discovery need names.

Following hands-on exploration, scientists often speak of mere handwaving, when a colleague fails to give a mathematical account. And we speak of handle-turning, from the turning of handles of mechanical calculating machines, to get answers automatically. This suggests a handy terminology for playful processes of individual and scientific discovery:

Three keys for discovery
- Hands-on   *Exploration*
- Hand-waving   *Explanation*
- Handle-turning   *Computation*

The suggestion is that, ideally, all three are needed for individual understanding of science and for science itself. Let us unpack them.

Hands-on exploration

This is knowledge by acquaintance, as Bertrand Russell put it – discovering properties of things by interaction. When highly developed, hands-on skill becomes craftsmanship.

Hand-waving explanation

This is the cauldron of scientific creativity. Examples in science are legion: Darwinian evolution by natural selection; Michael Faraday's lines of force; almost, if not all, theories in psychology. Taking off from hands-on exploration, we are free to create new possibilities. We wave our hands to communicate when language fails or is inadequate. Although hand-waving is not quite academically respectable, hand-waving mental models are extremely important for creative thinking. Presumably hand-waving explanations have a poor press in the academic world, because they are not quantified and are hard to test by examination. But informal intuitive explanations not only are the centre of seeing and thinking, but also give meaning to equations. Perhaps hand-waving is intimately related to the 'brain language' of thinking, which must be partly prior to language as we have some notion of what we want to say before we speak, and animals have considerable problem-solving ability without structured language (Pinker 1994). When highly developed, hand-waving explanations become philosophy and deep implicit concepts of science.

There is considerable evidence that creative scientists use hand-waving mental models, analogies and images, for their thinking. This is well described by Arthur Miller (1984), for physicists and mathematicians. Many, and most likely all, mathematical physicists start with hand-waving mental models, before they formulate equations. This is clearly so for Newton and for James Clerk-Maxwell, who made it clear that his equations for the electromagnetic theory of light started from mechanical models.

Handle-turning computation

This depends on following rules, or algorithms, of mathematics and logic. Although algorithms can be exceedingly hard to discover or formulate, once selected, answers may emerge automatically, by 'turning the handle'.

EXPLORATORY SCIENCE CENTRES FOR HANDS-ON SCIENCE PLAY

From Bacon's dream of 300 years ago, science centres should aim to make science and technology interesting; give confidence for individual discovery; introduce concepts and explanations which may be questioned and tested. So, children and adults may come to use, and sometimes create, science and technology more effectively, while appreciating potentialities and possible dangers.

A tricky question is how to move from hands-on experience to hand-waving explanations. For, how can we explore abstract concepts hands-on? A serious snag of science centres, in practice, is the bustle and noise of exuberant youth; so a necessity is oases of peace and quiet. What is needed are somewhat separate, quiet places for thinking and reading, perhaps with computer aids. We may call these Explanatories. Ideally, one should ask questions from the Exploratory – consider it in the Explanatory (perhaps formalizing logic and mathematics) and go back to the Exploratory for testing and getting new ideas.

Explanatories: how can counter-intuitive ideas be revealed to children and consenting adults? We are misled by much of day-to-day hands-on experience. For example Aristotle, and present-day children and most adults, think that heavy objects fall faster than light objects – because this is often observed, as for feathers and stones falling through water. Physics since Galileo tells us this is false for objects in a vacuum. Galileo's experiment on the Leaning Tower of Pisa is not easy to do, and for many objects (because of air friction) it does not work. When a spoon is placed in water it appears bent: one could easily be misled into believing that it truly is bent; except that when taken out of the water, clearly nothing has happened to it. Here we are not misled, because we often carry out (if implicitly) tests distinguishing reality from illusion. This leads to theories of the discrepancy – in this case bending of light by refraction or by reflection such as in mirrors. We are often (though fortunately not always) misled by day-to-day hands-on experience. A central problem is that a great deal of hands-on experience leads to incorrect hand-waving explanations. This is why, although children start off as observing and exploring like scientists, they often follow false trails. This is indeed true for science itself, which is why it has taken so long to formulate adequate theories, and effective unifying 'paradigms', such as evolution, universal gravitation, and much more recently quantum mechanics, which is highly counter-intuitive.

What concerns us, also, is how to move from hands-on experience and hand-waving understanding to the extremely useful, though for most of us difficult, skills of handle-turning mathematics. Computers now remove much of the sweat and tears of handle-turning. Their graphics reveal to the eye abstract principles with great beauty. They can be interactive, and so hands-on. It may be very useful in science centres to link computers to actual demonstrations and experiments, so the computer can, for example, draw dynamic graphs, to reveal underlying principles and functions in real-time.

It has been suggested, by Philip Davis and Reuben Hersh in *The Mathematical Experience* (1980), that computer interaction allows dimensions beyond the usual three of space and one of time to be visualized. A rotating computer-generated hypercube (a mathematical construct from extrapolating from one to two, to three dimensions, then to a fourth dimension, which can be defined only in terms of mathematics, though it can almost be displayed on a computer screen using movement) looks meaningless – but upon taking the controls:

> I tried turning the hypercube around, moving it away, bringing it close, turning it around another way. Suddenly I could feel it! The hypercube had leapt into palpable reality, as I learned how to manipulate it, feeling in my fingertips the power to change what I saw and change it back again. The active control at the computer console created a union of kinaesthetic and visual thinking which brought the hypercube up to the level of intuitive understanding.

This seems to have introduced a 'handle-turning' concept into 'hand-waving' intuitive understanding. How far this is possible – and more generally how we can learn to move with less effort and more freedom between hands-on exploration, hand-waving explanation, handle-turning computation – raises issues both for education and scientific creativity.

Many fundamental principles are usually masked by contaminations, such as friction; but can be experienced directly by 'purifying' them with carefully designed experiments and demonstrations. This, indeed, is how many basic discoveries have been made. This is important for science centres – where, for example, it is quite easy to remove air from around falling bodies, when we really do see that bodies of any weight fall at the same rate. Air tracks and air tables to reduce friction reveal Newton's laws of motion to direct observation. This has the great advantage over computer simulation or television or virtual reality, that it is the 'real world' of objects, in a simple defined situation, that is being observed and investigated interactively with possibilities for checking. It is not pre-programmed, but is entirely under the control of the explorer, who does, however, have to appreciate what is going on and what may be contaminating artefacts.

By playing with objects, static forces can be brought alive, with models of buildings and bridges, some of which *do* collapse. The inverted catenary for arches and domes is especially fascinating, revealing surprising underlying principles in familiar natural and human-made objects. Dynamic forces, and inertia and friction, lead to principles of mechanical devices such as balances, pendulums (with hints to problems of inertia and peculiarities of gravity), gears (and how gears are related to levers) and many devices of technology that become friends as one gets to know them and appreciate what they can do and how they work. The essential all through is to play with things, to get the 'feel' of levers, gears and gyroscopes, perhaps later to describe them formally with mathematics.

Differences may be brought out between Aristotle's mechanics, and Galileo's, which we now accept but which is counter-intuitive and so has to be individually discovered, with help. Chemistry is difficult to present hands-on. How far concepts of relativity and quantum mechanics can be appreciated through immediate experience remains to be discovered. Hidden forces of magnetism and electricity can be revealed by traditional means, such as iron filings (preferably in three dimensions) and by re-enacting historical experiments, such as Faraday's moving magnet in a coil of wire (1831). Sound waves can be shown with gas jets. In general it seems best to start with simple, directly experienced phenomena, before moving to sophisticated electronic displays or computer simulations; though how computers work, and the power of symbols in general, are as we now realize extremely important.

How to present mathematical ideas without appearing intimidating is a headache. To solve this problem, the Nuffield and the Open University experiences are invaluable. No doubt computer graphics combined with games and tangible examples will help; but just how children and adults generalize from examples and discover abstract principles is hardly understood. Research is particularly needed to work out ways for making principles of mathematics transparent – or rather visible to the understanding.

Adults, especially, can be surprised. In our first Exploratory exhibition, at the British Association for the Advancement of Science in the University of East Anglia in 1984, a professor of mathematics tried out the 'cycloid track' experiment, in which two identical toy cars run down a model car track in the form of a cycloid curve. A car starting from the top and the other starting simultaneously some way down, arrive at the bottom together. To non-mathematicians (including children) this is astonishing: the shorter track takes less time, and wherever the cars on the curved tracks start, they end together. The mathematician already knew this – Newton had proved it centuries ago – but he was amazed that it actually worked! He kept returning, and trying it out again, hardly able to believe his eyes as he thought friction would mask the mathematical truth. This experiment, using toy cars and toy racing tracks (with a graph paper design for the background) shows children that toys can have significance – as play and science are linked, with cars, and skates and tops and soap bubbles, and far more. It showed the professor of mathematics something in his own field that he found hard to believe – that the proof of the properties of a cycloid works in practice. And the working toys showed mathematics in action.

There are studies on visitor behaviour, such as time spent on each experiment ('Plores' as we call them in the Bristol Exploratory, as the museum word 'exhibit' is too passive for a hands-on science centre). I coined 'Plore' from explore, for hands-on exhibits and experiments. This word is used in the Exploratory, and now more widely, though perhaps not very generally. There are several studies on what children and adults can recall following visits to science centres.

But here we are more concerned with implicit learning, which may then be made explicit and so become scientific understanding. Measuring explicit knowledge can be done easily with quizzes and examinations; but implicit understanding is far more difficult to assess, though it is at least as important. It is likely that exams distort science teaching, towards what is easy to mark. So we need to discover how to recognize and assess implicit understanding. A first step is attempted with the suggested classification, about to be presented here.

A useful test of implicit and explicit understanding is power to predict. Thus, for the Bernoulli effect, blowing a hair dryer between freely suspended beach balls, most people expect them to move apart. In fact they are drawn together, which is highly surprising. The surprise shows the inadequacy of a mental model for understanding – signalling that an answer should be sought or invented – but at least the surprise is a sign that the mind is switched on. This hints at possible tests of implicit understanding – or misunderstanding.

SIGNS OF IMPLICIT UNDERSTANDING

Being surprised

Failed predictions can be clear evidence of inappropriate mental models. A classical example is Aristotle's rejection of the notion that the stars are seen as moving because the earth spins round. He jumped up – and landed in the same place – so how could the earth have been spinning under him? What Aristotle lacked was the concept of inertia. This shows both how important concepts are and how soon we depart from common sense in science.

A favourite science centre example of surprise (as already mentioned) is what happens when air is blown between a pair of freely suspended beach balls. Practically everyone expects them to fly apart – but they are drawn together by the flow of air between them. This failed prediction tells the explorers, as well as the teacher, their lack of appreciation of the situation. The failed prediction is a powerful internal signal of *not understanding*. From failed predictions we learn to examine assumptions; so we may correct our intuitions, or hand-waving mental models. As surprises show limits and failures of understanding, so they are pointers to discovery, for individuals and for science itself. For scientists, failed predictions may suggest the next step for advancing knowledge. Similarly for the child or for the aware but not especially knowledgeable adult – failed predictions can signal the need for further experiment, to see the phenomenon in a fresh way. They bring out implicit misunderstanding! But questioning and restructuring require effort which is not to everyone's taste.

Seeing analogies

If one understands, for example resonance, similarities are seen between what on the surface are quite different-appearing things: musical instruments, the divisions of Saturn's rings, tuned radio circuits, positions of spectrum lines from resonances within atoms, and far more. It is important to have many examples of diverse phenomena to practise seeing analogies. This enriches hand-waving understanding, and challenges and justifies handle-turning science.

Inventing

We may look for ability to invent novel solutions and fill gaps, for these require creative understanding. What Is In The Black Box evokes creative play. This can be observed sometimes to see processes of invention and for assessing originality.

Jokes

To appreciate and make jokes is clear evidence of understanding. With increased interest in science, and technology, we may expect more science 'in-group' humour, which should enliven life and literature.

Seeing small effects

Appreciating the significance of small, on the surface trivial phenomena shows that they are recognized as significant. So increasing understanding enriches experience far beyond sensory stimulation.

Appreciating nothing

The most dramatic evidence of understanding is seeing significance in *nothing*. This is the point of experimental controls, and a great deal comes from nothing happening in null experiments. Only when the situation is understood conceptually is it possible to appreciate nothing. So 'seeing nothing' is a strong sign of understanding.

If such signs as these could be used effectively – could we escape the tyranny of traditional examinations?

CONCLUSIONS

Play is important for individual learning and discovery in science; but unguided play is not *sufficient*. One can think of laboratories as scientists' playgrounds; but they have discipline and purpose to guide creativity. Children's games have something of this, but perhaps they are more for social and individual discovery, than for finding hidden principles of nature. It has taken thousands of years of technology – much based on hands-on trial and error, and explicitly formulated hypotheses of science, to see through appearances, and establish principles for prediction and control. We build upon the past. So it is a great help to appreciate something of the history of science. From history, we can see how hard it is to establish the significance of phenomena. To learn and discover from experience, we must classify phenomena, so that we can build up appropriate inductive generalizations. (It is important to know that a whale is a mammal, for it certainly looks like a great fish, though this is misleading.) Classification is also essential for deductions – for deriving logical conclusions – for deduction is from our symbols, not from nature's facts. This brings out a danger of hands-on teaching: it is extremely important to appreciate symbols of mathematics and language – it is important to read and play with words.

We have suggested that there are three key 'handy' classes, for considering – discovering – explaining: hands-on experience, hand-waving explanations, handle-turning computations. Exceptional scientists, especially Sir Isaac Newton, had abundant skills in all of these. Perhaps an aim of science education is to develop these three kinds of skills, and the overriding skill of how to move from one to the other freely, with imagination and sufficient discipline. To teach this, as anything else, motivation is essential. We speak of science centres as fun, which is motivating, but this is really pointing to a much deeper and non-trivial sense of the word – implying that the processes of learning and understanding can be immensely enjoyable for their own sake, as well as for practical gains to society and the individual.

15

SHARING SCIENCE

Sue Pringle

Science is a human activity and the best way to understand it is to
understand the individual human beings who practise it.

(Freeman Dyson, in Cornwell 1995)

Research scientists are increasingly encouraged to play a role in the public
understanding of science. All research councils now have public understanding of science (PUS) in their mission statements. In 1995 the Particle
Physics and Astronomy Research Council (PPARC) stated that grant
holders could spend 1 per cent of their grant, up to a maximum of £10,000,
on PUS, competitive award schemes have also been introduced by PPARC
and the other research councils.

Despite the increase in PUS activity, surprisingly few data are available
to find out which scientists are involved in PUS, why they do it, what
benefits they gain, what PUS activities are successful for them and, more
importantly, why some scientists are not involved in PUS and what
hurdles there are to being involved.

No one actually knows the extent to which scientists' attitudes [to
PUS] are changing. We have no idea how many activists are ready
and able to do something to improve public understanding, whether
they really know how to go about it, what activities they are willing
and equipped to carry out, what sort of training they would welcome.

(Bodmer 1985)

This chapter aims to address these questions by reviewing examples of
events and schemes where scientists and engineers have shared their
research with the public and in schools. But first we need to look at what
arguments exist for researchers themselves communicating with the public.

WHY SHOULD RESEARCHERS COMMUNICATE
WITH THE PUBLIC?

As Colin Blakemore (1990) asserts, if we are unwilling to go out and talk
about the excitement and significance of our work, especially about basic

research then we shall be the victims of our own elitism.

So how have we suffered from our own elitism? Dyson states (in Cornwell 1995) that

the image that scientists have traditionally presented to the public, the image of noble and virtuous dedication to the truth, is no longer credible. The public, having found out that the traditional image of the scientist as a secular saint is false, has gone to the opposite extreme and imagines us to irresponsible devils playing with human lives. It is our test now to dispel the fantasies with facts, showing the public that we are neither saints nor devils but human beings sharing the common weakness of our species.

The so-called 'anti-science' culture has caused concern among the government, scientists and industry. This concern was expressed most notably when the Royal Society decided, in 1985, to establish a working party on the public understanding of science chaired by Sir Walter Bodmer.

In the early 1990s *Realising Our Potential* (Office of Science and Technology 1993) included, for the first time in a government White Paper, a strategy for raising the public awareness of the contribution of science, technology and engineering to national wealth and well-being. The stated aim of the government's policy on PUS is to draw more of the best young people into careers in science and engineering and to strengthen the effectiveness of the democratic process through better informed public debate of issues of public concern in science, engineering and technology.

In 1995 the Office of Science and Technology (OST) set up the Wolfendale Committee to review the contribution of research scientists and engineers to PUS. The reason they give for researchers to be involved in PUS is 'Scientists, engineers and research students in receipt of public funds have a duty to explain their work to the general public'. Scientists were also expected to have a sense of duty in the Bodmer (1985) report. 'Learn to communicate with the public, be willing to do so and consider it your duty to do so'.

Surveys of Royal Society Research Fellows (Evaluation Associates 1995) and a group of MRC scientists (Pearson 1996) show overwhelmingly that the vast majority of researchers do believe they have a role to play in PUS: 'They [the scientists] are the best people to inform the public as they are the ones involved'.

However, I do not believe we can convince researchers to take an active role in PUS if we ask them only to consider the benefits to society, or if their only role is to counter negative public attitudes to science. We need to look at the benefits to scientists themselves, to assess the hurdles they face in being involved in PUS, and to share good practice, as well as exploring what special contribution sharing research can make to the public understanding of science. To quote from Evaluation Associates (1995): 'For Research Fellows the main issue is balancing personal return against the collective return from public understanding of science for society as a whole'.

TAKING RESEARCH TO THE PUBLIC

Research science in a shopping centre: the Bristol survey

During set95, the National Week of Science, Engineering and Technology, the University of Bristol took out its medical, scientific and engineering research to a shopping centre in the middle of the city. The exhibition 'Scientific Power To the People' was visited by over 100,000 people in the two days, who were mainly shoppers who just stumbled across the event. Shortly after the exhibition, 167 staff and students were asked to give their reactions to being involved, why they took part, what they enjoyed and disliked and how they felt face to face with the public (Pearson *et al.* 1995). Seven months after the event they were also asked whether they had seen any further benefits from the event.

The reasons given for being involved with the exhibition included 'were told to by senior members of staff' (20 per cent), 'group decision to publicize their own research' (30 per cent) and 'public duty' (10 per cent). To quote one participant, 'I am irritated by those in the University who moan about the lack of public esteem for engineering but do nothing'. Surprisingly, after the event 94 per cent of the exhibitors said they would like to be involved again. Almost 50 per cent of participants wanted to repeat the experience simply because they enjoyed it. Those not wanting to be involved again had enjoyed the event but were deterred by the amount of time needed to prepare and attend.

So what benefits and difficulties had the exhibitors experienced?

Benefits

Many participants were genuinely surprised by the interest the public showed in their work; it gave them an added sense that what they were doing was worthwhile and exciting. By explaining their work, they got a better understanding of their field and its relevance. Their comments included:

> It made me see my research in a wider context and gave me confidence communicating with people.

It's good for morale to know that people are interested in what
I am doing.

It gave me a lot of encouragement in my work.

In social situations I am not normally allowed to talk about my
work.

Supervisors commented that the exhibition was an excellent communication skills training event and good for team-building, both
within individual departments and in the university as a whole.

The materials produced for the exhibition have been used at many
other events. For example, the Alzheimer's research group produced
a leaflet which has been used extensively with the public; without the
focus of the event these leaflets would not have been produced. The
group has also agreed to give a one-day workshop for the public on
Alzheimer's. The Atomic Force Microscopy group produced a video,
Flying through Atoms, which has been at public lectures and open days.
United Artists, who set up a World Wide Web link for the event,
worked with the university to repeat the exercise in the Exploratory
hands-on science centre.

The exhibition generated very good publicity for the university and
enabled useful contacts to be made. There was also a private showing
of the event for industrialists, politicians and postgraduates which
generated excellent public relations.

The human fertility group was able to advertise its services, the
Alzheimer's group recruited volunteers and new members to the
charity, the back pain group made contacts with local osteopaths and
an occupational health adviser. During the event a visitor brought to
the World Wide Web exhibit the first edition of the pages of the
British Library, so they were seen for the first time at the exhibition;
one sports science PhD student was able to recruit for her research
into women, exercise and self-esteem. Every morning in the week
before the event, the local radio station covered a different research
group; the scientists were impressed that in their twenty-minute
broadcast slot they were given time to explain their research. It was
more difficult to get serious television coverage; they tended not to
cover the science but did publicize the exhibition. After the event
groups were subsequently asked to give radio interviews and schools
talks.

The public were invited to help researchers collect data and at the
same time find out something about themselves. For example two
psychology PhD students were able to use visual perception tests with
a 'random public' as opposed to those who normally volunteered for
the tests or patients in hospital conditions. They were able to use data

from 45 people; the noisy environment of the shopping centre did not create ambient conditions, but the sample was large enough to have significance. Other examples included the Track Analysis group, who invited the public to take part in the Polonium-210 pilot study: 130 forms were completed and 65 of these returned the results of their experiments. The public were also invited to test their colour vision. A number of the public, 10 of the 14 who showed colour vision problems, volunteered to go at a later date to the hospital for further tests under controlled conditions.

Contact with the public also provided ideas for research. The back pain group chose to assess neck muscle activity, a much more manageable test than the one during set94 on the lower back, but one which is not normally done. The test assessed the best way to reduce neck muscle activity and reduce tension headaches, and has the potential to be a new area of research for the back pain group. The bat echo location group found out about bat colonies in the area, in fact they were told of one bat roost which turned out to house 80 Leisler's bats – a very rare breed and an important find. The Interface Analysis group was told about old aeroplanes stored locally and now the group has started conservation research on these engines.

Difficulties

The event was very tiring for participants, a great deal of time went into preparation and many exhibitors were at their stands for over twenty hours over the two days. The public can be very demanding: people even telephoned the Sports Centre after the event expecting personal fitness assessments. Others visiting the medical stands expected private consultations, which was not only tiresome but also raised issues of medical ethics. For example, the Alzheimer's group, in showing members of the public the memory tests they used, had to ensure against the distress that could be caused by impromptu self-diagnosis.

The broad medical issues associated with animal experimentation had also to be considered. For the first exhibition in 1994 it was decided that to ensure the safety of the exhibitors and the public, 'sensitive' displays would be excluded; the policy was extended to the 1995 and 1996 events. In general, researchers using animals have not come forward to exhibit because of fears for their own safety. One or two thought that the university should face the problem and be proactive in countering the anti-vivisection arguments.

Public liability is a worrying problem when putting on hands-on exhibitions that involve so many staff, students and members of the public. In 1995, one person threatened to sue the university for a mild shock received from a display on electrostatics. The matter was dealt with promptly: the university was well aware that this single incident had the potential to counter all the public goodwill that the event had created.

Despite the recognition that the exhibition gained nationally and at the university, some exhibitors felt unsupported by their departments and penalized for spending too much time on PUS. The activity was seen as an extra to their 'real' work.

Dealings with the media irritated one or two participants. The diamond film group had spent some time with a television crew only to have the piece cut when the crew discovered that diamond-coated sun-glasses were not available. However, this story did have a happy outcome. A year later the same television company followed up the team's progress and made a programme about diamond films which went out at the start of set96. This was the result of the efforts of one BBC journalist who made good contacts with researchers as a consequence of the exhibition.

There were a few security and crowd control problems but considering the amount of equipment on show and the potentially controversial nature of some of the exhibits, these were minimal. There were also surprisingly few criticisms from the participants about the arrangements or organization; this was because the event had a team of people providing practical support who solved the problems of electrical supply, access, insurance, security, funding, advertising, and so on.

The Bristol survey highlights two important factors for the development of PUS. First, the scientists and engineers were talking with the public about what they knew best – their research. They were not trying to teach basic science or put on some bang-whiz popularizing event. No doubt some of the exhibitors would have had the skills and enthusiasm to talk about other aspects of science but this would not have provided them with the direct feedback from the public about their research.

Second, the scientists and engineers interacted directly with the public and were able to dispel the 'male lab-coated boffin' stereotyped image of the researcher. All too often science is communicated without 'seeing the whites of the eyes' of the public. The lack of real contact with the public often leads to misconceptions about what interests and concerns the public. At the exhibition scientists and engineers found the public better informed and less confrontational than they had expected. In fact, contact with the public was the very reason why exhibitors enjoyed the event so much.

211

Adult continuing education classes

It is interesting to compare the experiences of those involved in taking science out to the public with the experiences of tutors who volunteer to teach to a public that pay to hear about research at adult education classes.

Generally in university continuing education programmes, the sciences, especially the physical sciences, are not well represented. However, when scientists are appointed by continuing education departments to run programmes they are able to demonstrate interest in adult classes in science and, in the UK, there are pockets of activity resulting in some 35,000 students attending classes each year (Pringle 1995). Even so it is difficult to find examples of classes which address research topics. This case study looks at the experiences of four physicists from the same physics department, who present research to the public.

'Certainly not for duty' was the comment from one physicist explaining why he has given evening classes since the mid-1960s. Each week he gives a different presentation on a new area of research in astronomy and the classes have a loyal following, attracting between forty and sixty members of the public. He chooses topics that genuinely stimulate him; he excludes material that does not interest him, even though he suspects it may grip the public: 'I must be enthusiastic about the topic to enjoy presenting it'. This opinion was reflected by the other tutors. 'It is great to teach the bits I enjoy, unlike with the undergraduate classes'. Some tutors said that their initial involvement in adult classes resulted from wanting to justify the expense of particle physics or that they believed that it is important to share science with the public. One tutor, whose lectures are in demand, even turns down invitations to give general lectures to scientific societies in preference to speaking to lay audiences. However, without doubt, what now sustains the motivation of these tutors is the interaction of the audience and the feedback; this is what they enjoyed the most.

They all commented that teaching lay audiences has benefited their undergraduate teaching; it generates new ideas and materials, allows them to try out new teaching methods, and helps them to find new ways of presenting difficult concepts. One tutor now offers to teach the more difficult areas of the undergraduate syllabus because he actually enjoys the challenge of communicating difficult ideas and has more confidence.

They do feel the need for their continuing education work to be recognized and valued and have noticed that in the Physics Department the attitude to PUS work has become more positive, particularly since 1994. At his staff appraisal in 1992, one of the tutors was told he was doing too much PUS work, that it was getting in the way of his research; since 1994 he has been praised for his PUS activities. The tutors sense that the rest of the department are relieved that someone is doing something about PUS and thus relieving them of the burden. 'I don't think they realize that I actually enjoy teaching adult classes' said one tutor.

There are still colleagues who privately criticize those tutors giving adult classes, comments include 'you are wasting your talents', 'your research should be more important than all this messing around' and 'you don't present proper science, you oversimplify things and leave out the detail'. Other difficulties that result from doing adult classes include the attention from tiresome members of the public and trying to satisfy such a diverse audience, from those with degrees in physics to those who have no science background.

All these tutors were encouraged and given practical support from the Continuing Education Department, without which none of these classes would have started. However, currently the sad reality is that such courses are under serious threat nationally, as government funding for traditional courses is being transferred to accredited courses. Many classes that offer 'tasters' of topics do not lend themselves to accreditation; tutors, inspired to teach the public because of love of their subject, are understandably reluctant to assess. Some university staff from the Science Faculty, who previously saw efforts to popularize science as positive, are now suspicious about the value of the credits now awarded.

However, despite these worries, the experience reported here shows what can be done. When enthusiastic tutors receive good support, are encouraged to do what interests them, and feel they are valued by the audience and their colleagues alike, programmes can flourish. The experiences and difficulties of this group were therefore similar to those at the Bristol exhibition.

SURVEYS OF RESEARCH SCIENTISTS' ATTITUDES TO, AND ACTIVITIES IN, PUS

MRC research scientists

The Medical Research Centre (MRC), like all other research councils, has stated a commitment to PUS in its mission statement. In collaboration with Gillian Pearson from the Oxford Trust, it surveyed the research scientists from the MRC Radiobiological Unit about their involvement in PUS activities (Pearson 1996). The survey was returned from 88 of the 136 scientists located at three units: Radiobiological Mechanisms, Genetics and Experimental Oncology.

A surprisingly high percentage of scientists (75 per cent) had already been involved in PUS; however, this was partly due to the strong work experience programme at the units. Other activities included careers conventions, open days, lectures to the public and schools, schools projects and media interviews.

Reasons for taking part in PUS and how the scientists benefited were similar to those given in the Bristol survey. The majority (53 per cent) had taken part because they felt obliged to, either they considered it to be part of their job or they had been asked to contribute. They felt they had benefited from being involved, they enjoyed the experience and it helped them put their work in perspective. The concern about the lack of recognition and credit, which had been raised in both the previous case studies, was also echoed by the MRC scientists (see Pearson 1996): 'research time is interrupted and when the unit is reviewed this will not be taken into account'.

This survey was particularly interesting because it asked those not involved in PUS (25 per cent) why they had not been involved and what might encourage them to be involved. There were a number who did not see any reason or benefits from being involved with PUS: one person saw 'his job to conduct research, to achieve something, not to act as a salesman to a concept'. However, the main reasons for not being involved were either not being asked to or that no opportunity had arisen. In response to what would encourage them to be involved in PUS, 50 per cent said simply being asked.

The activities involving scientists working directly with older schoolchildren and teacher/scientists schemes were thought to be most effective, again highlighting the need for scientists and engineers to interact directly with the public, or to quote one MRC scientist: 'direct dialogue in the appropriate environments is best – it is difficult to convey any understanding otherwise'. However, some, particularly those who worked in the animal experimentation field, were very nervous about any dealings with the public.

Royal Society Research Fellows

It is interesting to compare the MRC survey with a similar survey on the 250 Royal Society Research Fellows, of whom 168 returned the survey (see Evaluation Associates 1995). The Research Fellows are aged 26–37 years old and are not located in one institution. Over 50 per cent had taken part in PUS activities; interestingly more than half of this group had initiated the science activities themselves. This may be because the Fellows are encouraged to be involved in PUS by the

Royal Society, for example they are required to mention PUS activities in their reports. The main activities that Fellows were involved in were lectures to schools and societies and radio interviews; not unexpectedly, work experience and school projects did not feature, as the Fellows would not have the infrastructure to organize them. Again the benefits were similar to those found in the MRC and Bristol surveys: satisfaction, improved communication skills, and increased interest and insight into their own work. Half of those involved in activities had not experienced any difficulties, while others found it difficult to interact with the media either having problems getting interest in their story or with the accuracy of reporting. Others found it difficult to describe scientific concepts and were uncertain they were getting their message across. As with the MRC scientists, those involved in animal experimentation were worried about jeopardizing their physical safety. The Fellows needed help in PUS with organizational support, publicity, media contacts and funding.

Of those who had not taken part in PUS 21 per cent said it was due to lack of opportunity while 59 per cent cited lack of time and 7 per cent quoted career pressures.

> Time is extremely short . . . the priority has to be advancing one's own research wherever possible.

> At present, the [university system] does not in practice recognize public understanding of science activities. In order to get grants, jobs, research fellowships, one must have papers to show, maybe teaching experiences. Public understanding of science activities don't count.

TAKING RESEARCH AND RESEARCHERS INTO SCHOOLS

Why take research into schools?

Morris Shamos (1995) suggests that while many students perform well in school science, this does not guarantee that they will become scientifically literate adults. Few people retain much of the information they learnt in school science lessons. He suggests a programme to improve scientific awareness which, as a minimum, would make it clear what science is and how it is practised.

Perhaps the best way to show 'how it is practised' is to engage people in scientific research projects. Brian Woolnough's (1994) studies on effective science teaching in schools have revealed the importance of student research projects.

I wish to stress the holistic nature of the scientific enterprise, in contrast to the reductionist approach in which learning becomes simply the acquisition of a number of scientific facts, principles, theories and skills – each of which when set into its natural context of scientific activity is important but which, when separated and isolated from it, becomes sterile.

(Woolnough 1994)

Effective science teaching needs to integrate all of those attributes, and one of the most genuinely scientific ways of doing this is through student research projects. Woolnough quotes from John Ziman (1992) and comments that no wonder students involved in such an activity find it highly motivating.

Real scientific research is very much like play. It is unguided, personal activity, perfectly serious for those taking part, drawing unsuspected imaginative forces from the inner being, and deeply satisfying.

Since the 1980s there has been an increase in the number of schemes designed to bring research into schools, and recognizing that many teachers themselves have not had experience of research, all of the schemes actively involve research scientists and engineers. However, currently the schemes have generally not monitored the reactions or benefits to the scientists involved, much of the feedback is anecdotal.

Scientific research in schools

Knowing science from within, 'owning science', is very different from knowing it from afar, from outside, from textbooks. It is also something different again from the hierarchically structured view of exploring and investigating science.

(Albone et al. 1995)

'Science for Real' is the motto behind the Scientific Research in Schools Scheme co-ordinated by the Clifton Scientific Trust. Projects involve schoolchildren actually researching, working with scientists (in some schools with 'Scientists in Residence'). A comprehensive report (Albone et al. 1995) outlines the various studies, ranging from exercise tolerance in adolescent schoolgirls to cadmium sulphide–cadmium telluride solar cells. Many of these studies currently take place outside the formal curriculum, and some of the projects use specialized equipment so the number of children involved is also restricted. However, the projects do benefit the teachers by updating their scientific knowledge and broadening their experience, so the projects can have a wider impact on the school community.

From the report there is no doubt that the experience of research is very beneficial to the pupils; it gives real value to the students' own ideas and creativity, they are inspired by solving real problems and are greatly motivated by having their ideas taken seriously. Often their work is reported at conferences which increases their confidence and opens their minds to much wider horizons. They also work in a team, each student valued for their own particular contribution.

It is interesting to reflect that the MRC survey revealed that of the range of PUS activities scientists were engaged in, student project work was considered the most rewarding. So what do the research projects offer scientists? They provide contacts with lively young minds un-hampered by preconceived ideas and able to approach problems from new angles and there are plenty of examples to show this. In one project a school was approached by a scientist, Dr Stenner, to help him sample the seaweed *Fucus serratus* from along the Welsh coastline to look at heavy metal pollution. The work of these students is due to be published in the *Marine Pollution Bulletin*. Meanwhile the work has been displayed at Cardiff University and an article is in preparation for *Education in Chemistry*. Professor Besant, who researches on computer-aided surgery on the spinal column, invited pupils to his department and explained the problems he faced in developing the robotic system. The pupil team was invited to suggest and develop ideas for the design. Professor Besant was impressed by the progress the students had made and was particularly interested in a non-contact guidance system one pupil suggested. When the director of Long Ashton Research Station approached a school to develop links with secondary education he was not expecting the liaison to result in research projects spanning five years which resulted in several discoveries. The scientists also benefit as they make contacts with teachers who have valuable experience in communicating science and they make the work of their institution better known and understood.

However, anyone who has carried out research knows that it is often unfruitful and a hard slog. This aspect of research, and the effect it has on teachers and pupils, is not addressed in the report except in one of the projects where it was stated: 'not all of the pupils enjoyed every aspect of the project, some found the pace of Research a little slow and one boy decided he had experienced enough after one week and went home early'. The report gives an optimistic view and considering the difficulties of time, resources and expertise in schools, it is actually surprising that so much has been achieved. The success is undoubtedly due to enthusiastic teachers working with willing scientists and pupils.

I believe that the real strength of those projects has been to bring the idea of 'research in schools' to the attention of educationalists, the research councils and the government. As a result new schemes have been initiated. Two schemes are outlined below; they do not necessarily aim to take research into schools but they are important to mention because they take researchers into schools and it is interesting to see the range of activities the researchers get involved with and what other role they can play.

Teacher Scientist Network

In 1994 the Teacher Scientist Network (TSN) was started in Norfolk, funded by the Gatsby Charitable Foundation. It copied a scheme first adopted in San Francisco in 1987 which brought teachers and scientists together. The core activity of the network is contact and communication between partnered pairs of scientists and teachers (see e.g. *TSNews* 1996). There is no set agenda: once the partnership is made after a 'blind date', the teachers and scientists negotiate the best ways of working together.

The scheme was set up to aid schools by bringing fresh up-to-date information and other resources, providing teachers with a contact for science advice, producing new investigations and materials and providing teachers with chances to work in professional laboratories. However, Bruce Alberts, President of the National Academy, said of the original US scheme that it is not all one-sided; scientists profit as well: 'I had no idea how much the scientists would learn from these teachers about effective teaching methods'.

Sixty partnerships have been set up and the amount of contact varies from occasional advice on the telephone to planning taste perception experiments with 6 year olds and explaining new experiments on DNA cloning to A Level students. The UK co-ordinator, Frank Chennell, has found that the scientists enjoy explaining their work to children; it helps them think carefully about what their work entails and why they are doing it; it is also rewarding and refreshing for them to see so much interest in science. At the end of the first year half the scientists involved answered a survey which showed that 70 per cent of them felt that the partnership had met their expectations, 70 per cent wanted to continue with the same partner, 20 per cent wanted to try a different partner and 1 per cent wanted to leave the scheme. The scheme has shown that careful matching of the partners is crucial.

One case from the USA clearly illustrated that enthusiasm from the scientists is not sufficient for things to succeed.

> We [scientists] may know about science, but most of us have precious little idea of how to teach it to young children or even high school students. The major San Francisco earthquake occurred during the first months of a science education program

218

for elementary schools initiated by the Carnegie Institution; it was easy to recruit a very eager young scientist from a Carnegie department to talk to the children about earthquakes. But it didn't work. With no training in how to talk to children the young scientist lost his audience within a minute, despite his obvious enthusiasm. The director of the program came to the rescue; in another minute we knew that some of the children who were immigrants from Central America had themselves memories of earthquakes. From their descriptions and after a few well-chosen questions, the children were considering what goes on under the surface of the planet. By the end of the hour they were comfortable with a rather sophisticated view of the structure of the Earth.

This does raise the question of training scientists before they communicate with the public. Currently communication skills training is piecemeal and despite the recommendation in the government White Paper *Realising Our Potential* (OST 1993), for communication skills to be part of postgraduate training this has not been made available. One strategy for disseminating good practice is explored in the next section.

Researchers in residence

The Pupil Research Initiative is a science curriculum development project aimed at 14–16 year olds funded by Engineering and Physical Sciences Research Council (EPSRC) and Particle Physics and Astronomy Research Council (PPARC); the project is based at Sheffield Hallam University (see Brodie and Hudson 1995).

A very important aspect of the project is the active involvement of up to a thousand EPSRC and PPARC research students, working in schools alongside teachers to assist in the development of youngsters' research, investigation and practical skills. It aims to provide research students with opportunities to pass on their interest and enthusiasm for science and engineering to young people, develop their communication skills and gain experience of the work of schools. Unlike the previous Scientific Research in Schools projects which often rely on the interest and enthusiasm of teachers to get projects started, this project particularly aims to involve schools with no record of research work, extracurricular science projects or clubs. It is similar to the TSN scheme in that the researcher and teachers form a partnership and negotiate the most effective way of working together, either within the curriculum or in extracurricular activities. It might be surprising that the young researchers were given such a wide brief but the pilot study revealed that this flexibility allowed some good ideas and ways of working to emerge.

The pilot study was carried out between December 1994 and April 1995 with twenty EPSRC and PPARC students. The researchers were placed in school for six half-days; in addition the researchers were given a half-day training with a further half-day for evaluation. The training includes advice on communication skills, though the re-searchers thought they also needed up-to-date information about life in schools. It was found that formal talks about their research generally did not work well, the most successful placements were where researchers used their expertise to help pupils with their investigations, that is with emphasis on the research process rather than the particular area of research. They also were good role models and one school was particularly pleased with the positive response of the girls to the female engineering researcher. Other ways in which the researchers were used was to give demonstrations, work with small groups on projects, give careers advice, create links with their research departments, help with school fairs, help students present work at conferences and support field work. All the researchers enjoyed the experience and want to repeat it and felt they had gained in confidence. The reason that researchers gave for being involved included: to improve their communication skills and confidence, to learn about science education today, to take a step back from research, to add the experience to their cv and for the, albeit small, financial reward (the students were paid at demonstrator rates).

The pilot was also considered to be a success for the schools. One particularly satisfying example was a school which had no history of research projects. After pupils from the school had been invited to a conference on school science projects, chaired by a researcher, they 'demanded' to present at the next conference. Enthused, their teacher received a bursary to go to Bradford University; he worked with a group on robotic telescopes and from this developed curriculum materials at Sheffield Hallam University. Since then he has organized a residential weekend to 'study the stars' with a group of pupils and two researchers. The results of this weekend were then displayed at a school fair.

ENCOURAGING RESEARCHERS TO BE INVOLVED WITH PUS

Carrots and sticks

Research scientists and engineers can, and are, making a contribution to PUS. As practitioners they can bring the process of science alive and share science as a human endeavour involving imagination. Their contribution is crucial if the image the public has of scientists is to be better informed and more balanced. There are, and have been, many scientists who have added colour to the drab stereotypical scientist image. People like Richard Feynmann, Carl Sagan and Richard Gregory not only have been excellent communicators but also, perhaps not uncoincidentally, are among our best scientists. They infect others with their enthusiasm to explore. Brian Woolnough (1994) in his studies of effective science teaching states that many scientists, recollecting the influential events that led to their liking for, and commitment to, science will point to one or two events that stimulated their imagination: meeting a real scientist, perhaps attending a spectacular lecture demonstration or being shown the wonders of the stars, the fossils in a quarry, or the life in a rock pool.

Examples of good practice (discussed in this chapter), have shown that researchers communicate best when they work with topics they enjoy and feel most comfortable with, that is their own research or the process of research. It is often projects which allow dialogue with the public or schoolchildren that are the most rewarding, as these provide immediate feedback, interest and appreciation from the audience. It is also interesting to note the success of schemes like 'researchers in residence', which allow negotiation and dialogue not only to decide the best 'use' of the scientists but also to match the needs of the audience with the interests of the scientist. But we must not be restricted by what has already been done. Since the mid-1980s there have been some new and exciting schemes for PUS, including 'science shops' (see Irwin 1995) which make the technical expertise of local universities available to the public or Consensus Forums (see Joss and Durant 1995) which elicit the opinion of the public about science issues and ethics.

Enthusiasm and the desire to communicate with the public does not guarantee success. A badly presented lecture will turn off an audience, and similarly a researcher who works hard to prepare for a PUS activity to find no audience, or a school unprepared for the visit, will be discouraged. Support and training are crucial.

The constraint of time limiting the involvement of scientists in PUS is a major issue which can be resolved only by allocating a greater priority to PUS. In the evaluation of the contribution of Research Fellows to PUS (Evaluation Associates 1995) it was suggested that participation could be encouraged by

- ensuring that time is available for activities
- according status to Research Fellows who participate
- rewarding participants through the appraisal and promotion system.

221

These sentiments were echoed by the Wolfendale Committee which was set up in 1995 to 'review the steps currently being taken to equip and encourage professional scientists, engineers and research students to contribute to improved public understanding of science, engineering and technology, and to suggest how these might be improved consistent with available funding.'

The committee recommended that:

1 Universities should increase the emphasis on the acquisition of communication skills and their use for the benefit of the public.
2 Increased responsibility should bring with it increased recognition for both individuals and institution.
3 Universities should develop cost-effective ways of measuring performance in public understanding.
4 Research councils should develop further their grant procedure to make PUS an integral feature.
5 The OST should produce a 'best practice' guide.

The committee recognized that not all scientists and engineers are equally skilled at communicating to a wider public but thought that extreme cases of inability to communicate are likely to be few. It advocated training in communication skills not only for postgraduates, as recommended in the 1993 government White Paper, but also for undergraduates. In the survey of MRC scientists 62 per cent said training would help them with PUS work, this figure was much lower (less than 30 per cent) when the same question was asked of those involved with the Bristol exhibition. However, this may be because the exhibition was in itself a good training exercise. So the quality and appropriateness of the training will need to be addressed.

The committee suggested that the Higher Education Funding Councils (HEFCs) should play a part in the assessment of university departments' work in the field of public understanding. It saw a need to link public understanding with research effort and suggested that the groups responsible for 'Research Assessment' should have a role in measuring the effectiveness of public understanding work.

Although many applaud the recommendations of the Wolfendale (1995) report, their enactment certainly requires commitments from a wide range of autonomous institutions. Key questions remain. Can the recommendations be brought into effect without earmarked funding? Where are the new sources of funding? Who will use the 'Best Practice Guide' and how will the extra activity it hopes to generate be resourced? As always, resources are a critical factor; if involvement in PUS activities increases, more and more people will be bidding for the small sums of money currently available. Diverting money from existing university teaching budgets will be difficult in these cash-strapped times.

PUS must become a mainstream activity, involving the majority of the scientific community. One way to realize the ambitions of the Wolfendale report would be to create Science and Engineering Communication Units. These units would be responsible for training all medical, engineering and science postgraduates in communication skills and report writing – presenting their work to other scientists. The units would also give further training in presenting science to the public and provide practical experience by staging events and capitalizing on links with local radio and television. Science and Engineering Communication Units would encourage an interdisciplinary approach to PUS, evaluate PUS events, disseminate good practice and provide good organizational support. It is envisaged that the units would be set up within universities and staffed mainly by seconded researchers from science and engineering departments.

The research councils currently have a commitment to PUS. Welcome as this stance is, there is as yet no overall coherent joint policy. Research councils could provide funding for Science and Engineering Communication Units directly to the universities in proportion to the number of research students and the amount of research council funding.

Providing the resource and infrastructure to promote PUS is a necessary step but more is needed. Above all scientists need to be convinced of the merits of communicating with the public. The best way to be convinced is by doing:

> When I have to prepare for a lecture to the general public, I drop the professional attitude and try to use fascination as my starting point. . . . By working in a popular vein, I think you get a broader perspective on your own research line – what is interesting? Really I think all research would improve if people tried to popularize it.
> (Professor Bengt Gustafasson – awarded the 1989 N. G. Rosen Prize for achievements in popular science)

REFERENCES

Agricultural and Food Research Council (AFRC) (1992) *Recent Advances in Plant and Microbial Biotechnology,* Swindon: AFRC.

Aikenhead, G.S. (1986) 'The content of STS education', *STS Research Network Missive* 1(3): 18–23.

Aikenhead, G.S. (1991) *Logical Reasoning in Science and Technology,* Toronto, Ontario: John Wiley.

Albone, E., Collins, N. and Hill, T. (1995) *Scientific Research in Schools: A Compendium of Practical Experience,* Bristol: Clifton Scientific Trust.

Allaby, M. (1995) *Facing the Future: The Case for Science,* London: Bloomsbury.

American Association for the Advancement of Science (AAAS) (1967) *Science: A Process Approach,* Washington, DC: AAAS.

AAAS (1993) *Benchmarks for Science Literacy: Project 2061,* New York: Oxford University Press.

Andersson, B. (1990) 'Pupils' conceptions of matter and its transformation (age 12–16)', *Studies in Science Education* 18: 53–8.

Appleyard, B. (1992) *Understanding the Present: Science and the Soul of Modern Man,* London: Picador.

Araos, A.C. (1995) 'Environmental education in Victorian Secondary Schools: constraints and possibilities', Master of Environmental Science thesis, Monash University, Clayton, Victoria, Australia.

Archenhold, F. (ed.) (1988) *Assessment of Performance Unit: Science at Age 15, A Review of APU Survey Findings 1980–84,* London: HMSO.

Armstrong, H.E. (1903) *The Teaching of Scientific Method and Other Papers on Education,* London: Macmillan.

Atkins, P. (1992) 'Will science ever fail?' *New Scientist,* 8 August: 32.

Atkins, P. (1995) 'The limitless power of science', in J. Cornwell (ed.) *Nature's Imagination,* Oxford: Oxford University Press.

Atkinson, P. and Delamont, S. (1977) 'Mock-ups and cock-ups: the stage management of guided discovery instruction', in P. Woods and M. Hammersley (eds) *School Experience: Explorations in the Sociology of Education,* London: Croom Helm.

Ayer, A.J. (1936) *Language, Truth and Logic,* London: Victor Gollancz.

Bader, R. (1993) 'Science and Culture in Germany: Is There a Case?', in J. Durant and J. Gregory (eds) *Science and Culture in Europe,* London: Science Museum.

Baez, A.V. (1980) 'Curiosity, creativity, competence and compassion: guidelines for science education in the year 2000', in C. McFadden (ed.) *World Trends in Science Education,* Nova Scotia: Atlantic Institute of Education.

Baggott, J. (1995) 'Too much phun can be bad for you', *New Scientist* 1970 (25 March): 47.

224

Baird, J.R., Fensham, P.J., Gunstone, R.F. and White, R.T. (1991) 'The importance of reflection in improving science teaching and learning', *Journal of Research in Science Teaching* 28(2): 163–82.

Bartle, I. (1991) *Herbicide-Tolerant Plants: Weed Control with the Environment in Mind*, Haslemere, Surrey: ICI Seeds (now Zeneca).

Barzun, J. (1994) 'Psychotherapy Awry', letter, *American Scholar* 63: 479.

Bauer, H.H. (1986a) *The Enigma of Loch Ness: Making Sense of a Mystery*, Urbana, IL: University of Illinois Press.

Bauer, H.H. (1986b) 'The literature of fringe science', *Sceptical Inquirer* 11(2): 205–10.

Bauer, H.H. (1988) *To Rise Above Principle: The Memoirs of an Unreconstructed Dean*, Urbana, IL: University of Illinois Press.

Bauer, H.H. (1990a) 'A dialectical discussion on the nature of disciplines and disciplinarity', *Social Epistemology* 4: 215–27.

Bauer, H.H. (1990b) 'Barriers against interdisciplinarity: implications for studies of science, technology and society (STS)', *Science, Technology and Human Values* 15: 105–19.

Bauer, H.H. (1992) *Scientific Literacy and the Myth of the Scientific Method*, Urbana, IL: University of Illinois Press.

Bauer, H.H. (1995) 'Two kinds of knowledge: maps and stores', *Journal of Scientific Exploration* 9: 257–75.

Bauer, M. (1995) 'Industrial and post-industrial Public Understanding of Science', paper presented at the International Conference on Public Understanding of Science, Chinese Association for Science and Technology (CAST), Beijing, October.

BBC (1995) *The Future of Radio: BBC Digital Audio Broadcasting*, Available from Broadcasting House, London, W1A 1AA.

Bernal, M. (1988) *Black Athena: The Afroasiatic Roots of Classical Civilization*, London: Free Association Books.

Berry, D.C. and Dienes, Z. (1993) *Implicit Learning: Theoretical and Empirical Issues*, Hove: Lawrence Erlbaum.

Bingle, W.H. and Gaskell, P.J. (1994) 'Scientific literacy for decision making and the social construction of scientific knowledge', *Science Education* 78(2): 185–201.

Biotechnology and Biological Sciences Research Council (BBSRC) (1994) *Biotechnology and You*, Swindon: BBSRC.

BBSRC (1995) *Microbial Friends and Allies*, Swindon: BBSRC.

Biotechnology Working Group (BWG) (1990) *Biotechnology's Bitter Harvest: Herbicide-Tolerant Crops and the Threat to Sustainable Agriculture*, Biotechnology Working Group, Environmental Defense Fund, 257 Park Avenue South, New York, NY10010.

Blades, D.W. (1994) 'Procedures of power and possibilities for change in science education curriculum discourse', Doctor of Philosophy thesis, University of Alberta, Edmonton, Alberta.

Blakemore, C. (1990) 'Who cares about science?', *Science and Public Affairs* 4: 97–119.

Bodmer, W. (1985) *The Public Understanding of Science: Report of an* ad hoc *Group endorsed by the Council of the Royal Society*, London: Royal Society.

Bourdieu, P. and Passeron, J. (1973) *Reproduction in Education, Society and Culture*, London: Sage.

Brickhouse, N.W. (1989) 'The teaching of the philosophy of science in secondary classrooms: case studies of teachers' personal theories', *International Journal of Science Education* 11(4): 437–49.

Brickhouse, N.W., Stanley, W.B. and Whitson, J.A. (1993) 'Practical reasoning and science education: implications for theory and practice', *Science and Education* 2: 363–75.

British Association for the Advancement of Science (BAAS) (1868) *The Best Means of Promoting Scientific Education in Schools*, Report of the Dundee Meeting 1867, London: Murray.

Brodie, M. and Hudson, T. (1995) 'Pupil research initiative', *Education in Science* November.

Bruner, J.S., Jolly, A. and Sylva, K. (1976) *Play: Its Role in Development and Evolution*, Harmondsworth: Penguin.

Brush, S. (1978) *The Temperature of History: Phases of Science and Culture in the Nineteenth Century*, New York: Burt Franklin.

Brush, S. (1988) *The History of Modern Science: A Guide to the Second Scientific Revolution, 1800–1950*, Iowa City: Iowa State University Press.

Bucat, R. and Cole, A. (1988) 'The Australian Academy of Science school chemistry project', *Journal of Chemical Education* 65(9): 777–9.

Burnham, J. (1987) *How Superstition Won and Science Lost*, New Brunswick, NJ: Rutgers University Press.

Calder, J. (1991) 'Biotechnology at the Forefront of Agriculture', in J.F. Macdonald (ed.) *Agricultural Biotechnology at the Crossroads*, Ithaca, NY: NABC.

Casti, J. (1992) *Science without Tears*, Third National Power and Open University on the Public Understanding of Science, Occasional Paper no. 4, Open University, Milton Keynes.

Chan, A. (1993) 'Science teachers and Science-Technology-Society (STS),' Doctor of Philosophy thesis, Monash University, Clayton, Victoria, Australia.

Chapman, B. (1991) 'The overselling of science education in the eighties', *School Science Review* 72(260): 47–64.

Claxton, G.L. (1990) *Teaching to Learn: A Direction for Education*, London: Cassell.

Claxton, G.L. (1991) *Educating the Enquiring Mind: The Challenge for School Science*, Hemel Hempstead: Harvester/Wheatsheaf.

Claxton, G.L. (1994) 'The next challenge for education', *Teacher's Post* autumn: 8.

Claxton, G.L. (1996a) 'Implicit theories of learning', in G.L. Claxton, T. Atkinson, M. Osborn and M. Wallace (eds) *Liberating the Learner: Lessons for Professional Development in Education*, London: Routledge.

Claxton, G.L. (1996b) 'A SMER campaign: combatting creeping contructivism', review of M.R. Matthews (1995) *Challenging NZ Science Education*, Palmerston North, New Zealand: Dunmore Press.

Clayton, A., Hancock-Beaulieu, M. and Meadows, J. (1993) 'Change and continuity in the reporting of science and technology: a study of the *Times* and the *Guardian*', *Public Understanding of Science* 2: 225–34.

Close, F. (1990) *Too Hot to Handle*, London: W. H. Allen.

Cohen, B. (1980) *The Birth of the New Physics*, Westport, CT: Greenwood (Harmondsworth: Penguin 1985).

Coles, M. (1989) *Active Science*, London: Collins Educational.

Collingridge, D. and Reeve, C. (1986) *Science Speaks to Power: The Role of Experts in Policy Making*, London: Frances Pinter.

Collins, H.M. and Pinch, T. (1993) *The Golem: What Everyone Should Know about Science*, Cambridge: Cambridge University Press.

Collins, H.M. and Shapin, S. (1986) 'Uncovering the nature of science', *Times Higher Education Supplement* 27 July, 1984 13, reprinted in J. Brown, A. Cooper, T. Horton, F. Toates and D. Zeldin (eds) *Science in Schools*, Milton Keynes: Open University Press.

Connell, R.W., Ashenden, D.J., Kessler, S. and Dowsett, G.W. (1982) *Making the Difference: Schools, Families and Social Divisions*, Sydney: Allen & Unwin.

Cornwell, J. (1995) *Nature's Imagination: The Frontiers of Scientific Vision*, Oxford: Oxford University Press.

Cosgrove, M. (1995) 'A study of science-in-the-making as students generate an analogy for electricity', *International Journal of Science Education* 17(3): 295–310.

Cresson, E. (1996) 'Adapt to survive in formidable form', *Times Higher Education Supplement* 23 February: 11.

Dart, E. (1988) *Development of Biotechnology in a Large Company,* London: ICI External Relations Department (now Zeneca).

Davis, P. J. and Hersh, R. (1980) *The Mathematical Experience,* Brighton: Harvester.

Dawkins, R. (1995) *River Out of Eden,* Weidenfeld & Nicolson.

Dearing, R. (1996) *Review of Qualifications for 16–19 year olds,* School Curriculum and Assessment Authority, London: HMSO.

Delamont, S. (1990) 'A paradigm shift in research on science education?', *Studies in Science Education* 18: 153–8.

Department for Education (DfE) (1994) *Science and Maths: A Consultation Paper on the Supply and Demand of Newly Qualified Young People,* London: DfE.

Department of Education and Science (DES) (1985) *Science 5–16: A Statement of Policy,* London: HMSO.

Department of National Heritage (1993) *National Museums and Galleries: Quality of Service to the Public,* London, HMSO.

Department of Trade and Industry/Laboratory of the Government Chemist (DTI/LGC) (1991) *Biotechnology: A Plain Man's Guide,* Laboratory of the Government Chemist, Queens Road, Teddington, Middx,TW11 OLY.

De Solla Price, D. (1986) *Little Science, Big Science . . . and Beyond,* New York: Columbia University Press.

Dewey, J. (1946) *Problems of Man,* New York: Philosophical Library.

Di Sessa, A.A. (1982) 'Unlearning Aristotelian physics: a study of knowledge-based learning', *Cognitive Science* 6: 37–75.

Doble, J. and Johnson, J. (1990) *Science and the Public: A Report in Three Volumes,* New York: Public Agenda Foundation.

Donaldson, M. (1978) *Children's Minds,* Glasgow: Fontana Collins.

Donnelly, J. (1994) 'Policy and curricular change: modelling science in the National Curriculum for England and Wales', *Studies in Science Education* 24: 100–28.

Doray, B. (1988) *From Taylorism to Fordism; A Rational Madness,* tr. David Macey, London: Free Association Books.

Driver, R., Guesne, E. and Tiberghien, A. (1985) *Children's Ideas in Science,* Oxford: Oxford University Press.

Driver, R., Squires, A., Rushworth, P. and Wood-Robinson, V. (1994) *Making Sense of Secondary Science. Research into Children's Ideas,* London: Routledge.

Driver, R., Leach, J., Millar, R. and Scott, P. (1996) *Young People's Images of Science,* Buckingham: Open University Press.

Dulskie, R.E., and Raven, R. (1995) 'Attitudes towards nuclear energy: one potential path for achieving scientific literacy', *Science Education* 79(2): 167–87.

Durant, J. (1996) 'Red faces, white coats, blue funk', *Times Higher Education Supplement* 5 April: 14–15.

Durant, J., Evans, G. and Thomas, G. (1989) 'The Public Understanding of Science', *Nature* 340: 11–14.

Durkheim, E. (1977) *The Evolution of European Thought,* London: Routledge

Duster, T. (1990) *Backdoor to Eugenics,* New York: Routledge.

Eijkelhof, H. and Kortland, K. (1988) 'Broadening the aims of physics education', in P.J. Fensham (ed.) *Developments and Dilemmas in Science Education,* London: Falmer.

European Federation of Biotechnology (EFB) (1994) 'Biotechnology in Foods and

Drinks', briefing paper 2, EFB Task Group on Public Perceptions of Biotechnology, London: Science Museum.

Evaluation Associates (1995) *An Evaluation of the SET95: The Second National Week of Science, Engineering and Technology,* privately published document.

Evans, G. and Durant, J. (1995) 'The relationship between knowledge and attitudes in the Public Understanding of Science in Britain', *Public Understanding of Science* 4(1): 57–74.

Fawns, R.A. (1987) 'The maintenance and transformation of school science', Doctor of Philosophy thesis, Monash University, Clayton, Victoria, Australia.

Fensham, P.J. (1973) 'Reflections on the social content of science education materials', *Science Education Research* 3: 143–50.

Fensham, P.J. (1980) 'Constraint and autonomy in Australian Secondary Education', *Journal of Curriculum Studies* 12(3): 189–206.

Fensham, P.J. (1985) 'Science for all: a reflective essay', *Journal of Curriculum Studies* 17: 415–35.

Fensham, P.J. (1986) 'Lessons from science education in Thailand', *Research in Science Education* 16: 92–100.

Fensham, P.J. (1995a) 'Curriculum emphases in conflict in science education', in D. Roberts and L. Ostman (eds) *The Multiple Meanings of a School Subject: Essays on Science and the School Curriculum,* New York: Teachers' College Press, Columbia University.

Fensham, P.J. (1995b) 'One step forward . . .', *Australian Science Teachers Journal.*

Fensham, P.J. and Corrigan, D. (1994) 'The implementation of an STS chemistry course in Australia: a research perspective', in J. Solomon and G. Aikenhead (eds) *STS Education: International Perspectives on Reform,* New York: Teachers' College Press, Columbia University.

Fensham, P.J. and May, J.B. (1979) 'Servant not master: a new role for science in a core of envirionmental education', *Australian Science Teachers' Journal* 25(2): 15–24.

Fensham, P.J., Gunstone, R.F. and White, R.T. (1994) *The Content of Science: A Constructivist Approach to its Teaching and Learning,* London: Falmer.

Flax, J. (1993) *Disputed Subjects: Essays on Psychoanalysis, Politics and Philosophy,* New York and London: Routledge.

Ford, H. (1923) *My Life and Work,* London: Heinemann.

Fox Keller, E. (1983) *A Feeling for the Organism: The Life and Work of Barbara McClintock,* San Francisco: W.H. Freeman.

Franklin, A. (1986) *The Neglect of Experiment,* Cambridge: Cambridge University Press

Geertz, C. (1977) *The Interpretation of Cultures,* New York: Basic Books.

Geertz, C. (1993) *Local Knowledge,* London: Fontana.

Gibbons, M., Limoges, C., Novotny, H. and Swartzman, S. (1994) *The New Production of Knowledge: The Dynamics of Science and Research in Contemporary Societies,* London: Sage.

Giere, R.N. (1991) *Understanding Scientific Reasoning,* 3rd edn, Fort Worth, TX: Holt, Rinehart & Winston.

Gillespie, R. (1976) 'Chemistry – Fact or fiction? Some reflections on the teaching of chemistry', *Chemistry Canada* 28(11): 23–8.

Goodman, D. and Redclift, M. (1991) *Refashioning Nature: Food, Ecology and Culture,* London: Routledge.

Görlitz, D. and Wohlwill, J.F. (eds) (1987) *Curiosity, Imagination: On the Development of Spontaneous Cognitive and Motivational Processes,* London: Erlbaum.

Gregory, R.L. (1983) 'The Bristol Exploratory: a feeling for science', *New Scientist* 100: 484–9.

Gregory, R.L. (1988) 'First-hand science: the exploratory in Bristol', *Science and Public Affairs* 3: 13–24.

Gregory, R.L. (1989) 'Turning minds on to science by hands-on exploration: the nature and potential of the hands-on medium', *Sharing Science*, London: Nuffield Foundation.

Gregory, R.L. (1993) 'Exploring Science Hands-on', *Science and Public Affairs* Spring: 34–7.

Grint, K. and Woolgar, S. (1995) 'On some failures of nerve in constructivist and feminist analyses of technology', *Science, Technology and Human Values* 20(3): 286–310.

Gross, P. and Levitt, N. (1995) *Higher Superstition: The Academic Left and its Quarrels with Science*, Baltimore, MD: Johns Hopkins University Press.

Hacking, I. (1992) 'Statistical language, statistical truth and statistical reason: the self identification of a state of scientific reasoning', in E. McMullin (ed.) *The Social Dimensions of Science*, Notre Dame, IN: University of Notre Dame Press.

Hansen, A. (1994) 'Journalistic practices and science reporting in the British press', *Public Understanding of Science* 3: 111–34.

Hansen, M. (1990) *Biotechnology and Milk: Benefit or Threat?*, Mount Vernon, NY: Consumer Policy Institute.

Haraway, D. (1985) 'A manifesto for cyborgs: science, technology and socialist feminism in the 1980s', *Socialist Review* 80: 65–107.

Haraway, D. (1989) *Primate Visions: Gender, Race and Nature in the World of Modern Science*, New York: Routledge.

Harding, J.M. (1983) *Switched-off: The Science Education of Girls*, London: Longman (for The Schools Council).

Harding, J.M. and Donaldson, J. (1986) 'Chemistry from issues', *School Science Review* 68(242): 49–59.

Harding, S. (1986) *The Science Question in Feminism*, Ithaca, NY: Cornell University Press.

Harding, S. (1991) *Whose Science? Whose Knowledge?: Thinking from Women's Lives*, Milton Keynes: Open University Press.

Harré, R. (1986) *Varieties of Realism*, Oxford: Blackwell.

Hart, C. (1995) 'Access and the quality of learning: the story of a curriculum document for school physics', Doctor of Philosophy thesis, Monash University, Clayton, Victoria, Australia.

Hawking, S. (1988) *A Brief History of Time*, London: Transworld Bantam.

Hein, H. (1987) 'The museum as teacher of theory: a case study of the Exploratorium Vision Section', *Museum Studies Journal* 2(4): 30–9.

Heisenberg, W. (1971) *Physics and Beyond*, London: Allen & Unwin.

Hobbelink, H. (1991) *Biotechnology and the Future of World Agriculture*, London: Zed.

Hodgkin, R.A. (1985) *Playing and Exploring*, New York: Methuen.

Hodson, D. (1988) 'Towards a philosophically more valid science education', *Science Education* 72(1): 19–40.

Holton, G. (1993) *Science and Anti-Science*, Cambridge, MA: Harvard University Press.

House of Commons (1995a) *Human Genetics: The Science and its Consequences*, House of Commons Science and Technology Select Committee, London: HMSO.

House of Commons (1995b) *Science and Technology in Schools*, vol 1, House of Commons Education Select Committee, Fourth Report, London: HMSO.

Howe, M.J.A. (1988) 'Intelligence as an explanation', *British Journal of Psychology* 79: 349–60.

Hurd, P. DeH. (1990) 'Challenge and change in science education', guest editorial, *Journal of Research in Science Teaching* 27(5): 413–14.

INRA (Europe) (1993) *European Co-ordination Office for the Commission of the European Community DG XII, Eurobarometer 39.1, Biotechnology and Genetic Engineering: What Europeans Think About It*, Brussels: Commission of the European Community.

Institute of Medicine (1990) *Consensus Development at the NIH: Improving the Program*, Washington, DC: National Academy Press.

Irwin, A. (1995) *Science at the Service of the Community?*, The Nuffield Foundation Science Shop Initiative, London: Nuffield Foundation.

Irwin, A. and Wynne, B. (eds) (1996) *Misunderstanding Science*, Cambridge: Cambridge University Press.

Irwin, A., Dale, A. and Smith, D. (1996) 'Science and Hell's kitchen: the local understanding of hazard issues', in A. Irwin and B. Wynne (eds) *Misunderstanding Science?*, Cambridge: Cambridge University Press.

Jenkins, E.W. (1996) *Innovations in Science and Technology Education*, vol. VI, Paris: Unesco.

Jones, S. (1996) *In the Blood*, London: HarperCollins.

Joss, S. (1995) 'Evaluating consensus conferences: necessity or luxury?' in S. Joss and J. Durant *Public Participation in Science: The Role of Consensus Conferences in Europe*, London: Science Museum.

Katz, J. and Satelle, D. (1991) *Biotechnology for All*, Cambridge: Hobsons (an updated version of *Biotechnology in Focus*, 1988).

Kelly, A. (1981) *The Missing Half: Girls and Science*, Manchester: Manchester University Press.

Kelly, A., Whyte, J. and Small, B. (1984) *Girls into Science and Technology (GIST)*, Department of Sociology, University of Manchester.

Kinsey, T.G. and Wheatley, J.H. (1984) 'The effect of an environmental course on the defensibility of environmental attitudes', *Journal of Research in Science Teaching* 21(7): 675–83.

Knight, D. (1986) *The Age of Science*, Oxford: Blackwell.

Knorr Cetina, K. (1993) 'Strong constructivism – from a sociologist's point of view', *Social Studies of Science* 23: 555–63.

Koertige, N. (1981) 'Methodology, ideology and feminist critiques of science', in P.D. Asquith and R.N. Giere (eds) *Proceedings of the Philosophy of Science Association 1980*, Ann Arbor, MI: Edwards.

Kuhn, D., Amsel, E. and O'Loughlin, M. (1988) *The Development of Scientific Thinking Skills*, London: Academic Press.

Kuhn, T. (1963) *The Structure of Scientific Revolutions*, Chicago: University of Chicago Press.

Labinger, J. (1995) 'Science as culture: a view from the Petri dish', *Social Studies of Science* 25(2): 285–306.

Ladd, E.C. and Lipset, S.M. (1972) 'Politics of academic natural scientists and engineers', *Science* 176: 1091–100.

Langer, E., Hatem, M., Joss, J. and Howell, M. (1989) 'Conditional teaching and mindful learning: the role of uncertainty in education', *Creativity Research Journal* 2: 139–50.

Latour, B. (1987) *Science in Action*, Milton Keynes: Open University Press.

Latour, B. (1993) *We Have Never Been Modern*, Cambridge, MA: Harvard University Press.

Latour, B. and Woolgar, S. (1979) *Laboratory Life: The Social Construction of Scientific Facts*, London: Sage.

Lave, J. (1988) *Cognition in Practice: Mind, Mathematics and Culture in Everyday Life*, New York and Cambridge: Cambridge University Press.

Lawrence, R.H. (1988) 'New applications of biotechnology in the food industry', in *Biotechnology and the Food Supply*, Washington, DC: National Academy Press.

Layton, D. (1973) *Science for the People: The Origins of the School Science Curriculum in England*, London: Allen & Unwin.

Layton, D. (1984) *Interpreters of School Science*, London: John Murray.

Layton, D. (1991) 'Science education and praxis: the relationship of school science to practical action', *Studies in Science Education* 19: 43–79.

Layton, D., Jenkins, E., Macgill, S. and Davey A. (1993) *Inarticulate Science? Perspectives on the Public Understanding of Science and Some Implications for Science Education*, Driffield: Studies in Education.

Layton, E. (1987) 'Through the looking glass or news from lake mirror image', *Technology and Culture* 28: 594–607.

Levidow, L. (1991) 'Cleaning up on the farm', *Science as Culture* 2(4): 538–68.

Levidow, L. (1995a) 'Agricultural biotechnology as clean surgical strike' in S. Elworthy, K. Anderson, I. Coates, P. Stephens and M. Stroh (eds) *Perspective on the Environment II*, 31–44, London: Avebury.

Levidow, L. (1995b) 'Scientizing security: agricultural biotechnology as clean surgical strike', *Social Text* 13(3): 161–80.

Levidow, L. (1995c) 'Whose ethics for agricultural biotechnology?', in V. Shiva and I. Moser (eds) *Biopolitics: A Feminist and Ecological Reader on Biotechnology*, London: Zed.

Levidow, L. and Tait, J. (1991) 'The greening of biotechnology: GMOs as environment-friendly products' *Science and Public Policy* 18(5): 271–80.

Levidow, L. and Tait, J. (1992) 'Which public understanding of biotechnology?', *Biotechnology Education* 3(2): 102–6.

Levidow, L. Carr, S., von Schomberg, R. and Wield, D. (1996) 'Bounding the risk assessment of a herbicide-tolerant crop', in Ad van Dommelen (ed.) *Coping with Deliberate Release: The Limits of Risk Assessment*, Tilburg: International Centre for Human and Public Affairs.

Lijnse, P. (1990) 'Energy between the life-world of pupils and the world of physics', *Science Education* 74(5): 571–83.

Lock, R. (1996) 'What do GCSE students know and think about biotechnology and genetic engineering?', *Issues in Science Teaching*, Proceedings of the 1995 ASE INSET Services Annual Conference, Association for Science Education, Hatfield, Herts.

Lundgren, U.P. (1981) 'Education as a context for work', *Australian Educational Researcher* 8(2): 5–29.

McClean, M. (1995) *Education Traditions Compared: Content, Teaching and Learning in Industrialised Countries*, London: David Fulton.

Macgill, S.M. (1987) *The Politics of Anxiety: Sellafield's Cancer-link Controversy*, London: Pion.

Macgill, S.M. and Funtowicz, S.O. (1988) 'The "pedigree" of radiation estimates: an exploratory analysis in the context of exposures of young people in Seascale as a result of the Sellafield discharges', *Journal of the Society of Radiological Protection* 8: 77–86.

Malcolm, C.K. (1987) *The Science Framework P-10*, Melbourne, Victoria: Ministry of Education, Schools Division.

Marks, J. (1983) *Science and the Making of the Modern World*, London: Heinemann.

Martin, S. and Tait, J. (1992) 'Attitudes of selected public groups in the UK to biotechnology', in J. Durant (ed.) *Biotechnology in Public*, London: Science Museum.

Marton, F., Fensham, P.J. and Chaiklin, S. (1994) 'A Nobel's eye view of scientific intuition: discussions with the Nobel prize winners in physics, chemistry and medicine (1970–86)', *International Journal of Science Education* 16(4): 457–73.

Matthews, G.B. (1990) *Philosophy and the Young Child*, Cambridge, MA: MIT Press.

Matthews, M.R. (1994) *Science Teaching: The Role of History and Philosophy of Science*, London: Routledge.

Matthews, M.R. (1995) *Challenging NZ Science Education*, Palmerston North, New Zealand: Dunmore Press.

Medawar, P. (1974) *Plato's Republic*, Oxford: Oxford University Press.

Mellar, H., Bliss, J., Boohan, R., Ogborn, J. and Tompsett, C. (eds) (1994) *Learning with Artificial Worlds: Computer-Based Modelling in the Curriculum*, London: Falmer.

Merton, R. (1943) *The Sociology of Science*, Chicago: University of Chicago Press.

Miles, R.S., Alt, M.B., Gosling, D.C., Lewis, B.N. and Tout, F.A. (eds) (1988) *The Design of Educational Exhibits*, London, Allen & Unwin.

Mill, J.S. (1859) *On Liberty*, London.

Millar, R. and Driver, R. (1987) 'Beyond processes', *Studies in Science Education* 14: 33–62.

Millar, R. and Wynne, B. (1988) 'Public understanding of science: from contents to processes', *International Journal of Science Education* 10(4): 388–98.

Miller, A.I. (1984) *Imagery in Scientific Thought: Creating 20th century Physics*, Cambridge, MA: MIT Press.

Miller, J. (1982) 'Attitudes towards genetic modification research: analysis of the views of the Sputnik generation', *Science, Technology and Human Values* 7(39).

Miller, J. (1983) 'Scientific literacy: a conceptual and empirical review', *Daedalus* 112(2): 29–48.

Monsanto (1984) *Genetic Engineering: A Natural Science*, St Louis, MO: Monsanto Company.

Moulton, J. (1983) 'Against the adversarial method in philosophy', in S. Harding and M. Hintikka (eds) *Discovering Reality: Feminist Perspectives on Epistemology, Metaphysics, Methodology and Philosophy of Science*, Dordrecht: Reidel.

Mulkay, M. (1995) 'Galileo and the embryos', *Social Studies of Science* 25(3): 499–532

Murphy, P. (1985) (ed.) *The Exploratorium*, Bristol: The Exploratory.

National Research Council (NRC) (1989) *Alternative Agriculture*, Washington, DC: National Academy.

National Science Board (1993) *Science and Engineering Indicators*, Washington, DC: Government Printing Office.

National Science Foundation (1983) *Educating Americans for the Twenty First Century, Report of the National Science Board Commission on Pre-college Education in Mathematics, Science and Technology*, Washington, DC: National Science Foundation.

Needham, J. (1986) *Science and Civilisation in China*, Cambridge: Cambridge University Press.

Nehru, P. (1960) Speech, reprinted in *Proceedings of the National Institute of Science of India* 27.

Nelkin, D. (1987) *Selling Science*, W.H. Freeman: Basingstoke.

Nott, M. and Wellington, J. (1996) 'Ethics and morals in the science classroom', *Issues in Science Teaching*, Proceedings of the 1995 ASE INSET Services Annual Conference, Association for Science Education, Hatfield Herts.

Nye, A. (1990) *Words of Power: A Feminist Reading of the History of Logic*, London: Routledge.

Office of Science and Technology (1993) *Realising Our Potential*, Cm 2250, London: HMSO.

Ogborn, J. (1995) 'Recovering reality', *Studies in Science Education* 25: 3–38.

Ogborn, J. (nd) 'The nature of science, and its implications for science for all', unpublished paper.

Osborne, R. and Freyberg, P. (1985) *Learning in Science: The Implications of Children's Science*, Auckland, New Zealand: Heinemann.

Panos (1993) 'Genetic engineers target Third World crops', *Media Briefing* no. 7 (December), London: Panos Institute.

Parker, L.H. (1986) 'The choice point: a critical event in the science education of girls and boys', in B.J. Fraser and G.J. Giddings (eds) *Gender Issues in Science Education 13–18*, Perth, Western Australia: Curtin University of Technology.

Pearson, G. (1996) 'Survey of MRC scientists', *MRC Today* 10.

Pearson, G., Pringle, S. and Thomas, J. (1995) 'Sore feet and public goodwill', *Science and Public Affairs* autumn: 38–43.

Perlas, N. and Hobbelink, H. (1995) *Biopolitics: A Feminist and Ecological Reader on Biotechnology*, London: Zed Books.

Pfundt, H. and Duit, R. (1994) *Bibliography: Students' Alternative Frameworks and Science Education*, 4th edn, Kiel, Germany: IPN.

Pickering, A. (1984) *Constructing Quarks*, Chicago: University of Chicago Press.

Pimentel, D. (1987) 'Down on the farm: genetic engineering meets ecology', *Technology Review* January: 24–30.

Pinker, S. (1994) *The Language Instinct*, London: Allen Lane.

Pomeroy, D. (1996) 'STL in a culturally diverse world', in E.W. Jenkins (ed.) *Innovations in Science and Technology Education*, vol. VI, Paris: Unesco.

Posch, P. (1993) 'Research issues in environmental education', *Studies in Science Education* 21: 21–48.

Postgate, J. (1995) 'Public Understanding, did you say?' *Science and Public Affairs* autumn: 8–10.

Price, H. (1992) 'CD by radio', *IEE Review* 16 April: 131.

Prigogine, I. and Stengers, I. (1984) *Order Out of Chaos: Man's New Dialogue with Nature*, London: Heinemann.

Pringle, S.M. (1995) 'Don't take the pleasure out of learning', *New Scientist* 1997: 61–2.

Quinn, F. (1996) 'Cultural adaptation in science', manuscript in preparation, Virginia Polytechnic Institute and State University.

Ravetz, J.R. (1971) *Scientific Knowledge and its Social Problems*, Oxford: Clarendon.

Redner, H. (1987) *The Ends of Science: An Essay in Scientific Authority*, Boulder, CO: Westview.

Roberts, D. (1982) 'Developing the concept of "curriculum emphases" in science education', *Science Education* 66(2): 243–60.

Rodgers, M. (1992) 'The Hawking Phenomenon', *Public Understanding of Science* 1: 231–4.

Rogoff, B. (1990) *Apprenticeship in Thinking: Cognititve Development in Social Context*, New York and Oxford: Oxford University Press.

Rose, H. (1994) *Love Power and Knowledge: Toward a Feminist Transformation of the Sciences*, Cambridge: Polity.

Roszak, T. (1972) *Where the Wasteland Ends*, London: Faber & Faber.

Rowell, P.M. and Gaskell, P.J. (1986) 'Tensions and realignments: school physics in British Columbia', in I. Goodson (ed.) *International Perspectives in Curriculum*, London: Croom Helm.

Ryle, G. (1949) *The Concept of Mind*, London: Hutchinson.

Satelle, D. (1988) *Biotechnology . . . in Perspective*, Cambridge: Hodsons.

Schiebinger, L. (1993) *Nature's Body: Sexual Politics and the Making of Modern Science*, Boston, MA: Beacon.

Science Council of Canada (1984) *Science for Every Student: Educating Canadians for tomorrow's world*, Summary of Report 36, Ottawa: Supply and Service.

Screen, P.A. (1986) 'The Warwick Process Science Project', *School Science Review* 68(242): 12–16.

Scriven, M. (1987) *The Rights of Technology in Education: The Need for Consciousness Raising*, a paper for the Education and Technology Task Force, Adelaide, South Australia: Ministry of Education and Technology.

Semin, G.R. and Gergen, J.K. (eds) (1990) *Everyday Understanding: Social and Scientific Implications*, London: Sage.

Senior Advisory Group on Biotechnology / CEFIC (SAGB) (1990) *Community Policy for Biotechnology: Priorities and Actions*, Brussels: SAGB and Hodsons.

Shamos, M.H. (1988) *Great Experiments in Physics*, New York: Dover.

Shamos, M.H. (1995) *The Myth of Scientific Literacy*, New Brunswick, NJ: Rutgers University Press.

Shapin, S. (1992) 'Why the public ought to understand science-in-the-making', *Public Understanding of Science* 1(1): 27–30.

Shapin, S. (1995) 'Here and everywhere: sociology of scientific knowledge', *Annual Review of Sociology* 21: 289–321.

Sheldrake, R. (1994) *Seven Experiments that could Change the World*, London: Fourth Estate.

Shiva, V. (1989) *Staying Alive: Women, Ecology and Development*, London: Pluto.

Shiva, V. (1995) *Biodiversity: Social and Ecological Perspectives*, London: Zed Books.

Shortland, M. (1987) 'No business like show business', *Nature* 328: 213.

Sivanandan, A.N. (1995) 'La traison des clercs', *New Statesman* 14 July: 20–1.

Skinner, B.F. (1973) *Beyond Freedom and Dignity*, Harmondsworth: Penguin.

Smail, B. (1987) 'Encouraging girls to give physics a second chance', in A. Kelly (ed.) *Science for Girls* 13–18, Milton Keynes: Open University Press.

Smith, A. (1996) *Software for the Self*, London: Faber & Faber.

Smith, N. (1988) 'In support of an application-first chemisty course: some reflections on the Salters' GCSE scheme', *School Science Review* 70(250): 108–14.

Smith, W. (1987) 'COMETS: career-orientated modules to explore topics in science', in K. Riquarts (ed.) *Science and Technology Education and the Quality of Life*, Kiel, Germany: IPN.

Snow, C.P. (1965) *The Two Cultures: And a Second Look*, Cambridge: Cambridge University Press.

Solomon, J. (1988) 'Science technology and society courses: tools for thinking about social issues', *International Journal of Science Education* 10(4): 379–87.

Solomon, J. (1992) *Getting to Know about Energy*, London: Falmer.

Solomon, J. (1994) 'Towards a notion of Home Culture', *British Education Research Journal* 20(5): 565–77.

Solomon, J. and Aikenhead, G. (eds) (1994) *STS Education: International Perspectives on Reform*, New York: Teachers' College Press, Columbia University.

Speedy, G., Annice, C., Fensham, P.J. and West, L.H.T. (1989) *Discipline Review of Teacher Education in Mathematics and Science, vol. I, Report and Recommendations*, Canberra: Australian Government Printer.

Staudenmaier, J. (1985) *Technology's Storytellers: Reweaving the Human Fabric*, Cambridge, MA and London: Society for the History of Technology and MIT Press.

Stephan, P.E. and Levin, G. (1992) *Striking the Mother Lode in Science*, Oxford: Oxford University Press

Stevenson, J. (1991) 'The long-term impact of interactive exhibits', *International Journal of Science Education* 13(5): 521–31.

REFERENCES

Stove, D. (1982) *Popper and After: Four Modern Irrationalists*, Oxford: Pergamon.

Taverne, D. (1990) *The Case for Biotechnology*, London: Prima.

Taylor, F.W. (1914) *The Principles of Scientific Management*, New York: Harper.

Thier, H. and Hill, T. (1988) 'Chemical education in schools and the community: the CEPUP project', *International Journal of Science Education* 10(4): 421–30.

Third World Network (1986) 'Modern science in crisis: a Third World response', in S. Harding (ed.) *The 'Racial' Economy of Science*, Bloomington, IN: Indiana University Press.

Thomas, G. and Durant, J. (1987) 'Why should we promote the public understanding of science?', *Scientific Literacy Papers*, University of Oxford Department of External Studies, summer: 1–14.

Thompson, T. (1993) 'Characteristics of self-worth protectiveness', *British Journal of Educational Psychology* 63: 469–88.

Tolstoy, I. (1990) *The Knowledge and the Power: Reflexions on the History of Science*, Edinburgh: Canongate.

TSNews (1996) Newsletter of the Teacher Scientist Network. Available from Frank Chennell, Hurdle Cottage, Brisley Road, North Elmham, Norfolk, NR20 5DL.

Turney, J. (1996) *To Know Science is to Love It?*, COPUS publication, London: Royal Society.

Unesco (1983) *Science for All*, Bangkok: Unesco Regional Office for Education in Asia and the Pacific.

Unesco (1994) *Science and Technology Education for All: The Project 2000+ Declaration The Way Forward*, Paris: Unesco.

Van Berkel, B. (1995) 'A conceptual structure of school chemistry', in P. Janich and N. Psarros (eds) *Proceedings of the Second Erlenmeyer Colloquy*, Marburg, Germany.

van den Brul, C. (1992) 'Why the "arts Mafia" is guilty of loading the dice', *Daily Telegraph* 29 June.

van den Brul, C. (1995) 'Perceptions of science: how scientists and others view the media reporting of science', *Studies in Science Education* 25: 211–37.

Van Lawick, J. and Goodall, J. (1974) *In the Shadow of Man*, London: Fontana.

Vincenti, W. (1982) 'Control-volume analysis: a difference in thinking between engineering and physics', *Technology and Culture* 23: 145–74.

Walgate, R. (1990) *Miracle or Menace? Biotechnology and the Third World*, London: Panos.

Wellington, J.J. (1981) '"What's supposed to happen, sir?" Some problems with discovery learning', *School Science Review* 63(222): 167–73.

Werskey, G. (1988) *The Visible College*, London: Free Association Books.

White, R.T. and Gunstone, R.G. (1993) *Probing Understanding*, London: Falmer.

White, S., Evans, P., Mihill, C. and Tysoe, M. (1993) *Hitting the Headlines*, Leicester: British Psychological Society.

Williams, R. (1961) *The Long Revolution*, Chatto & Windus.

Wolfendale, A. (1995) *Report of the Committee to Review the Contribution of Scientists and Engineers to the Public Understanding of Science, Engineering and Technology*, London: Office of Science and Technology, Department of Trade and Industry.

Wolpert, L. (1993) *The Unnatural Nature of Science*, London: Faber & Faber.

Woolnough, B.E. (1994) *Effective Science Teaching*, Buckingham: Open University Press.

World Bank (1992) *Development and the Environment*, Washington, DC: World Bank.

Wynne, B. (1991) 'Knowledges in context', *Science, Technology and Human Values* 16(1): 111–21.

REFERENCES

Wynne, B. (1994) 'Public Understanding of Science', in S. Jasanoff, G.E. Markle, J.C. Peterson and T. Pinch (eds) *Handbook of Science and Technology Studies*, London: Sage.

Yearley, S. (1989) 'Bog Standards: science and conservation at a public enquiry', *Social Studies of Science* 19(3): 421–38.

Yount, J.R. and Horton, P.B. (1992) 'Factors influencing environmental attitude, defensibility and cognitive reasoning level', *Journal of Research in Science Teaching* 29(10): 1059–78.

Yoxen, E. (1981) 'Life as a productive force: capitalizing the science and technology of molecular biology', in L. Levidow and R.M. Young (eds) *Science, Technology and the Labour Process*, London: CSE Books.

Yoxen, E. (1983) *The Gene Business: Who Should Control Biotechnology?*, London: Pan.

Ziman, J. (1978) *Reliable Knowledge: An Exploration of the Grounds for Belief in Science*, Cambridge: Cambridge University Press.

Ziman, J. (1984) *An Introduction to Science Studies: The Philosophical and Social Aspects of Science and Technology*, Cambridge: Cambridge University Press.

Ziman, J. (1991) 'Public Understanding of Science', *Science, Technology and Human Values* 16(1): 99–105.

Ziman, J. (1992) *Puzzles, Problems and Enigmas*, BBC Broadcast, reprinted by Cambridge University Press.

Ziman, J. (1994) *Prometheus Bound*, Cambridge: Cambridge University Press.

Ziman, J. (1995) 'Postacademic science: constructing knowledge with networks and norms', Royal Society Medawar Lecture, 29 June.